THE

FEMINIZATION

OF

AMERICA

Also by Elinor Lenz:

SO YOU WANT TO GO BACK TO SCHOOL (coauthor)

EFFECTIVENESS TRAINING FOR WOMEN (coauthor)

ONCE MY CHILD, NOW MY FRIEND

Also by Barbara Myerhoff:

PEYOTE HUNT: THE SACRED JOURNEY OF
THE HUICHOL INDIANS

NUMBER OUR DAYS

CHANGING IMAGES OF THE FAMILY (coeditor)

THE FEMINIZATION OF AMERICA

HOW WOMEN'S VALUES ARE CHANGING OUR PUBLIC AND PRIVATE LIVES

Elinor Lenz & Barbara Myerhoff

JEREMY P. TARCHER, INC. Los Angeles

Distributed by
ST. MARTIN'S PRESS New York

The authors would like to thank the following for their permission
to reprint:

Excerpt from "For Colored Girls Who Have Considered Suicide
When the Rainbow Is Enuf," by Ntozake Shange, reprinted by
permission of Russell & Volkening, Inc., © 1975, 1976, 1977.

LIBRARY OF CONGRESS CATALOGING
IN PUBLICATION DATA

Lenz, Elinor.
  The feminization of America.

  Bibliography: p. 257
  Includes index.
  1. Feminism—United States. 2. United States—Social
conditions—1900– . I. Myerhoff, Barbara G.
II. Title.
HQ1420.L46 1985   305.4'2'0973   85-9752
ISBN 0-87477-369-5

Jeremy P. Tarcher, Inc.
9110 Sunset Blvd.
Los Angeles, CA 90069

Design by Cynthia Eyring
Manufactured in the United States of America
10 9 8 7 6 5 4 3 2 1
First Edition

CONTENTS

CONTENTS

The girl and the woman, in their new, their own unfolding, will but in passing be imitators of masculine ways, good and bad, and repeaters of masculine professions. After the uncertainty of such transitions, it will become apparent that women were only going through the profusions and vicissitudes of those (often ridiculous) disguises in order to cleanse their most characteristic nature of the distorting influences of the other sex. Women, in whom life lingers and dwells more immediately, more fruitfully and more confidently, must surely have become more fundamentally riper people, more human people, than easygoing man, who is not pulled down below the surface of life by the weight of any fruit of his body and who, presumptuous and hasty, undervalues what he thinks he loves. This humanity of woman, borne its full time in suffering and humiliation, will come to light when she will have stripped off the conventions of mere femininity in the mutations of her outward status, and those men who do not yet feel it approaching today will be surprised and struck by it. . . . Some day there will be girls and women whose name will no longer signify merely an opposite of the masculine, but something in itself, something that makes one think, not of any complement and limit, but only of life and existence: the feminine human being.

—Rainer Maria Rilke, *Letters to a Young Poet*

PREFACE

We began this book as an exploration of women's friendships, a subject we felt had suffered from not-so-benign neglect; while men's friendships had been ennobled, women's had been either ignored or ridiculed. But we soon discovered that women's friendships could not be extricated from the totality of women's lives: their values, behavioral style, world view—in short, their culture, which had evolved from earliest human history.

Before long, we realized that we were on to a much bigger theme than we had started with, a theme with momentous implications not only for women but for all Americans living at this time of sweeping social transformation. Our subject had grown in stages from women's friendships to women's culture to the head-spinning changes now occurring in American life as a result of women's transition from their historic domestic world to the public world of business, industry, and the professions. These changes are truly revolutionary; some of them could not have been predicted even a decade ago. They represent nothing less than the feminization of America.

Despite the floodtide of books in recent years on feminism and related subjects, no other book to our knowledge has dealt with this theme. So far, there has been no attempt to synthesize the transformations occurring along the entire spectrum of contemporary culture and to interpret what these changes mean to individuals, families, work, relationships, the economy, politics, and social institutions in America today.

In our exploration, we discovered an America that, spurred on by the feminizing influence, is moving away from many archaic ways of thinking and behaving toward the promise of a saner and more humanistic future. There are, of course, many problems and barriers along the way, but we believe ultimately in the human ability to adapt and survive, and the history of our species supports this optimistic view. We believe, moreover, that the force of feminization has been set in motion by the primal human drive to survive through adaptation; for feminine culture, with its commitment to creating and protecting life, is our best and brightest hope for overcoming the destructive, life-threatening forces of the nuclear age.

There is no attempt here to claim scientific truth or an all-inclusive coverage of this vast, volatile, and infinitely complex process of social change. We have had to gloss over or omit, often reluctantly, some aspects of cultural feminization, such as changing attitudes toward lesbianism and abortion. We could not possibly have done justice to all of the issues that might be encompassed by our theme, and several of these, we felt, had been dealt with more than adequately by others. Our concentration has been on the process of feminization as a "little-noticed revolution," in historian Daniel Boorstin's phrase, out of which we see the emergence of a new social consciousness and a growing awareness of the need for a more balanced, more compassionate society.

The perceptions and insights that are the grist of the book have emerged through hundreds of interviews with women and men of a variety of ages, occupations, family, marital and sexual arrangements, social stations, religions, education. We have not talked as much with various ethnic groups and races or with as many people in rural areas as we would have wished. The subject is boundless and open-ended, which is as it should be.

It would take another book simply to acknowledge all those who have generously and with uncommon candor shared with us their time, their thoughts, their experience. We have been especially fortunate in the support and enthusiasm we have had throughout the development of the book from our publisher, Jeremy Tarcher, and our editors, Janice Gallagher and Laura Golden. The editorial assistance we received often went beyond the call of duty and at times crossed that fine, invisible line between editing and creating.

Researching and writing the book has deepened our respect for the women and men in America today who are confronting with courage and intelligence the often daunting problems and challenges of cultural change. To these new women and men who are helping to shape a more enlightened, more humane society, we dedicate this book.

1. ON THE THRESHOLD

Women have an opportunity today to change the course of American cultural history. The conditions for bringing about such change have never been more favorable, and women, because of their cultural orientation through the ages, are particularly fitted to act as agents of change. The familiar litany of disorders and discontents in American life—the loneliness, alienation, rootlessness—have converged with fear of nuclear war to engender a widespread yearning for a more humane, more enlightened way of living together. Never before have so many people been engaged in what often seems like a desperate search to find out who they are, what they believe in, and how to relate to each other.

Woman's historic responsibility for protecting life has endowed her with a set of adaptive characteristics: a strong nurturing impulse that extends to all living things; a highly developed capacity for intimacy that fosters her need for relatedness; a tendency to integrate rather than separate; an ability to empathize; a predilection for egalitarian relationships together with a resistance to hierarchy; an attachment to the day-to-day process of sustaining life; a spirituality that transcends dogma and sectarianism; a scale of values that places individual growth and fulfillment above abstractions; and a preference for negotiation as a means of problem solving, which springs from her antipathy to violence.

These are the very qualities that are so desperately needed in today's increasingly divisive and dangerous world. They offer the possibility for the kind of humanizing, life-enhancing relationships that both men and women are seeking and that so often elude us in the impersonal, bureaucratic, self-aggrandizing, high-tech society of America in the 1980s.

It is our claim that the values and behavioral style that women have developed over the centuries as a cultural adaptation have equipped them with a special propensity for effecting the personal and social transmutations so urgently needed today. Women's subordinate position, which throughout history and across the cultural spectrum has kept them outside the mainstream, can now be seen as their most reliable source of strength. Since they have not been programmed to act or react according to the conventions of the male-dominated public world, they can bring fresh and innovative perceptions to traditional, entrenched modes of thinking.

"Any existing culture can only reach and develop a certain amount of human creativity," Elizabeth Janeway reminds us. "The rest is suppressed because the terms of life don't demand its use, or are even hostile. In times of change, however, the old repertory of action will turn out to be insufficient; then the untapped reservoir of creativity belonging to hitherto overlooked groups and classes of society may be called on."[1]

Today, the mass movement of women into the public world of action and achievement is functioning as a revitalizing force. And, as in the case of other outside groups, this subtle dynamic is working its way into the mainstream, often below the level of public consciousness. In their traditional domestic role, women have not been able to fit their experience into tidy categories, nor have they been in a position to create enduring structures or arrangements. They have lived too long with the disorder, with the shift and flux of family life. Thus, women's culture poses a challenge to the masculine mainstream by acting as a constant irritant, forcing the dominant culture to confront itself from time to time with uncomfortable questions.

What we are witnessing is an evolutionary development as two cultures—one subordinated and disdained, the other dominant and controlling—come into contact. The concept of men and women as two cultures emerged out of the post-'60s questioning of some of our basic assumptions about how the world functions. A sense of impending disaster together with a feeling of helplessness brought on by the nuclear arms race began to be translated into a conviction that the world was dangerously out of control and that fundamental change was urgently needed. Both men and women began questioning a system based upon a set of values and strategies identified with a specific masculine perception that was bringing us all to the brink of extinction.

The women's movement, as part of a new humanism, began calling for a restructuring of society more in accord with feminine principles. As the world view moved away from androcentrism, it became apparent that a more positive direction for the future was linked to a combination of both the masculine and feminine sensibilities: ways of talking, personality, style, desires, and dreams encompassing and describing our whole being, which is commonly summed up as culture.

WHAT DO WE MEAN BY CULTURE?

Since the concept of culture is central to our discussion of the feminization of America, we begin with a definition of culture and what it encompasses. Culture is a way of life, transmitted from one generation to another, a collective set of agreements about how to perceive and interpret the world. It is an adaptive arrangement, consisting of solutions to common problems, with an enduring though by no means unchanging pattern. Though it is functional it is not necessarily or even largely rational. Much of culture is arbitrary, but it has the power to convince all who embrace it of its innate rightness and desirability. The better a culture functions, the less awareness its members have of its power over them, because much of it is unconscious, its dictates operating through the individual psyche. It is not until aspects of a culture have been made conscious that they may be examined and possibly revised. Culture is identified by what people say and do, the objects they invent, the symbols with which they present and interpret themselves, the social relationships provided for and prohibited.

When we speak of masculine culture or feminine culture, we are using a metaphor, since these are not fully developed, entirely separate systems. Technically they are sub- or partial cultures, and their overlap is substantial. Nevertheless, it is reasonable to speak of a distinctive sensibility, a style of life, set of values, as well as activities, relationships, and cognitive and emotional predilections that are present among women but absent when men and women are together, or when men are together.

Of course, women can be and often are participants in men's culture and vice versa. We are speaking not of gender per se but of rules of conduct usually but by no means always associated with gender. Certainly, more women participate in men's culture than the reverse, for men's culture is associated with the "real" world: success, seriousness, matters of consequence, maturity. It is associated with what the sociologists have called the instrumental dimension: purposive, firm, efficient, impersonal, specialized, evaluative, hierarchical.

Women, particularly in families, often take charge of the opposite function, providing the expressive dimension. In this capacity, they are responsible for matters dealing with the quality of life, with relationship and relatedness; with emotions and diffuse, universal concerns—the whole human being. The style is egalitarian, accepting, and compassionate. The underlying impulse is toward integration rather than separation: mind and body are a unity, the political and the personal are one.

These cultural attributes have been regarded as at best charming but irrelevant to traditional mainstream values and purposes. Other minorities in our society—Jews, Slavs, Asians, Hispanics— have found themselves in a similar situation. The minority member displays characteristics viewed as marginal to the mainstream but signifying a fuller, freer humanity than is available to those on the inside. The blacks have "soul," implying subtle, rich possibilities that are nonetheless regarded as irrelevant to white mainstream culture; the Latinos, *corazón*, or heart; the Jews, *menschlichkeit*, or humaneness—all terms that suggest a robust vitality missing from the bloodless, goal-dominated narrow pursuits of WASP middle-class mainstream society. Like these outside groups, women have enjoyed the privileges and suffered the penalties of minority subcultures: disdain and, paradoxically, greater freedom—the same freedom allowed children, artists, the insane, and all those less-than-full members of society who mirror and exaggerate the least valued dimensions of society.

WOMEN'S CULTURE:
An Ethnographic View

In tracing the impact of feminine culture on the mainstream, we used an ethnographic lens; that is, we looked at women's culture in America as anthropologists look at a culture that is unfamiliar to them. This enabled us, who have lived all our lives in feminine culture, to bring a fresh perspective to the subject. At times we had only sketchy clues to guide us, and as archaeologists sometimes draw conclusions from fragments of bone or utensils, we included a certain amount of educated guessing in our interpretation of the shards of women's changing culture that became available to us through our interviews and documentary research. For the most part, the evidence was clear enough to speak for itself.

An anthropologist looking at traditional female culture must be immediately struck by its fundamental transience. It is a culture rooted in the tending of life: the producing of children; the care for the sick and dying; the nurturance of the elderly; the gathering, cleaning, preparation, and serving of food; the tending of hearth and home; the sweeping, sponging, chopping, mending, wiping that is ceaseless and evanescent. In their long domestic history, women's energies have been devoted to process, the repetitive doing and redoing that invisibly, often unconsciously, attempts to impose order on the chaos of daily living.

Whatever else women do or do not do in the world, almost everywhere they are primarily responsible for creating human beings out of the raw material of biology. Women, even those without children, express as if with one voice a deeply felt sense of this responsibility for life. In their life-producing and life-supporting work, women need other women. For long periods of time (for some throughout their life cycle) women are restricted in mobility and freedom in the carrying and caring for small children. (Several anthropologists have suggested that the first "tools" may have been invented by mothers to carry their offspring who could not cling or walk.) At such times, cooperation among women, practically and emotionally, is essential. Women in many cultures can and do suckle each other's children, serve as midwives to each other, and coparent one another's infants.

Directly linked to woman's maternal function is her strong sense of personalism. Much of the time, women are tied to their children's well-being. In cases of conflict, there is a good chance a mother will demonstrate her allegiance to her child over the norms of society. Her orientation to the personal predisposes her toward the individual more than the group. When the military establishment speaks of "body counts" and "heroic deaths" for noble causes, women think of the husbands and sons who are mutilated or killed and of the agonies of their wives and mothers.

The responsibility for nurturing and preserving life imbues women with feelings of empathy toward the struggling, suffering individual that transcend abstract legal or political issues. "The moral imperative that emerges repeatedly in interviews with women," asserts Carol Gilligan, Harvard professor of education, "is an injunction to care, a responsibility to discern and alleviate the 'real and recognizable trouble' of this world. For men, the moral imperative appears rather as an injunction to respect the rights of others and thus to protect from interference the rights to life and self-fulfillment."[2]

Because of their role in early child care, women perform the function of culture carriers. Scientist-author Lewis Thomas notes, "Family education is something women are better at than men. . . . All the old stories, the myths, the poems comprehended most acutely by young children, the poking and nudging and pinching of very young minds, the waking up of very small children, the learning what smiles and laughter are all about, the vast pleasure of explanation, are by and large gifts of women to civilization. It is the women who remember and pass along the solid underpinnings of culture, not usually the men.''

We are dealing here with a psychic mode that combines a commitment to cooperation with a subjective orientation to the personal and specific. Intimacy, emotional expressiveness and responsiveness, personalism, flexibility—these qualities, generally identified with feminine culture, are the psychological forces that have shaped women's perceptions and out of which women have developed their own special brand of individualism. We call it "cooperative individualism," a form of association which, instead of pitting individuals against each other, merges the individual self-interest with that of the group. It is an associative style resembling that of a family closing ranks to protect or advance the interests of one of its members. In his classic work, *Democracy in America,* Alexis de Tocqueville identified this modus operandi as the principle of enlightened self-interest which, "rightly understood, produces no great acts of self-sacrifice, but . . . suggests daily small acts of self-denial''—a cogent description of the way most women have lived out their lives.

Cooperativeness, as women have practiced it through the ages, is one of women's hidden sources of power. Power carries special nuances of meaning in the feminine psyche. Psychologist Jean Baker Miller distinguishes between the traditional view of power as control and domination over others and "empowerment," which is personal power that develops in the context of self-support and the support of others. From Miller's perspective, personal power can be enhanced by redefining, discovering, and valuing so-called feminine traits, summarized in the following way: an ability and affinity for emotional/relational matters; acceptance of one's vulnerability; skill in and attraction for cooperative work; and pleasure in helping others learn and develop.[3] These traits have been the source of women's power in their private world, across cultures and throughout the ages.

"We are not really comfortable talking about power," says Ginny Mullin, a psychotherapist whose patients are mainly women, "because power in women has been seen as manipulative, dangerous, too impassioned and uncontrolled to be given full expression." The four elements she identifies as the amalgam of feminine power overlap with Miller's analysis: acknowledgment, the willingness to admit one's weaknesses as well as strengths; vulnerability, the recognition that our defenses are not impregnable and cannot protect us from the pain that is part of living; self-trust, the belief in one's own strength and integrity; and self-acceptance, the ability to live in peace with oneself.

TWO CULTURES IN TRANSITION

In dynamic societies such as ours, change is an ongoing process that sweeps individuals, groups, and subcultures relentlessly along in its path. The tremors and turbulence of recent years have left their mark on all of us and have displaced deeply ingrained knee-jerk patterns of thought and behavior in men as well as women. Both cultures are in transition, but it is women's culture that is acting as the catalyst for change, as it pushes against the boundaries within which it has been confined throughout history.

As is generally the case when a weak culture has an impact on a stronger one, the "soft areas" of the dominant culture—food, fashion, the arts—are more readily penetrated than the "hard areas"—heavy industry, the military, the government bureaucracies—although in the course of time, a changing public consciousness affects even these megainstitutions. We see this happening today; it is a process of change that is long overdue, a much-needed feminizing influence, and it is pervading our homes, workplaces, political institutions, even the food we eat and the cars we drive.

It was inevitable, of course, that so momentous a development as women's transition from the domestic to the public world would have social consequences, but the extent of the feminizing influence has gone largely unnoticed as the shocks and convulsions of the post-'60s era have occupied most of our attention. Moreover, this feminine-inspired process of social and psychological change has been so subtle, even subliminal, that its absorption into our thoughts, actions, and interactions has been as inconspicuous as the absorption of nutrients from the soil by plants in the forest.

Historian Daniel Boorstin, in describing the transformation of America into a "new civilization" held together by the "apparatus of daily life," has referred to the "little revolutions" that, since the Civil War, have occurred "not in the halls of legislatures or on battlefields or on the barricades but in homes and farms and factories and schools and stores, across the landscape and in the air—so little noticed because they came so swiftly, because they touched Americans everywhere and every day."[4] The feminization of America is one of these little revolutions, and it offers us, we firmly believe, our best hope for a safer, saner, more humane world.

RESTORING THE BALANCE

Wherever we look today, we see a world out of balance, teetering precariously on the edge of an abyss. Children die of hunger while nations pour billions into terrifyingly destructive weapons. Perishable resources, the heritage of the future, are sacrificed to the voracious demands and pressures of the present. Family values are extolled while one in every two marriages ends in divorce and child neglect and abuse assume the dimensions of a national scandal. Our educational and health-care systems are showing signs of serious erosion, even while the costs of maintaining these services continue to escalate.

The roots of these and related problems are deep and tangled, but a fault line that extends throughout the system points to an imbalance that has developed over the centuries, in which the values and perceptions of half of humanity have been excluded from public decision-making and action. This is now being corrected as women take their place in the public world, and though the rebalancing process is still in its early stages, some salutary effects are already in evidence, while other promising possibilities loom on the horizon.

In exploring the feminizing influence, we have given special attention to those aspects of feminine culture that are often over-looked or distorted in the sound and fury of ideological debates about gender and society. The nature-nurture controversy; the biological determinism that draws heavily on man as hunter, predisposed to aggression and war by his early evolutionary role; the Freudian, Jungian, Eriksonian analyses of woman's nature—these are well-worn paths of inquiry that others will, no doubt, continue to tread.

We have taken as our turf the deeply inbred patterns of culture that can be distinguished as "feminine" and that are slowly but surely making their way into the public consciousness. These patterns, akin to Boorstin's little revolutions, are transforming, in much the same way as the changes Boorstin cites in post–Civil War America, "human experience itself, the very meaning of community, of time and space, of present and future. . . ."

We begin our exploration of these patterns of change in chapter 2 with women's language, which in its vocabulary, grammar, and timbre, expresses the feminine need for human warmth and connection. Language, deeply inbred in our consciousness, is one of the more stubborn areas of cultural change, and as with other immigrants, women, in this early phase of their transition to the public world, continue to speak their own language among themselves. Yet if, as some linguists have suggested, language can produce a world, it is conceivable that the language spoken by women will produce some changes in the worlds of business, the professions, and politics, as well as in personal relationships. Those changes, already occurring in both verbal and nonverbal language, provide intriguing clues to an evolving style of communication that will no longer require women to be bilingual.

In chapter 3, we move on to women's friendships, those intimate and enduring bonds that have always been essential to women's lives. In women's mutually supportive relationships there is a model for men, who readily admit that developing close friendships is difficult for them. We examine the quality of intimacy that is integral to women's relationships and that is usually lacking among men, and we address such rarely-talked-about issues as why men in Western societies fear intimacy and how the feminization of our culture can overcome this fear.

In chapter 4, we look at one of the oldest and newest forms of feminine association: the network. The networks women have been developing in recent years represent a blending of their traditional values and perceptions with their emergent cultural adaptations to the public world. Out of this private-public fusion has come a new definition and new applications of feminine power that project a fundamental change in the way careers are built and decisions arrived at in business and politics.

Chapter 5 takes us into the workplace, where some of the more conspicuous results of feminization are to be found as the number of working women has increased until it now exceeds half of the work force. Observing women performing in virtually every type of job and profession, plus the opportunity to work with them as peers, has probably done more to change masculine consciousness than any other development in our history. We are witnessing a major shift in working styles and relationships with long-range implications for humanizing the workplace and enhancing our working lives.

In chapter 6, we examine how the basic social unit, the family, is responding to the changing working lives of men and women. The feminizing process is altering the family in ways that could not have been imagined even a few decades ago. As the family is redefined, we are seeing the emergence of new attitudes toward mothering and fathering and the reordering of relationships all across the social spectrum.

Chapter 7 reviews the impact on medicine and health care of women's changing attitude toward their bodies. As women become informed consumers of medical and health services, the shock effects are being felt throughout the health-care system, particularly in obstetrics and gynecology. The return of the midwife, the new doctor, new definitions of health and sickness, a reevaluation of high-tech medicine and of the exaggerated specialization that treats the human being as a collection of unrelated parts—these are among the developments being spawned by the feminization of health care.

Similarly, women's spiritual search, the theme of chapter 8, is shaking up centuries-old theological concepts and clerical practices, forcing people of all religions to question some of their most deeply held beliefs. Feminine spirituality has generated an awareness of the inability of institutionalized religion to fulfill our spiritual needs in a nuclear age. Archaic dogmas and practices are giving way to a personal, earthbound spirituality that celebrates human experience and our relationship with nature.

Chapter 9 offers a tour of the lively arts—music, painting, theater—where women's experience is being expressed in new forms. Women are revitalizing and redefining creative activity, providing alternatives to obscurantism and arid abstractionism. The feminine voice and vision are leading the way to artistic frontiers that represent a sharp break with tradition; it can be argued, of course, that casting aside time-hallowed conventions in the arts is easier for women than for men, since women have not been part of the "great tradition" in the arts, and are therefore not as burdened by two thousand years of artistic tradition.

In chapter 10, we see how women are overcoming boundaries and barriers in their determination to bring a unified effort to the protection of life. The issue of war and peace is one on which women differ sharply from men, and women are investing their special skills and values in the antiwar and environmental movements. Feminization has been particularly effective in dramatizing these life-and-death concerns and in demonstrating a new kind of leadership that transcends national boundaries.

Chapter 11 profiles the new women and new men who are the precursors of an emerging era in which relationships will be based on true equality and cooperative individualism. We identify three stages in the development of women's gender identity during this time of cultural transition: the new feminine woman, the masculinized woman, and the hybridized woman. These identities are shifting, and our prognosis is that ultimately the hybridized identity will prevail—among men as well as women.

Chapter 12 takes us beyond feminism to a new era in which feminism merges into humanism. Following the feminization process as it moves toward this inclusive vision and extrapolating from current trends, we map out some pathways to the future, suggesting both the opportunities and the dangers that lie ahead.

THE TWO FACES OF CRISIS

Social commentators, whatever their philosophy or point of view, are virtually unanimous in labeling the time we live in as an age of crisis; but if this is so, it is crisis as represented by the Chinese ideograph for the word, which is made up of two images, one for danger and the other for opportunity. In a world bristling with weapons that are capable of instant and total destruction, the danger is undeniable, and one does not have to be a prophet of doom to fear for the future. But when we look back at the past, we can snatch some hope out of the human species' almost uncanny ability to save itself again and again.

At times of extreme social breakdown and disarray such as the present, countervailing forces of recovery are often set in motion by a confluence of cosmic events, scientific discoveries, and spiritual awakening that sets the stage for a dramatic transformation of public consciousness, the necessary prelude to sweeping public change. We are at such a turning point in our history today, and fortunately, the emerging temper of the time is on our side. The prospect for restoring health and wholeness to our culture through feminization is enhanced by a series of shifts in consciousness that can be summarized as follows:

The women's movement, gathering steam from the civil rights movement in the late 1950s, forced a questioning of some basic assumptions about the roles and relationships of men and women, particularly in terms of the conventional division of sexual responsibilities and rewards.

In the realm of science, Thomas Kuhn coined the term *para-*

digm shift, defining paradigm as a "universally recognized scientific achievement that for a time provides model problems and solutions to a community of practitioners." Kuhn's analysis sharpens the challenge to the immutability of scientific truth, posed earlier by Einstein's theory of relativity and Heisenberg's uncertainty principle. By shaking up the longstanding belief in final, testable truths arrived at empirically through deductive reasoning and testing, Science and Reason, the twin gods of secularism, have been stripped of their ability to resolve questions of not only meaning and morality, but now of survival as well—in confronting issues of world peace and ecology. Since faith in science was the modern replacement for the moral absolutes of religion, the loss of faith in scientific absolutes has engendered a renewed yearning for spiritual as well as interpersonal and global connectedness.

An androcentric world view has been losing its hold, with the growing recognition that the world, largely made by males, has become increasingly unbearable to both sexes. A new synthesis has been introduced as a replacement for the old analytic method of interpretation. Ludwig von Bertalanffy's general systems theory has influenced the study of peace as well as biological, behavioral and social research. Barbara McClintock's breakthrough discovery of genetic dynamism, challenging the long-accepted concept of a static genetic structure, is the outcome of her integrated approach to her materials, her feeling for the whole organism. Scientists of both sexes and various nationalities are coming together to work on common problems.

The human connection to Mother Nature and Mother Earth, which was sundered in the eighteenth-century Age of Enlightenment, is being restored in the wake of the environmental movement.

Further, we are redefining our relation to time, change, death, the unconscious, myth—above all, to our sense of power and control. Rampant, ruthlessly competitive individualism, androcentrism, and the subjugation of nature are proving dangerously inadequate to the critical needs of our present world. We are becoming aware of another sense of power and sensibility—a mythopoeic or synergistic mentality, which held sway in ancient times and which in its contemporary form is more in harmony with our current cultural development.

THE COST OF ASSIMILATION

This shifting public sensibility is encouraging to the rebalancing trend that can lead to a healthier, more secure society. But the feminizing process is incipient, and there is a very real possibility that in the years ahead it will be overwhelmed by the more powerful forces of the masculine mainstream. We have had some indications of this already in the defeat of the ERA and the watering down of affirmative action.

Yet the greatest threat to the cultural counterbalance so urgently needed at this time comes not from courts or legislatures but from women themselves. The question at the heart of the women's revolution is whether women can take their place in the public world, a place too long denied them, without becoming alienated from the feminine culture that has nourished and sustained them and that is now so necessary as a source of renewal for a society desperately seeking an infusion of new energy. For if, like immigrants rushing to assimilate, women, in their zeal to prove themselves in the public world of action and achievement, surrender all that is uniquely feminine, the result will resemble a revolution in which only the personnel have changed.

If women surrender their culture in a blind exchange for worldly official power or allow it to be trivialized out of existence, if feminine culture cannot be viewed as a serious, alternative world view, then all of us, men and women, are in jeopardy. As women move into the public world, they must accommodate this once-exclusive masculine domain to their own style and shape, so that the process of feminization can continue to revitalize American culture.

2. FEMININE AS
A SECOND LANGUAGE

The feminization of American culture has intensified our awareness of the difference between male and female styles of communication and of the linkage between this linguistic dualism and social change. The realization that men and women speak different languages is as ancient as the spoken word, but it is only in recent years, as women have been entering public life, that systematic research has begun to shed light on the role of language in the age-old problem of male-female misunderstanding.

The language gap between men and women has been attributed to a mix of biological and cultural factors. The biological explanation is derived from research in left brain–right brain functioning, the left brain being the hemisphere controlling visual-spatial skills, the right brain governing language ability. "The female [brain] may be less lateralized and tightly organized than the male brain," says Jerre Levy, biopsychologist at the University of Chicago. "The hemispheres of the female brain seem to be less functionally distinct from each other and more diffusely organized. And switching between them seems easier." This would account, at least in part, for women's greater flexibility and integrative aptitude.[1]

The cultural explanation proceeds from the relations between the sexes and their socialization into male-female roles and behavioral styles. Language reflects the social position of men and women; as linguists Barrie Thorne and Nancy Henley state,

> It is intimately bound up with the social differentiation of the sexes, with the structure of male dominance, expressed and maintained through language *about* women and men, as well as in the ways men and women use speech, and with the division of labor by sex. The fact of male dominance—built into the economic, family, political and legal structures of society —is also central to speech. Language helps enact and transmit every type of inequality, including that between the sexes; it is part of the "micropolitical structure" which helps maintain the larger political-economic structure.[2]

Most researchers agree that culture outweighs biology in the development of language. According to Jacques Lacan, the French psychoanalyst, it is through the acquisition of language that we are located as female or male into a social structure. As we learn our language, we become aware of the preexisting culture into which we were born—its values, its laws, and how the masculine-feminine polarity functions. Lacan argues that the "symbolic order" governs the total pattern of social relatedness, superimposing culture upon nature.

As Lacan and other sociolinguists maintain, language is more than a means of communication. It is a mirror of how a society thinks, what it values, how it structures relationships. Through language, we shape and articulate experience, transform reality, weave complex webs of social interaction. Language signals who we are: our age, social position, education, occupation, ethnic origin, gender—in short, our personal and cultural history. Language has the power "to realize a world," write Peter Berger and Thomas Luckman in their study of the social construction of reality, "not only to apprehend it but actually to produce the world."

When Shaw's Henry Higgins proved that he could pass a cockney girl off as a duchess through speech training alone, he made the mistake of treating language as nothing more than a technical skill. Eliza knew better. In her face-off with her mentor, she reminded him that language is a vehicle for conveying humanness, for exchanging affection and respect. For Professor Higgins, Eliza's successful phonetic emulation of an upper-class woman was simply a feather in his professional cap. For Eliza, it was a means of establishing a relationship between them: "I did it because we were pleasant together and I come [correcting herself]—came—to care for you."

Eliza discovered what many women have long suspected, that men and women use language differently, that there is a special female language. As one woman we interviewed said: "With men, you're always translating." Rebecca Novelli, a West Coast marketing executive, explains it this way: "When I want to discuss a situation with a woman, I ask her questions like What does this mean? Why is it happening? Why do I feel this way? If I were talking to a man, I'd say, Here's the situation . . . what do you think? I wouldn't discuss how I feel about it as I would with a woman."

THE BILINGUAL WOMAN

> The way the female world uses language in speech reflects a characteristic style of bonding, collaborative rather than competitive.
> —JESSIE BERNARD, *The Female World*

"American-English not only is sexually denigrating of women but is also a vehicle for asserting male superiority," says sociologist Jessie Bernard. She describes it as a "sexually inadequate language . . . inadequate for expressing a wide gamut of female experience, which puts women at a great disadvantage in understanding themselves, let alone in communicating with others."[3]

Since language and culture are closely intertwined, women

have developed their own style of communication, a language of liminality—subtle, covert, wary, deferential, egalitarian. The talk is diffuse, fragmented, interrupted again and again by a child's cry or the soup boiling over on the stove, yet the fragments fit together in a pattern of communication that is unmistakably feminine. Women talk to each other to establish contact; the connection itself has value, which is why the feminine discursive style often seems to be rambling, chatty, open-ended.

Masculine language, by contrast, is firm, crisp, purposeful. Men, long identified with authority and power, use language assertively. Their talk is uninterrupted by hesitant qualifiers ("I think," "maybe"), and their sentences almost never end with the tag question, "Don't you think so?" that marks women's speech. In masculine speech, words are frequently used as power tools: "I made a killing on the market"; "When I'm closing a deal, I go for the jugular."

Of course, competitiveness is not entirely lacking in women's talk. In the domestic world, women's language has always included an element of what one woman calls "comparativeness"—my children, my cooking skills, my husband's achievements versus yours —that bears a striking resemblance to competitiveness. But since women have been socialized to regard competition as unfeminine, it does not intrude into their talk as frequently or as blatantly as in masculine discourse. For the most part, women tend to build on rather than challenge others' statements.

Because of women's long dependence upon the masculine system, which has excluded them even from its language, they have been forced to become, in effect, bilingual—to communicate in a particular style when they are participating in the public world and in a very different style when within their own feminine world. The shift from one mode of discourse to another is performed through a kind of simultaneous translation that is part of a woman's thought processes, developed as a result of socialization beginning in childhood.

Until the age of five, with the mother as the dominant influence, both boys and girls speak the "mother language," the natal tongue. The fact that the mother tongue (there is no "father tongue'') is our earliest source of linguistic nourishment testifies to the potency of feminine imprinting upon the child. Psychoanalyst Ralph Greenson has suggested that ''speech is on the one hand a means of retaining a connection with the mother as well as a means of becoming separated from her. The child who suckled at the mother's breast now replaces this by introjecting a new liquid of the mother—sounds. It can easily be imagined, therefore, that the earliest relationship between child and mother's breast will have a decisive influence on the relationship of the child to the mother tongue.''

From the age of five, the linguistic separation between male and female begins. Boys are encouraged to adopt the masculine style of speech, while girls are admonished to speak politely, keep their voices down, avoid ''rough talk.'' Boys learn to drop their g's (throwin', runnin') and acquire a basic vocabulary of profanity. Their talk is direct, forceful (''Watch where you're goin' '' . . . ''Get outta my way'' . . . ''Gimme that ball''). Little girls, by contrast, talk politely (''Could I please play with you?''). As they grow older, girls also begin learning what Jon Stewart, an editor of the ''California Living'' supplement to the *San Francisco Sunday Examiner*, describes as ''womanwords that would burn the tongue of a boy or man: the lexicon of non-primary colors, such as 'mauve,' 'magenta,' and 'puce,' and the wonderful empty adjectives that are *so* feminine like 'dear,' 'stunning,' 'darling,' 'adorable.' ''[4]

By the age of ten, according to linguist Robin Lakoff, the male and female languages are already present; at this age, girls begin demonstrating superior linguistic abilities, outscoring boys in all tests involving language skills. (One explanation for this disparity is that girls are more affiliative and spend more time interacting with their friends.)

But this superior language facility that girls demonstrate does not, as we might expect, set a standard for boys' linguistic development. In fact, while boys continue speaking in the socially approved masculine mode in both same-sex and male-female interactions, girls, as they discover that feminine speech is held in low esteem outside the female world, begin developing a second language patterned after the masculine style for communicating with the dominant culture. As women become more and more absorbed into the mainstream, the masculine style of speech becomes their first language, and feminine speech takes second place in their linguistic scale of priorities, relegated to increasingly infrequent all-female social occasions.

LANGUAGE AND GENDER

In cultures where language segregation by sex is formally sanctioned, the marking off of female from male speech is symbolic of the social order. More than forty years ago, anthropologist Mary Haas reported systematic differences between the speech of men and women (middle aged and older) using Kosati, an American Indian language spoken in southwestern Louisiana. In another instance, women of the Laymi Indians in the Central Bolivian highlands are excluded from politics and are not permitted to speak directly to the spirits, because as women they are considered to be incapable of the formal speech commanded by men. In Arabic, pronunciation of certain words denotes masculinity or femininity. Women in Darkhat Mongol pronounce back and mid vowels differently from men.

In our technologically advanced society, which subscribes overtly to an ideology of egalitarianism, language segregation by sex is unrecognized as such, and there are no formal syntactic constructions that set women's speech apart from men's. Anthropologist Stephen Tyler has suggested that, in general, the systematic marking off of social relationships through language structure can be maintained only in societies in which roles are clearly delineated and social identity is relatively unambiguous. In fluid social systems such as ours, language segregation, whether based on social distinction or gender, is informal and unofficial, reflecting, as in masculine and feminine speech, cultural differences that shape perception and group identity.

Systematic study of the language-gender connection has affirmed a long-suspected phenomenon, that since gender is a major component of identity, the acquisition of masculine or feminine speech patterns has a significant effect on the perception of the self, or what linguists refer to as the "language ego." Children, for example, who have not yet firmly marked themselves off from the rest of the world as separate entities, possess ego boundaries that are far more flexible, and they are therefore readily receptive to acquiring a new language culture. As one matures, however, a concept of self is more and more carefully outlined, essentially by means of language that plays a fundamental role in the emergence of consciousness, the development of a sense of self, and the establishment of conscience.[5] So language, in effect, helps to create and perpetuate both the self in its singular form and the interaction of selves that we call culture.

Because women's ego boundaries in traditional feminine culture have been more flexible than men's—reflecting the ambiguity of the feminine as compared with the masculine role—women have been better able to develop bilinguality. The effect of this ambilinguistic facility upon the formation of feminine identity is a matter of dispute, but a growing body of evidence suggests that women undergo an inner shift as they switch from one language to the other.

"I feel strong and capable when I'm having a discussion with women, but when I'm talking to a man or I'm in a meeting with several men, something in me shuts down and I become soft, weak, incompetent." This theme with minor variations came through in our interviews with women of various ages and occupations. "Women tend to have low self-esteem among men and high self-esteem among women," says Patrice French, a specialist in the psychology of communication.

The male tendency to monopolize the conversation belies what is probably the most persistent myth about women's speech, that women are more talkative than men. In fact, in male-female discourse, studies show that it is men who constantly interrupt women. Dale Spender in *Man Made Language* reports on a study that found that "when women talked to men, they experienced a reduction in their overall talking time, a restriction in the range of topics they could talk about as they attempted to cater to men's interests, and restrictions in their style as they attempted to speak in a manner which was acceptable to men. These limitations do not seem to apply when women talk to women.'' (Susan Brownmiller suggests that tonal quality may have something to do with why women are interrupted more than men: the low-pitched masculine tones sound more authoritative, as if they are conveying something important enough to override whatever is being conveyed in the softer, higher-pitched feminine tones.)

Women agree, almost without exception, that their hidden and authentic selves emerge fully in woman-to-woman talk but rarely when they interact with men, even men with whom they have close and loving relationships. A common refrain is, ''I love my husband [or boyfriend] but there are many things I can't discuss with him.''

''Women have an astonishing capacity for bringing truths to each other,'' comments theater producer Naomi Pollack,

> holding up hard truths that are normally not looked at. Women are dedicated to growth—it goes with their responsibility for life—and growth requires facing up to yourself and others with honesty and courage. I think that's why women are such good listeners. It's important for us to hear, really hear, what's being said to us.
>
> Men do not get into the energy of what I would call participatory listening, the kind of listening that adds intelligence to the conversation. But this happens frequently with women. They look at an experience and share their understanding of it with me, and I feel I've gained something from the exchange. Even with the most brilliant men I know, I end up feeling stupid when I talk to them. The way they listen simply does not contribute, so I feel left alone in the talk.

The special way women listen—the eye contact, nods of the head, responsive facial expressions and gestures, these communication patterns that reflect traditional feminine attributes of nurturing and supportiveness—has been ascribed to the historic male-female behavioral pattern: he acts, she reacts. In their study of nonverbal communication, Marianne La France and Clara Mayo support this thesis: "Considering the fact that this society assigns the responsive role to women, you might well expect that women are better at tuning in to others' emotional states. Research consistently bears this out. In order to be responsive and reactive to others, it is necessary to sense what the other person is feeling. This sensitivity is perhaps less important if your stance is proactive, and that may be why men don't show as much decoding skill."[6]

THE UNSPOKEN LANGUAGE

Language encompasses not only the spoken and written word but also nonverbal communication, or body language, clothing, even the way we walk and style our hair—the totality of what sociologist Erving Goffman refers to as "the presentation of self." In all of these aspects of communication, the feminine style differs from the masculine. Women and men occupy not only two different semantic systems but also two different semiotic systems—semiotic being the mode of communicating by signs and symbols, which often speak louder than words.

Because the desire to make contact is so important to women, they express their affiliative need throughout their communicative style: they talk in a soft voice, lean toward each other, establish heightened eye contact. They smile more frequently than men, nod their heads encouragingly, and participate actively in the conversation even when others are speaking through gestures and facial expressions.

Tests of nonverbal sensitivity have shown that women have a higher response level to visual cues than men and are, therefore, more accurate in interpreting the meanings behind nonverbal behavior. The reasons are not hard to find.

From their early years onward, women are trained to decode nonverbal behavior. As little girls, they observe how their mothers and other women in the family interpret and respond to behavioral cues in their interaction with each other, and particularly with the male world. Their budding awareness is shaped by social expectations that convey the message that femininity is synonymous with supersensitivity to the needs of others.

Motherhood is, of course, a valuable training ground for translating and interpreting body language. During the infant's early preverbal stage, a woman must learn to decipher cues from the infant's body, facial expressions, and vocal tones. She must learn to read her child's responses in endlessly changing, exceedingly subtle signs—the web of facial expressions, body states, temperatures, tension, sounds, the smell and texture of bodily emissions that comprise a nonverbal vocabulary; her child's survival ultimately depends on her ability to comprehend these signs and respond appropriately.

But whether or not she has children, a woman's feminine sensibility equips her with special sensory antennae to pick up the meanings behind facial and body expressions; it is an evolutionary adaptation common to outsiders who are dependent upon the approval of those inside the system. As with verbal communication, feminine nonverbal communication also is bilingual, shifting from same-sex to cross-sex encounters. In all-female situations, women assume relaxed postures—they sprawl, sit with legs apart, gesticulate, touch each other frequently, hug, grin broadly, and generally exhibit the behavior of people who are, for the moment, free from constraints. Since women report feeling less "feminine" when in the company of other women, in the sense of not having to adhere to sex-typed roles, their behavior shifts from reactive to active, and their body talk strips away facades and pretenses, revealing their authentic sense of who they are.

TOWARD A LANGUAGE OF EQUALITY

The constitutional right to freedom of speech does not include a provision for equal speech, a consideration that would hardly have occurred to the founding fathers. But equality of speech, it can be argued, is as important for a democratic society as freedom of speech; in fact, one can hardly exist without the other.

The inequality of our language surfaced as a public issue during the late 1960s, borne aloft by a rising feminist consciousness. Linguist Ethel Strainchamps emphasized the need for linguistic reform in her indictment of English, a language spoken in the most thoroughly technological society, "which retains more vestiges of archaic sexual attitudes than any other civilized tongue." In *Language and Woman's Place*, Robin Lakoff identifies two ways in which women experience linguistic discrimination: in the way they are taught to use language and in the way language treats them, both tending to relegate them to subservient functions.[7]

A widely accepted linguistic principle is that, as culture changes, so will language. And changes *are* occurring, particularly in the direction of equalizing verbal communication, an important first step in humanizing the language. With women going public, many words and expressions in common usage have begun to strike our ears with a dissonance that has sent reverberations throughout the public realm: such titles as "Miss" and "Mrs." (versus the neutral "Mr."); "mankind" for "humanity"; "postman" and "chairman" regardless of gender; "girl" regardless of age; the indiscriminate use of the masculine pronoun. By the mid 1970s, it was generally acknowledged that these usages were out of touch with the reality of our society. The time was ripe for a change in the language that would rid it of its centuries-old misogyny.

The degenderizing of the language, officially as well as informally, has been a momentous development; for the first time in our history, there has been a conscious effort to narrow the language gap between men and women. A milestone in this reform movement was the 1974 convention of the National Council of Teachers of English, when that organization gave its blessing to a new linguistic era by adopting a set of guidelines for the nonsexist use of language. The resolution was prefaced by a statement that defined sexism as "words or actions that arbitrarily assign roles or characteristics to people on the basis of sex. Originally used to refer to practices that discriminated against women, the term now includes any usage that unfairly delimits the aspirations or attributes of either sex.''

The statement went on to make an eloquent plea for a more feeling, more humanistic language:

> Neither men nor women can reach their full potential when men are conditioned to be only aggressive, analytical, and active and women are conditioned to be only submissive, emotional, and passive. The man who cannot cry and the woman who cannot command are equally victims of their socialization. Language plays a central role in socialization, for it helps teach children the roles that are expected of them. Through language, children conceptualize their ideas and feelings about themselves and their world. Thought and action are reflected in words, and words in turn condition how a person thinks and acts. Eliminating sexist language will not eliminate sexist conduct, but as the language is liberated from sexist usages and assumptions, women and men will begin to share more equal, active, caring roles.

Examples of nonsexist usage offered by the guidelines follow:

SEXIST TERM	ALTERNATIVES
Mankind	Humanity, human beings, people
Man's achievements	Human achievements
Man-made	Synthetic, manufactured, crafted, machine-made
The common man	The average person, ordinary people

Today, the use of nonsexist terminology is accepted as a matter of course. Many publishing firms require authors to write in nonsexist fashion and provide guidelines for the purpose, similar to those of the NCTE. Dictionaries, newspaper-style guides, advertising copy, and English handbooks have quickly followed suit. Sexist terminology has been virtually eliminated from state constitutions and both state and federal documents. A new translation of the Bible issued by the National Council of Churches in 1983 refers to God as both the mother and father of mankind and to the Son of God as the Child or the Human One. Writers, teachers, speakers, business executives of both sexes have begun using language that is gender-neutral. Most business letters no longer begin with the salutation "Gentlemen"—it has either been eliminated or replaced by "Ladies and gentlemen." Pejorative terms like "old maid" and "spinster" are being replaced by "single woman."

The use of sexually discriminatory language in the courtroom —for example, addressing female judges, witnesses or litigants by their first names or as "honey" or "sweetie"—has diminished considerably with the tripling of women judges between 1970 and 1980. The elimination of such denigratory language in court is a goal of the National Association of Women Judges, whose members include Supreme Court Justice Sandra Day O'Connor.

The divisive language of sexism is on the wane, and within a brief period of time we have made remarkable strides toward achieving a language of equality. New studies reported by the American Psychological Association in 1983 revealed a number of ways in which reforms have entered our lives:

Forty-four percent of the people surveyed said they had tried to change their language to make it less sexist, and 31 percent said the English language needs a new sex-neutral pronoun.

The use of computer programs as "sexist-language watchdogs" is growing, and some professional organizations, including the APA, have enacted stringent guidelines against using pseudogeneric terms such as "he."

Teachers and others who serve as role models and forbid

students to use sexist language have a strong impact and often change their students' language patterns.

These linguistic reforms may not in themselves transform the fundamental power structure, but they are providing men and women with new cultural definitions of who they are and with a language that is expressive of their changing relationships.

HUMANIZING THE LANGUAGE

In recent years, with the growing feminization of our culture, it has become apparent that the linguistic subordination and denigration of women has worked to men's disadvantage as well as women's, depriving men of the use of language as it was intended to be used: to make connection and promote understanding. Masculine power talk is often concealing rather than revealing. The process of developing a facade of superior strength and control results in a style of speech that, along with its sexism, is guarded and flattened out, so that it tends to frustrate rather than promote communication. Tom Wolfe, in *The Right Stuff,* calls it an ''amputated language,'' a language that distances and divides.

A system of communication that brings clarity out of confusion and reduces levels of tension is a critical need in our complex, angst-ridden society, and a language of sexual equality is a significant step in that direction. But the feminizing of our language can take us beyond degenderization toward a more humanistic mode of communication, a language of understanding and empathy. We are witnessing some evidence of a reevaluation by men of the concealing, competitive power talk of masculine culture.

With women working alongside them, men are beginning to listen to what women say and how they say it—and linguistic change registers in the ear before it travels to the tongue. Thorne and Henley report from their review of the research that ''men who are discontented with traditional notions of masculinity often refer enviously to the greater ability of women to express emotions and to engage in personal self-disclosure.'' In newspaper and magazine articles, men express envy of women's style of communication, a longing for what Jon Stewart calls ''the rich and sensual language our mothers taught us. I like womantalk,'' he says, ''I love to listen to women talk to one another. How they speak, as much as what they say, reminds me that they live in another world, one which sometimes makes my own look rather barren.'' Novelist Irving Wallace says, ''Listen to women and you touch many new discoveries. Many women are never given a chance to talk. They're seldom given points for being whole persons with working lives.'' Several men told us that, through increasing contacts with women as peers in the workplace, they are beginning to notice a change in their own speaking style: it is becoming less constrained, more open and energetic.

We believe it is more than mere coincidence that, as women have moved into executive ranks, corporations have discovered information flow to be as important to a company's health as cash flow and have been promoting the style of intimate, informal communication associated with feminine culture. At Walt Disney Productions, everyone including the president wears a name tag bearing his or her first name. Corning Glass has installed escalators instead of elevators in its new engineering building to promote face-to-face contacts among its employees. In one company, four-person round tables in the company dining room have been replaced by long, rectangular army mess tables; the president of the company has explained, ''At a little round table, four people who already know each other will sit down and eat lunch with each other, day in and day out. With long mess tables, strangers come in contact.''[8]

If this trend toward closer, more authentic discourse continues, we may even see in the not-too-distant future a concerted effort to clear away the ''bureaucratese'' emanating from the traditionally masculine domains of business and government, that language of evasion that has settled over our communication environment like a thick cloud of verbal smog. Such terminology as ''team play'' instead of ''working together,'' ''secondary labor market'' for "unemployed," or "peacekeeper" for "nuclear missile" represent the extension of language as a coverup. Feminization, with its predilection for talk that reveals and connects, can protect our communication system from verbal distortion and restore it to its intended function as human connective tissue.

PRESERVING THE MOTHER TONGUE

The development of a more humanistic language is dependent upon the preservation of the warm, nourishing "mother tongue" of feminine culture and its continuing infusion into the mainstream. But despite encouraging signs of progress, there are those who are not entirely optimistic about the future of women's language. Robin Lakoff, for example, takes a dim view of woman's bilinguality. "Shifting from one language to another requires special alertness to the nuances of social situations, special alertness to possible disapproval. It may be that the extra energy that must be (subconsciously or otherwise) expended in this game is energy sapped from more creative work, and hinders women from expressing themselves as well, as fully, or as freely as they might otherwise."[9]

Other problems in feminine bilingualism are coming to the fore as women leave their private domestic world and join men in the public sphere. The "double talk" that is a product of a two-tier society, in which feminine and masculine interests and activities are widely divergent, becomes a barrier to effective communication in an integrated social and economic system, the ideal toward which American society is steadily moving. In such a society, with men and women sharing equally in family, community, and economic responsibilities, it is essential that they be able to communicate with each other in a common language.

When immigrants become assimilated into a society, they are usually quick to discard their native tongue in favor of the language of their adopted country. Longstanding controversies over "black English" and bilingualism in schools with large Hispanic populations testify to the depth of feeling that surrounds the loss of linguistic culture. Nevertheless, the dominant language invariably wins out as the immigrants are absorbed into the mainstream, and the native language is confined to ever-decreasing pockets of ethnic populations.

Is this the linguistic future that awaits feminine language, the style of discourse that has evolved through the centuries as an expression of women's warm and nourishing culture? One doesn't have to look far to find evidence of feminine talk patterning itself after the masculine mode. The executive suites, expense-account restaurants, and other formerly all-male habitats today echo with profanity, scatological terms, and a Hobbesian vocabulary of self-aggrandizement and competitiveness, all uttered in unmistakably feminine voices. In her book on corporate gamesmanship, *Games Mother Never Taught You,* Betty Harragan advises women to "learn the men's language and translate *to* them. Theoretically men shouldn't object; they keep saying that women aren't assertive or aggressive enough in business."[10] If women become convinced that using a style of speech devalued by the mainstream works to their disadvantage, is there not a real danger that womantalk will disappear or be relegated to the outer fringes of linguistic usage, a "quaint dialect" like Yiddish?

The danger is there, of course, just as it exists wherever women adopt male values uncritically and unselectively in the hope of shedding their "otherness" and gaining acceptance in the public world. But in discarding their language of empathy and connection, it is not only women who will be the losers but men as well, and with them very possibly our hope for achieving more egalitarian, more compassionate male-female relationships.

In an impersonal and isolating world, it is a matter of urgency for women's language not only to be preserved but to be granted the recognition it has so long been denied. Certainly, the feminine style of communication will undergo change as women adapt themselves to the public world; some of this adaptation is necessary and desirable and in keeping with women's new roles and responsibilities. But as men develop a deeper understanding and appreciation of feminine language, there is reason to believe from what we are seeing in the early stages of this process that they will absorb its affiliative, self-revealing nuances into their own style of discourse. The result will be a blended language that is truly egalitarian and that expresses the full human experience. When that comes to pass, the need for woman's bilinguality will disappear, and men and women will finally, for the first time in history, be speaking the same language.

3. FEMININE FRIENDSHIP:
The Art of Intimacy

*Friendship, which in our society is most highly
developed in women, is the finest possible human
work. Not directly necessitated by those primal,
biological or social drives which generate family,
work or love relationships, friendship arises from
the human ability to enact the love for another
for its own sake.*

—DEENA METZGER, *writer, teacher*

Friendship is being examined today from a variety of perspectives: as a key to the development of sexuality, as a barometer of social change, even as a therapeutic tool. This growing interest, stimulated by the feminization of our culture, has been fostering a changing attitude toward women's friendships. Once ignored or even ridiculed, these feminine affiliations are now being viewed as a possible antidote to the alienating, depersonalizing effects of the dominant, male-controlled culture.

By all accounts, there is in America today a desperate and growing loneliness. We are a people who pride ourselves on our openness, warmth, sincerity, enthusiasm—qualities that people in other cultures often mistake for friendship. But the high divorce rate, postponed marriages, decline of extended families and neighborhoods add up to more and more people living alone—and as longevity is extended, more and more people dying alone.

"The Search for Intimacy" and "The Broken Heart: Medical Consequences of Loneliness" are topics of books, seminars, support groups, workshops, and studies. Current research and analyses are confirming what women have always realized, that intimacy is absolutely critical to human existence. Infants do not survive without touching, fondling, and cuddling, however ideal the environmental conditions. For the development of self-worth and the establishment of personal identity, intimacy and friendship are requisite.

However, American mainstream culture has not encouraged intimacy. Rugged self-reliance has been deeply embedded in our national self-image. The American hero is revered for his solo achievements, single-handedly defeating the forces of evil (the classic example being Gary Cooper in *High Noon)*. Examples of group heroism are rare in American mythic thought.

The cult of self-aggrandizing individualism not only sets the individual above the group, it disconnects the communal ties that in most societies have bound people together. Mobility, competitiveness, the emphasis on the self—what Christopher Lasch calls "the narcissistic personality"—these attributes of contemporary American life intensify the individualistic impulse.

Sociologist Philip Slater, in his classic study, *The Pursuit of Loneliness,* locates the roots of this extreme form of individualism in "the attempt to deny the reality and importance of human interdependence," a denial that ignores the fact that the individual, like a group, "is a motley collection of ambivalent feelings, contradictory needs and values and antithetical ideas."[1] Slater's contention is confirmed in a recently released five-year study conducted by sociologist Robert Bellah and other scholars in sociology, theology, and philosophy, which found, in interviewing white middle-class Americans, that many people in this country have been swept away by "radical individualism," which makes them incapable of commitment to our most basic institutions of marriage, family, religion, and politics. As a result, according to one psychotherapist they interviewed, "In the end you're really alone, and you have no one to answer to but yourself."[2]

To be really alone, however, is unbearable for most of us. Human beings are social animals, to paraphrase Aristotle. Our earliest societies were tribal, and survival was linked to interdependence. Throughout history, people in most parts of the world have been part of a larger collectivity—a clan, a polis, a commune. Though the forms of social aggregation have varied at different times and in different cultures, the need for some kind of association appears to be as universal as the need for food or sex.

FRIENDSHIP, FEMININE STYLE

> Sartre: With men I was quite ready to stop talking once what had to be said on politics or something of that kind had been said. It seems to me that two hours of a man's company in a day, and without seeing him the next day, is quite enough. Whereas with a woman it can go on all day long and then start tomorrow.
>
> de Beauvoir: Yes, because it's based on that intimacy, of the near-possession of her being by means of the feeling she has for you.
>
> —SIMONE DE BEAUVOIR, *in Adieu: A Farewell to Sartre,*
> *Recorded Conversations with de Beauvoir and Sartre in 1974*

Today, voluntary ties of friendship are emerging as the form of bonding most compatible with contemporary American culture; friendship makes a better fit with our society's commitment to individual choice than the associations of kinship or religion that bound the individual to the social unit in premodern times. Unlike these formal, institutionalized relationships, friendship is based on choice, affection, trust, and equality. It can be terminated without legal consequences and often without accountability. It can be expanded to include others but it is usually most intense when confined to a two-person bond, that privileged connection between "best friends."

Though it has many distinctive characteristics, feminine friendship takes place within the larger context of our contemporary culture, a context in which intimacy is languishing. But women, the major providers of intimacy, do not want to, perhaps cannot, live without it; hence they turn to each other, to their women friends. When pressed, women will mention disappointments in their friendships, betrayals, abandonments, competitition, and envy, but these negative aspects never seem to outweigh their enthusiasm and gratitude. Constancy, trust, freedom, acceptance, exhilaration, and psychological support are the themes they return to as they talk eagerly and in detail about their friendships with women.

As far back as the records go, we see that women have been the archetypical givers—of emotion, attention, nurturance, nonjudgmental love; it is women who have been responsible for restoring the exhausted, the injured, the needy man or child. Being needed became woman's justification, her profession, and in many instances her bondage. But whatever the cost as she gave herself away to others, it seems women have always been able to turn this back to one another, and never more so than now, when the social underpinnings of women's domestic world are giving way under the pressures of changing sex roles and relationships.

Some scholars feel that women turned away from each other during the decades between the beginning of this century and the new women's movement of the 1960s; they were isolated from one another due to the growing insularity of the nuclear family and the popular image of a woman's husband as her best friend. Others maintain that women never grew indifferent to friendship with other women; it was rather that without the social support of the women's movement, feminine friendships were either unnoticed or devalued.

Certainly, the chronic underreporting of the female realm has left large gaps in our understanding of those day-to-day activities and relationships among women that have structured and maintained family and community life from earliest human history. But as the course of feminization has taken scholars into what historian Fernand Braudel calls "the structures of everyday life," these previously unexplored areas are yielding ample documentation of women's friendships, particularly as we move toward the modern era.

In the nineteenth century, friendships were an indispensable source of sustenance for women. Many of these friendships began in early adolescence and, despite subsequent marriages and geographic separation, continued throughout the women's lives. The diaries of eighteenth- and nineteenth-century women reveal a depth of emotional attachment and dependency that reflects a social system of rigid gender-role divisions within family and community and a pattern of emotional segregation of the sexes. Within this tightly constricted social structure, friendships among women provided a support system that bound them together through the biological cycle of frequent pregnancies, childbirth, child-rearing, menopause, and old age.

Nineteenth-century women expressed their feelings for each other unrestrainedly. Letters between close friends contained such effusions as, "How do I love you . . . you are the joy of my life. . . . My darling, how I long for the time when I shall see you. . . . If the day should come when you failed me either through your fault or my own, I would forswear all human friendship, thenceforth. . . ."[3]

The radical segregation of male and female worlds that followed the industrial revolution segregated human capabilities, dividing them up between the sexes. Women took charge of everything left over from the world of work. The development of what Jessie Bernard calls "the female world" and its ideology, "the cult of domesticity," was the arena in which women became professional and full-time caretakers. For the first time in history this became possible, since before that women had been "so busy contributing to the family's subsistence income that they could not be restricted to the household."[4]

As men were pulled into the factory and marketplace and as physical mobility intensified, previous forms of human bonding began to crumble. Mechanization, urbanization, secularism, the growing cult of individualism and free enterprise, intense competition, a diversification in the division of labor—these developing economic forces disrupted the kin-based local communities in which human beings had lived throughout history. Life was never again to be lived among a limited number of known, related people, integrated by common ways and beliefs. The social form known as *Gemeinschaft,* community, gave way to *Gesellschaft,* congeries of strangers relating to each other piecemeal, impersonally, as role players instead of as familiar beings bound by a common moral sense.

Today as in the past, women look to their friends for sympathy and assistance with personal or family-related problems. The mother of small children today may be divorced or unmarried, or she may be remarried and coping with the problems of a blended family. Whatever her marital situation, she is likely to be working full- or part-time, struggling to balance work and motherhood. The working mother feels a special sense of isolation; she is cut off from her single or married but childless colleagues and is also removed from full-time mothers who learn from each other and lend support over the backyard fence or at the sandbox.

Working mothers, therefore, gravitate to each other and develop ties that serve as their communication channels to vitally needed information about child care. They use their lunch hours and coffee breaks, and they linger in the rest room to exchange funny baby stories and discover that their children's problems are not unique. These casual encounters frequently develop into strong and lasting friendships that move beyond the original child-related bond, establishing themselves on a broad sense of mutual interests and empathic ties.

The friendships of single women have also gained new importance as a result of the breakdown of the traditional family structure. The single childless woman may value her independence, as many do, but her financial self-sufficiency and her wide range of social and sexual options do not mitigate her need for the closeness and nonjudgmental understanding that is special to feminine friendship. The single woman looks to her friends for the kind of caring and emotional support that had previously been provided by either her family or her husband. The woman with an absorbing, fulfilling, high-paying career shares with the domesticated woman of the past the lifelong need for intimacy. For many women, it is a need that cannot be satisfied even by a loving relationship with a man.

THE NATURE OF INTIMACY

> Of course, I have moments of incredible intimacy with
> my husband, but I have to say these are usually sexual.
> And they are just moments. I have that kind of inti-
> macy with my women friends all the time, whenever
> we meet and talk. I feel so hungry for that kind of talk
> with my husband, and I've told him. He tries. He lis-
> tens to my problems and soothes my hurts, but he
> doesn't know how to give back and forth. He's afraid
> to take off his armor except for a few minutes at a
> time.

The woman quoted above speaks for many we interviewed who
admitted, often reluctantly, that something was missing from their
otherwise satisfying marriages. The "something," it usually turned
out, was the quality of intimacy, that ineffable interflow of understanding and empathy that appears to be indigenous to women's
friendships while foreign to personal relationships among men, and
often lacking between men and women. In the geography of gender, this female predisposition toward intimacy is the Great Divide
between the two cultures. A thirty-year-old woman in a middle
management position offers an example: "I was talking to a male
colleague recently about a friend of his, a man he'd known for
years. Since it had some relevance to his friend's problems, I asked
what he knew about the man's mother. 'I don't know anything
about his mother,' he said. 'I've never asked him and he's never
told me. We don't usually talk about these things.' I was incredu-
lous. I can't imagine a close friendship with a woman without intimacy at the deepest level, which means knowing who she is and
where she comes from.''

Women's affinity for the emotional dimension, the quality that
more than anything else distinguishes feminine from masculine language, is also an essential element in women's friendships; it combines individualism with cooperativeness through the mutual recognition of each other's uniqueness together with their commonality.

The ability to "feel what the other is feeling," as one woman described it, provides a sense of reassurance that they will always be there for each other and can be counted on at difficult times. Without this form of sustenance, many women say they do not know how they would have survived the crisis points in their lives.

A woman who went through a devastating divorce attributes her ultimate recovery from a mental breakdown to a woman friend with whom she has had a longstanding relationship. "She literally saved my life. She gave me a place to stay, she was my refuge. She'd known me long enough to be able to pinpoint my problems, and she helped me deal with them. I can't imagine a male friend doing this for me."

This fine-tuning to others, the ability to listen without judging, to understand without words, to defer one's own requirements to others' needs—why have these qualities, which are just beginning to be valued by the public world, traditionally been associated with women? Why are women often unable to keep themselves from empathy and identification, even when it is not in their best interest to do so?

Most often cited in answer to these questions is woman's experience with and programming for her task in assuring the perpetuation of the species in the form of care for her infant. A woman's mastery of interpersonal skills, like her aptitude for nonverbal communication, is acquired from the body-to-body experience that dominates the beginning of a mother's life with her child.

But women and girls who have not had the experience of nurturing an infant still show proclivities for intimacy in their relationships. Some biologically oriented interpretations point to the differences between men and women in brain functioning and morphology. The corpus callosum, the bundle of fibers that separates left- and right-brain hemispheres, is larger and more developed in the female brain, suggesting, as we mentioned in connection with women's language, that women use both sides of the brain more than men do, hence are less specialized in their thinking. This could incline women toward an integrated, intuitive understanding of the world instead of the either-or thinking and visual-spatial problem solving in which males excel.

Psychoanalytic research suggests that the difference between male-female and same-sex friendship behaviors may be rooted in the beginnings of gender identity. The eminent child psychiatrist Margaret S. Mahler and her colleagues found that mothers responded differently to the bodies of their girl babies than to those of their baby boys: the bodies of their infant girls felt more cuddly. The Mahler study does not take a position on "whether this feeling of mothers was culturally determined, or whether it was due to the fact that baby girls actually mold in a more pliable way than do boys; probably both. In any case, the feeling of the mother about her child's body may well have some early patterning influence."[5]

The adolescent stage, according to some psychoanalytic theorists, reinforces these early influences on the formation of gender identity. In order to establish his masculinity, the boy must reject his original identification with his mother and deny his original attachment and neediness for her. His erotic attachments continue to be through her to other women, as they must if he is to achieve heterosexual adulthood. But he must reject his erotic attachment to her, and in so doing, he also denies his emotions toward her and along with that toward all things associated with femininity.

The girl's psychosexual developmental requirements are the opposite. She must deny her erotic bond with her mother and shift it to a man, but her greater emotional investment remains with the mother, and the girl's identification with her as an appropriate role model remains intact. This switch in identity required for boys but not girls is one of the reasons men turn to women for nurturance and at the same time refuse to allow themselves to fully experience the dependence, vulnerability, and intimacy that came to them originally through the mother, the rejected parent.[6]

Another explanation for feminine friendship skills, which has been gaining support from recent anthropological studies, concerns a possible evolutionary adaptation predisposing women to close cooperation. It has been shown that women in Paleolithic times participated in the hunting technique of "stampede and surround," a practice that survives in contemporary hunting-and-gathering bands. And it has now been established that, far from being economically dependent on men for food, women have, in their gathering activities, provided the staples of the diet in band societies.

These findings contravene the androcentric man-the-hunter theories that attribute to males a superior bonding capability due to their early coordinated hunting and fighting activities. Once feminist scholars began looking for clues to women's early history, new questions and observations began appearing that challenged and amplified theories long regarded as final and unrefutable. We now have a much more complex picture than that suggested earlier; to the theory of man the hunter as the origin of male-female interpersonal differences we must now add woman the gatherer, woman the cohunter, woman the tool maker, woman the provider of most of the food, and woman the friend.

FEAR OF INTIMACY:
The Male Dilemma

Though male friendships have been glorified in Western history and legend—Achilles and Patrocles, David and Jonathan, Oliver and Roland—in reality, the lifelong friendships so common in feminine culture are rare among men in Western cultures, among whom friendships appear to be relatively short-lived and in many cases nonexistent. A team of social scientists who had studied a cross section of American men for ten years reported in 1978 that "in our interviews, friendship was generally noticeable by its absence. As a tentative generalization, we would say that close friendship with a man or woman is rarely experienced by American men." The researchers conclude from this portion of their study that there is a need to understand why friendship is so rare among men and what the consequences of this deprivation are for male adult life.[7]

In many non-Western cultures, male friendships are emotional and even passionate, and often last throughout the men's lives. Friendships in these societies are considered to be as important as marriage and are cemented with oaths, ritual, and ceremony. Ethnographer Robert Brain, in his study of the Chinautleco Indians of Guatemala, found that friendship, *camaradia,* reached its highest intensity at that stage of life when "young men achieve adult status without acquiring its emotional rewards. Most adolescents and young men have 'best friends' with whom they share secrets and ambitions and plan love affairs. Friendships are made and broken almost with the formality of a betrothal between a youth and his fiancée."[8]

The fear of intimacy among males in Western societies, confirmed in a number of similar studies, is bound up with the complex sociohistorical evolution of an asymmetrical relationship of men and women: men as economic custodians, women as emotional custodians. Psychotherapist Lillian Rubin reports, drawing on her research on the social psychology of intimacy, that interactions between men "are emotionally contained and controlled—a good fit with the social requirements of manly behavior." Rubin has found that even when a man claims a best friend, the two "share little about the interior of their lives and feelings. . . . When asked to explain their failure to speak of more personal matters with their friends, some men were quick to acknowledge that they couldn't share the pain they felt, couldn't risk allowing another man to see the vulnerability."[9]

The embarrassment that men feel about revealing intimate emotions comes through in the masculine style of expressing affection; the back thumping, punching, joking, and ritualized insults that men mete out to other men they care about can be understood as signs of regard. But these mannered forms of communication are a poor substitute for self-disclosure, asking for help, or sharing insights about one another. It is not simply that these are women's forms; men select and esteem the same terms for intimacy that women do and themselves indicate dissatisfaction with their friendships. But men are burdened with the impedimenta of a lifetime, which prohibit them from knowing how to establish intimacy and from finding other men who are willing to cooperate.

Intimacy, which means "to make known" and "innermost," by definition involves vulnerability, but American men have been taught from their earliest socialization to be outer-active, in control.

[47]

Vulnerability is seen as weakness, unmanly. Small boys play in groups where interactions tend to be less affective and intense, and this may lay the groundwork for a lifetime of diffuse emotionality. Their games are competitive; aggression and wariness are important, and expressions of pain, grief, disappointment are discouraged. As early as the age of three, boys organize themselves into hierarchical dominance systems, whereas girls of preschool age play in clusters that are devoid of any patterns of linear dominance.

When they begin attending school, girls pair up in their play activities, and in the safety of these twosomes practice loyalty, disclosure, spontaneity. At this time, the boy turns to his peer group and to competitive team sports for validation. He spends his time in highly sociable activities but does not learn to share personal concerns. His friendships with other boys are uncommitted, self-centered, and emotionally neutral. This guarded attitude toward friendship among adolescent boys has received official sanction from boys' preparatory schools, those exclusive enclaves that have served as the training ground for many of the nation's leaders. Choate, the New England school Jack Kennedy attended, had a strict code of behavior which, as described by David Michaelis in an account of Kennedy's boyhood friendship with Lemoyne Billings, scorned originality and sincerity. "In athletics, rivalry was the highest form of complementary affection. Emotional candor was suicidal. Digging for any level of intimacy was tantamount to digging a grave."[10]

It is not surprising that the adolescent boy sometimes feels isolated and seeks out a female companion, but he is uncomfortable revealing his inner self while she feels that anything else constitutes a superficial relationship. She is accustomed to long talks with a best friend, pledging commitment, exchanging confidences, smoothing out hurt feelings, exchanging gifts, talking about the relationship. Since childhood, she has easily declared her love for her friend; he cannot bring himself to tell his best friend that he likes him.

From the beginning, boys are trained to occupy the public world, to compete and fight in public arenas and avoid everything that threatens that preparation. Consequently, it becomes difficult, at times impossible, to extricate the private person from the public role; this total identification of the man with his occupation is what can make retirement so devastating for men, whereas women in later life have their friendships and a repertoire of personal and social resources that can serve to sustain them.

The identification of a man with his work tends also to undermine the trust and integrity forming the basic planks in the structure of friendship. A history professor who some years ago resigned as provost of a midwestern university in order to return to teaching recalls, somewhat ruefully: "The day after I handed in my resignation, people I had thought of as my friends disappeared." The experience taught him that "when you're in a position of power or influence, you have no way of knowing what motivates your friendships. In the past, women didn't have this problem, since they didn't occupy positions of public power. Their friendships were based entirely on personal factors. But now that they're taking on those positions, their friendships are coming under the same influences."

In a study of friendships between men and women, Robert Bell found that men "frequently see persons not as total human beings but as persons filling particular roles. They may see another man as a lawyer, a competitor in tennis, a coworker or a drinking partner. In this sense, many men do not see women as full human beings. Rather, they turn to their sets of role expectations and assign them to the woman in the light of the role in which they see her."[11]

"Therein lies the difference, I think, between my friendships with men and with women," says novelist-screenwriter Steve Tesich. "I can tell women I love them. Not only can I tell them, I am compulsive about it. I can hardly wait to tell them. But I can't tell the men. I just can't. Emotions are never nailed down. They run wild, and I and my male friends chase after them, on foot, on bicycles, in cars, keeping the quarry in sight but never catching up."[12]

It takes persistence, courage, *and* understanding of what intimate friendship looks like, as Stuart Miller discovered in his difficult quest for a close friend. In his book on men's friendships, he quotes a male friend who helped him learn the techniques: "As a psychiatrist and as a person, I would say the most important aspect of making a friendship is getting down. It's hard to get a man down. They want to stay on top, to avoid feelings, to avoid confrontation. They want to stay rational, professional, protected, and important. In analytic terms, they are afraid of the unconscious—the things that are never said, barely thought, shadows that haunt, the jealousies, the yearnings for depth.''[13]

Another haunting fear is the interpretation that our homophobic culture would be likely to place on a show of affection between men. In a *Newsweek* article on the scarcity of close and nurturing relations among men, the writer comments, ''Suddenly to be male and vulnerable is to be utterly acceptable—but only to women. . . . Let one male approach another with talk of needing a kindred spirit and the listener will start looking for the closet from which the speaker must have emerged.''[14]

Intimacy is viewed in masculine culture as a threat to personal privacy, and in the competitive, power-driven, male-controlled arenas of big business and government, the concern with privacy and secrecy amounts almost to an obsession. The personal life of every individual is based on secrecy, Anton Chekhov wrote; ''Perhaps it is partly for that reason,'' comments John Bayley in a review of Chekhov's *The Lady with the Little Dog*, ''that civilized man is so nervously anxious that personal privacy should be so respected.'' But privacy, carried to an extreme, shuts off channels of communication and imprisons the individual within a carefully guarded fortress of the self. Charles Fried, in *An Anatomy of Values*, casts the privacy-intimacy relationship in terms of a moral investment: ''To be friends or lovers, persons must be intimate to some degree with each other. Intimacy is the sharing of information about one's actions, beliefs or emotions which one does not share with all, and which one has the right not to share with anyone. By conferring this right, privacy creates moral capital which we spend on friendship and love.''

But there is one time in men's lives when the barriers to intimacy give way to friendship and love, the time of their military service. The nostalgia with which some men recall their war experience is usually induced by memories of their army buddies with whom, under conditions of extreme fear and tension, they shared their most intimate thoughts and feelings. "In the front lines, the friendships were deeper and closer," Freeman Dyson comments in *Weapons and Hope,* "the shared dangers and hardships brought men together as comrades and brothers."

Ever since the Trojan Wars, when Patrocles took Achilles' place in the battle lines, sacrificing his life for his friend, the war buddies theme has been grist for countless novels, plays, and films. It is a theme that has a special resonance for men: in confronting a common danger, carefully erected barriers to intimacy disappear, inhibitions evaporate, and as the men's authentic selves emerge, they experience the closeness and empathy that escape them in their civilian lives.

And when the fighting is over? Most of these wartime friendships end with the signing of a peace treaty. This is perhaps the most poignant aspect of the male dilemma, that in the loss and suffering of war, men learn to give and receive intimacy, something women have known and practiced throughout their lives.

CHANGING CONNECTIONS

The decade of the '80s is emerging as the era when, as feminization extends its influence, men are beginning to seriously question masculine culture in relation to its effect on the quality of their lives. Testifying to this upsurge of interest and concern is the spate of books, magazine articles, seminars, and full-length courses with such titles as "The Hazards of Being Male," "Men and Friendship," "Why Can't Men Open Up?," "Male Liberation," "The New Man." The relatively staid Sunday *New York Times Magazine* has instituted a regular one-page feature devoted exclusively to an exploration of men's changing lives. And now there is a syndicated newspaper column, by Jim Sanderson, "The Liberated Man," in which male angst is a favorite theme.

Moreover, men's groups, most of them supporting feminism and nonsexist roles, have begun appearing here and there. At a meeting last year in Washington, D.C., of the National Organization for Changing Men, workshop themes include Emotional Support and Intimacy; Men and Abortion Clinics; The Feminine Side: A Model or a Reality?; Healing the Wounded Father; Our Sons, Ourselves; Competition and Men: Sports Versus Play; and Masculinity and Survival. Although the meeting was described as having a "gay flavor," most of the men attending were heterosexual. One of them said, "I came here because I have a real desire to learn more about how to get men to open up, be emotional, stop abusing women, and stop killing themselves."

A fledgling men's movement, modeled after women's consciousness-raising groups of the '60s, emerged in the mid '70s and has continued into the '80s, coalescing into the National Congress for Men. This umbrella organization for 200 groups in the United States, Europe, and Australia has already had two national conferences. The organization's major concerns include nonsexist military; equality in law enforcement; prison reform; joint custody; veterans' problems; and flexible working hours. But discussions often center on personal concerns. A New York accountant whose marriage broke up after nineteen years found "support and guidance" in a seven-man support group. "Over the course of the last year we've really been able to talk about our feelings, and it's something that men, I've found, really needed."

A recurring motif in this search for the masculine self is male envy of women's intimacy. Stuart Miller discusses the yearning for his own kind of close attachments that his wife's friendships have aroused in him.

> What is it like not to have a close friend? Most men don't even notice. Docile, we have learned to accept our separation. But circumstances may arise that make us notice. A wife, touched by the women's movement perhaps, begins to form serious engagements with other women. You hear her talking on the phone as you watch television at night. Politely, she gets up and closes the door so you won't be disturbed. But you

are, somehow, even more disturbed. Occasionally, you hear the sound of a peculiarly hearty laughter that you don't have in your own life, laughter of a kind that your wife doesn't even share with you. A shadow falls across your consciousness but you don't know exactly what to do about it. You respect her new friendships but you are envious.[15]

Another man, an engineer married for twenty years, says:

Before I was married, I had a few friends, mostly men I worked with. But as the years went by, I lost touch with them. I figured my wife was my friend, I didn't need any others. I can talk to her about anything that's on my mind. And I'm not the outdoor-athletic type, so I don't need golf or fishing buddies. But it's not the same for her. She says she needs her women friends, that she doesn't expect from me what she gets from them. It makes me feel as though something's missing in my life.

In admitting that they envy women's friendships, men are acknowledging the damage they have suffered in relinquishing that part of their beings that has to do with what Jung calls the feminine principle. They are beginning to take a long, hard look at the experiences they have with each other and with women and are comparing them with what women have with each other. The same discrepancies appear again and again: women are intimacy givers and men are intimacy takers; women confide in each other and men confide in women or don't confide at all. Men are growing restless and embarrassed by the inescapable fact that, in this area at least, the sex roles are reversed: it is the men who are dependent, patronized, and indulged.

But changes are in the air that augur well for the development of intimacy in masculine culture. Some of this change is due to the growing appreciation, especially in the sciences and in management, of intuition and other nonrational approaches to knowing and solving problems. Philip Goldberg, business consultant and author of *The Intuitive Edge,* believes that the respect for inner feelings, which he attributes to the women's movement, has made it easier for men to have friendships with other men that are intimate and self-disclosing.

Men are also learning the art of intimacy through the experience of nurturing their children. As women have been combining work with motherhood, men—in some cases with no choice in the matter—have been trying to balance work with fatherhood. The father whose wife has a full-time job and the divorced father sharing custody are, often for the first time, experiencing the pleasures and burdens of parenting. They are also discovering that nurturing is not the exclusive domain of women, but can be developed with those one loves. Ciji Ware, author of a book on shared custody, saw her ex-husband transformed into a highly competent and devoted father when, in his own words, "I had to learn to be a mother after my divorce."

In researching her book, Ware came across a number of other divorced fathers having a similar experience. She found that these men, in learning to take a child's temperature, to dress, feed, and chauffeur the youngster to school, piano lessons, and dentist appointments, not only developed a new closeness with their children but also acquired a sense of competence and self-esteem. This proved to have an additional advantage: a father assured of not losing the bond with his child can relax the tension in the relationship with his ex-wife.[16]

Many of these "new fathers" are acquiring insights about feminity from their daughters and new definitions of masculinity from their sons, insights that can be transmitted to their friendships. The children can benefit too. As motherhood and fatherhood come into better balance, and as children's attachments to both parents become more evenly divided, separation anxiety may not necessarily be fixated on one or another parent. This may ease the separation trauma, which some psychologists believe can particularly help adolescent boys ameliorate, or perhaps even eliminate, one of the developmental barriers to male intimacy.

BRIDGING THE GENDER GAP

The fact that men are beginning to recognize that something important has been lacking in their lives is one of the more hopeful signs today. For the first time in our history, instead of women adapting themselves to the male style, men are looking over their shoulders at women's culture and finding in it some possible models for themselves. This is a promising development for both sexes, for so often the source of miscommunication between men and women that surfaces in their language differences resides in the disparity between the feminine ability to express intimacy and the masculine inability to do so. A standard feminine complaint is that, for men, sex makes for intimacy, while for women, intimacy leads to sex. This is why we believe that men who are willing to make even a tentative, groping effort to come to terms with the place of intimate friendships in their lives are on their way toward improved communication with women.

Based on interviews with several dozen men from California to New England, men widely varied in style and attitude, David Behrens was most impressed with "the care and caution with which many men examined problematic relationships, even if they often hesitated at the brink of self-revelation. Most of them seemed to be trying to unravel their feelings and to see the 'new woman' more clearly."[17]

With men and women working side by side and sharing responsibilities in both public and private worlds, men are beginning to see women as complex, many-faceted people rather than as unidimensional sexual creatures. Both men and women have been so heavily sexualized in our society that it is often difficult for them to reach beyond mutual suspicion and cynicism and see each other as whole human beings, capable of engaging in caring, supportive, nonjudgmental, nonmanipulative relationships. Basic inequalities between men and women make it difficult for them to communicate without sex intruding itself. A sexually separatist society fosters the "flight from feeling" that Christopher Lasch speaks of in *The Culture of Narcissism*.

[55]

But with feminization bringing about a sexually integrated society, men and women are seeing each other as vulnerable people, with depths and dimensions that transcend gender. Among the changing connections that are altering the social landscape are nonsexual friendships between men and women. Since the industrial revolution, the lives of men and women have intersected mainly at mealtime and bedtime. But today, with new focus on gender equality, Washington psychiatrist James Lieberman sees friendships between the sexes as a "broad-based social change in the ways men and women are relating."

It is the "sublime differences between men and women" that George Santayana in his *Little Essays* gave as the reason for seeking friends of the opposite sex. "Platonic friendships among men and women appear to be growing," says writer Barbara Mathias, who is researching a book on the subject. And Chicago journalist Michael Davis says, "Some of my best friends are women. . . . I have several loyal, loving, lifelong female friends, in addition to my wife, Sam. She has never been resentful of any of my female friends from work or elsewhere. To cut myself off from women simply because I said 'I do' one day would be to lose contact with roughly half the population of the planet. And wouldn't that be stupid?" Psychiatrist Anne Seiden adds, "Just as it's wonderful for a white person to have a close friend who is black and vice versa, it's great for a woman and man to be close friends. They can learn things about the other's life experience they'd never discover otherwise."

With feminine friendship serving as a model and guide for men, the bond of friendship is bridging the gender gap, and cross-sex friendships are growing along with same-sex friendships. The day may not be too far off when intimacy will be as much a part of men's lives as it is of women's, and impersonality and alienation will be replaced by more varied and vital interconnections throughout the social spectrum.

4. NEW NETWORKS:
Feminine Power Goes Public

Women used to consider networking unclean; it was synonymous for them with using people, "making contacts." It was morally pure to contact women for information on finding a pediatrician or for a bread recipe . . . but to do the same thing to advance your career—that was frowned upon. That's changing. Women are learning that there's a lot of satisfaction in making connections for people, bringing people together who have common interests and goals and having them do the same for you.
　　—SALLIE O'NEILL, *Director, LA Learning Network and founding member, Women in Business*

Women's friendships are being radically transformed by new linkages, or networks, and this cultural change is having a ripple effect, like a stream that gathers force as it flows through narrows and over waterfalls, slowly and steadily altering the landscape in its path. The feminization of American culture probably owes more to the growth of these new women's associations than to any other recent development in our history. Women's networks are affecting business and industry, the professions, health care, policy making at local and national levels, the peace movement; perhaps even more important, they are changing women's self-image and overcoming centuries of feminine passivity and deference. Commenting on the rapidity of this development, David Broder says, "Almost overnight, the range of people who can be considered for the policy-making jobs in the public sector has been doubled."[1]

In the past, when women lived almost exclusively in their private domestic world, friendships grew and were nourished in the organic soil of family and community. These friendships, as we saw in the last chapter, were grounded in personal compatibility and usually in a commonality of ethnic and socioeconomic backgrounds. David Broder in *Changing the Guard* refers to these associations as "vertical networks," many of which were inherited. "Membership was acquired by being born in a certain place in a certain time, of a certain family, religion, race, or political affiliation. They were handed down from generation to generation and thus served to stabilize the larger society."

By contrast, the new "horizontal" networks bring together women who are widely diverse in personality and background and who connect with each other across these differences for the express purpose of achieving a specific goal or set of goals. Some of these connections never go beyond work relationships; others develop into close personal friendships. In either case, what is occurring is a shift from passive to active association, as women overcome the tendency to think of friendship in purely social terms.

These new friendships, which are emerging out of a developing sense of self-directedness, represent a cultural adaptation to the masculine style of achieving and managing power in the public world; they are purposeful relationships resulting from a conscious choice or series of choices that women are making as they add new dimensions to their lives. Unlike traditional male work-related relationships, however, women's networking attachments formed in the public world can be as nurturing as those that sustained women in the *Gemeinschaft* world of family and community. A woman who describes herself as "an overpressured sales manager and single parent of two teenagers" puts it this way: "I now have two different sets of women friends—personal and business. With my personal friends, we talk about our kids, our plans for redoing the kitchen, the scarcity of attractive men, and our problems at work, roughly in that order. With my business friends, we talk about pretty much the same things, in reverse order. The emphasis is different. We're occupying two different kinds of space, but the spaces flow into each other through our friendships.''

Since the double pressure of work and family commitments makes it difficult for women to spend as much time in purely social friendship as they would like, their business or professional networks tend to become intimacy providers. This may account for the warmth and emotional openness that are characteristic of women's networks, which are serving as replacements for the traditional institutions of family, religion, and community that no longer form the bulwark of women's lives.

THE EVOLUTION OF WOMEN'S NETWORKS

Though women's networks are being greeted as a new development, they can be traced all the way back to human beginnings. A network is essentially an association, formal or informal, through which people exchange information and, at times, services in which they have a common interest. From primitive gathering groups in which women traded information about where to find the best supply of nuts, fruits, and edible wild plants to women's social clubs where domestic and community politics are brought up to date, women have depended on these lifelines, sometimes for their very survival. Women on the American frontier, isolated by vast distances and worn down by the relentless day-to-day struggle for existence, nevertheless managed, as we learn from their letters and diaries, to knit together a women's support system, a web of social interactions and mutual assistance that helped them cope with the harsh conditions of their lives.

The urge to cluster, whether with like-minded people for purely social purposes or in order to achieve certain goals, was identified as typically American by Alexis de Tocqueville in the early nineteenth century. In his classic study, *Democracy in America,* he noted that "in no other country in the world has the principle of association been more successfully used or applied to a greater multitude of objects than in America. Besides the permanent associations which are established by law . . . a vast number of others are formed and maintained by the agency of private individuals.'' In premodern agrarian society, private individuals joined together for a variety of purposes—social, political, and economic. Farming communities routinely shared information about weather, soil conditions, harvests, animal husbandry. These were family-to-family contacts, involving males and females who worked the soil in common. The binding ties were those of kinship, of extended families relating at certain points of mutual need or interest with other extended families.

During much of our history, in fact, the family network was at the center of the social structure for people at all economic levels and especially for immigrants and working-class people. As depicted in many novels and other accounts of immigrant and working-class life, the family served its individual members as employment agency, loan office, marriage bureau, child-care center, refuge for the unfortunate, and caretaker of the elderly.

In the aftermath of the industrial revolution, with the growth of urbanization and suburbanization and the divergence in the daily lives of men and women, the network of the extended family began giving way to new forms that were dependent less on kinship bonds than on personal and occupational commonalities. The development of the nuclear family, with its sharply differentiated male-female roles, together with increasing mobility and dispersion of family members, further weakened traditional ties. The new relationships that replaced family ties were based on common economic and occupational interests and were, for the most part, sexually segregated.

The women's networks of today were spawned in the early years of the women's movement, and like those of the past, they grew rapidly in a changing social climate. In the 1960s and 1970s, women came to realize that their traditional, socially prescribed dependence on men and marriage was ebbing into the past and that they must now find new ways to survive. Though economic survival was paramount, especially for the growing number of women heads-of-households, taking care of their emotional needs was also a priority as they moved into an unfamiliar and often incomprehensible male system.

The forerunners of today's women's networks were the professional organizations established by female doctors, lawyers, and college graduates who, in the late nineteenth century, comprised a small but cohesive group. Other women, Lois Banner writes in *Women in Modern America,* "flocked into women's clubs seeking education, cultural uplift, a better understanding of women's nature, and a chance to involve themselves in civic concerns that went beyond the home."[2] In their clubs and professional organizations, women shared an experience that would in the 1960s come to be known as consciousness raising. Even those clubs with no feminist or political orientation brought about a change in women, by making them aware of their common stake in issues beyond home and family, which had been considered as exclusive masculine concerns. It was a change, barely noticed in the larger society at the time, that held within it the seeds of the feminization trend that is transforming much of our culture today.

Between the early 1870s and the end of the century, women's organizations proliferated at a remarkable rate, their goals ranging from moral betterment (the Women's Christian Temperance Union) to women's suffrage (the National American Woman's Suffrage Association) to children's welfare (the Congress of Mothers, which later became the National Parent-Teachers Association). Women's organizing efforts have been most successful in these areas of moral reform, morality being generally accepted as women's turf. The "Declaration of Rights and Sentiments" drafted at the Seneca Falls Convention of 1848, which mobilized women like Lucy Stone and Susan B. Anthony, was an outgrowth of women's earlier antislavery efforts. At the beginning of this century, feminists expanded their agenda and began agitating for prison reform, tax reform, prohibition, free libraries, and public transportation; again, these were considered moral issues, in relation to which women were regarded to have a natural superiority, and most of these feminine-supported aims were in time achieved. The leading moral issue for women today is being tackled by the peace movement, which is gaining support not only from women's organizations but from a grass-roots and worldwide reaction to the proliferation of nuclear weapons.

The women's associations of the late nineteenth and early twentieth centuries, though predecessors of today's networks, were very different in their structure and function. While structures then tended to be relatively tight, with a set of officers and clearly defined goals, today's typical network, male or female, is a much looser agglomeration of individuals, often with no formal leadership and with fluctuating goals and schedules. But there is a basic and significant similarity between yesterday's and today's women's associations that sets them apart from the old-boy networks and other male groups: For women, political relationships tend to become personal, so that regardless of the composition, structure, or commitment of the organization, be it a church auxiliary or a sophisticated alignment of media executives, its members find the kind of intimacy and affirmation often missing in their personal and professional lives. As a woman involved with a health professionals' network said, "Our networks give us the group support that enables us to function better independently."

This blending of individual enterprise with cooperativeness—the cooperative individualism that we noted earlier—is present among women in cultures far removed in geography and way of life from the American woman's experience. In Tanzania, when a Turu bride comes to live in her husband's village, she is incorporated into a group of all the women in the village, which functions very much like a network. One of the male informants explained that "women must more actively cooperate than men, because they come from many different places and need a special bond that men, who live among those with whom they were born, acquire through their relatedness."[3]

It may seem that the expensively dressed urban entrepreneurs who are members of networks such as Women in Business would have little in common with Nairobi women in a squatter area called Mathare Valley who survive by brewing and selling a local form of maize beer called *buzaa*. But both groups of women depend on their networks for the solidarity that promotes and protects their economic interests in an uncertain market. Brewing buzaa is a precarious economic activity, made more difficult by the fact that it is illegal in Kenya. But it provides a subsistence for women who have few other economic options. Although the women operate as individual entrepreneurs, their networks provide the linkages that make it possible for them to cope with the life of a buzaa brewer. Network members will rally to a woman when she cannot raise the money to pay a bribe or when she calls for help with an unruly customer or a thief. Information is circulated among members of the network about the credit worthiness of male customers or the tendency of certain customers to become drunk and disorderly.[4]

As is the case in American women's business and professional networks, women tend to bond across age differences, joining forces to further a common purpose. Anthropologist Alan Lomax describes this as a "gatherer style, which makes a tightly woven texture of independent and equal parts," adding, "I take it to be symbolic . . . of a feminine preference for egalitarian interaction."[5] By contrast, men's associations across cultures tend to be age-homogeneous.

But more significant than the distinguishing features mentioned in comparing these emerging networks with those of the past is the fact that they represent the first organized bonding of women in a determined effort to adapt a male process to the feminine style. It was an effort that grew out of women's awakening to the fact that a subterranean structure, the old-boy network, was an important source, possibly the most important source of male power. Women began to understand that what happened in corporate boardrooms and legislative assemblies often had its origins in the locker rooms or golf courses of exclusively male clubs.

FEMINIZING A MALE POWER PROCESS

The very texture of American politics—its folkways and byways—militates against women's entry into the mainstream. The smoke-filled rooms, bourbon-and-branchwater friendships and all-night poker games

exclude women from the fellowship and cronyism that
seal the bonds of power.
—SUSAN AND MARTIN TOLCHIN, *Clout: Womanpower and*
Politics, as quoted in Broder, The Changing of the Guard

Since 1974, the year the Tolchins' book was published, the
cultural barriers keeping women out of full partnership in our democracy have been giving way under the steady and relentless pressure of feminization. The male-only networks are still in place, but
from all indications they are not what they used to be: for one thing,
they no longer have the field of economic and political action all to
themselves.

At this time, all over the country, women each day meet to
swap business cards, fill each other in on the latest developments in
their respective fields, exchange information about job opportunities, seek advice from experienced executives and entrepreneurs,
find reliable firms for personal and business use, and generally gain
support from each other. In neighborhood and civic groups, women
who work in the public world are meeting with women who are
full-time homemakers to discuss the problems of their communities. Women with political ambitions are pooling information on
voting patterns, fund raising, and related topics in networks that
have been springing up in state capitals and in Washington, D.C.
Career-oriented women are gathering in such far-flung and diverse
associations as the Women's Media Group, National Alliance of
Homebased Working Women, Women in Design International,
Women in Mining, and the Women's Bond Club of New York. In
the members' commitment to advancing their professional goals
through information sharing, these associations resemble the all-
male groups.

But the resemblance is only superficial. John Naisbitt, in describing networking as a megatrend more in accord with an information society than the hierarchical structure, says, "The Old Boy
Network is a clubbish, fraternal conspiracy that protects the self-
interest of a limited few."[6] By contrast, most women's networks
are unrestricted, and members treat each other as peers. Two of the

few exceptions are the Los Angeles–based Women in Business, limited to women who show leadership in the community and whose annual earnings are at least $30,000, and the Women's Media Group in New York, which restricts its high-powered membership to 140; both have been charged with elitism. But Donna Shalala, president of Hunter College and founder of the Washington Women's Network, one of the most influential in the country, sees a difference between the elitism of women's and men's networks. "I think most women's networks, even the most elitist ones, are more open than men's networks. They may have much more of an emotional-reinforcement aspect because you're talking about women in positions that they have never been in before. There's this tendency to look around a room full of women of achievement and to feel good about how far we've come."

In all-male groups, business takes first place, and the sociability, which revolves mainly around sports, rarely assumes personal dimensions; women's networks tend to serve as forums for sharing and solving problems, personal as well as occupational. Women in their networks discuss child care along with stock market trading, exchange information about pediatricians and hairdressers along with inside tips on job openings. "Their conversations are an odd combination of gossip, personal minutiae, and professional concerns," is how *New York Times* columnist Anna Quidlen describes the talk at meetings of the Women in Media Group. "Nobody makes deals, but they do find out whom to call if they want to place a book, sell subsidiary rights, generate a feature story, or find an agent. If someone needs a job, this could well be the place to find one."[7]

This typically feminine style of association is emerging as the new network model for the increasingly mixed male-female groups, a change that has come about partly as a result of the opening up to women of clubs that were formerly closed to them. The Yale and Princeton clubs, for instance, now admit women because the schools they represent are enrolling them. Similarly, as corporate hierarchies become sexually integrated, the younger women becoming part of them have formed "old school ties" with their male classmates in college or business school.

[65]

The contrast between these new integrated networks and the old-boy model is striking, according to men who have experienced both types. Basically, the difference appears to consist of a marked change in atmosphere. "There's more informality, more personal interchange, less ego-tripping," says a tax attorney who has been involved in networking since his graduation from law school ten years ago. The feminine style of networking, it appears, is capable of transforming a process that in the past was one of the most effective male strategies for keeping women out of the public world.

WOMEN'S NETWORKS IN ACTION

The heart and soul of the networking process is *information*, and access to the kind of information that drives the public world of action and power is what women have long been denied and are now gaining through their networks. A simple exchange of information can be helpful to a woman's career. Word of one member's imminent job change gives another member an early shot at applying for the job about to be vacated. Career transitions and entrepreneurial endeavors, generally more difficult for women than for men since women are not encouraged to be risk takers, are also often facilitated by networking. Women's networks have lent money to members to help them start a business or to keep a business going when it ran into financial difficulties.

Women's networks are "personalizing business," says Carolyn Desjardins, founder of the Women's Center at Mesa Community College in Phoenix. Desjardins and her networkers make it a point to assist women who are trapped in low-paying jobs for which they are overqualified or who are trying to start up a business of their own. The networkers believe their efforts are changing the attitudes as well as the composition of the community's business leaders, thus "causing business to be more caring, have more responsibility to their customers and clients," claims Desjardins.

The women's networking process, she continues, can humanize business, helping it regain an integrity lost in the ruthless, competitive power struggles that have characterized much of American business.

Networking success stories multiply along with networks. Arlene Hurwitz, secretary of the Barnard Business and Professional Women's Network in New York, met someone through the network who introduced her to executives at a management consulting firm where she became a department head. In turn, she hired a woman she met through the network to do translations for her company. Kathryn Power, former director of the Pennsylvania Coalition Against Rape, recently became a partner in a counseling firm and a senior associate at a computer firm. She gives credit to the Monday Club, a women's network in Harrisburg modeled after the city's all-male Tuesday Club. Suzy Ells organized a network at Polaroid that succeeded in persuading the male-run company to treat time out for childbirth equally with disabilities and to develop a recruiting plan complete with timetables for moving women up in the company.[8]

Helping women find positions in top management and government is a networking function that is gradually feminizing these male bastions. It is an incremental process that often seems to move at a snail's pace, and we are still a long way from anything like gender balance in business and politics, but during the past decade, significant changes have occurred in both arenas. The increasing concern of big business with the quality of working life among the people on staff has developed during the span of time when women began occupying influential positions in business corporations and in government. Moreover, during this time such attributes as intuition and relationship skills (long tagged as "feminine") have begun gaining recognition from business and are now included in new books, courses, and seminars on successful management.

The fact is that men, especially those who have networked their way to top positions, are paying close attention to women's networks. Peter J. Solomon, managing director at Lehman Brothers Kuhn Loeb, suggests that when the same ten women keep showing up on every board, it's safe to assume that some kind of network is in operation. "Ten years from now it will be the same 100 women. You have to look at evolution. There were not that many women in business five years ago. . . . But that's all changing."[9]

One change that is a significant outcome of feminization is the demise of the "token woman," hired during the early days of affirmative action as a gesture of appeasement to the women's movement and who, in her isolation, felt constrained to conform so as not to rock the boat. Backed up by their networks, women are now more comfortable speaking out and taking positions not always in line with organizational policy. "The most important thing we do is communicate to those women out there that they are not alone," says Janice Blood, director of public information for Working Women, a Boston-based network of 12,000 office workers across the country.

The message appears to be coming through loud and clear. It was network support that encouraged Doris Brunner, a chemist for the Pennsylvania Department of Environmental Resources and a member of the Monday Club network, to appeal a job ruling concerning a dispute over authority through a labor relations attorney she had met at a network meeting. "I don't think I would have had the confidence to initiate something like this," she said, "prior to my association with the people here." In another case, when a Boston legal secretary was fired for bringing her boss a corned-beef sandwich for his lunch that was on white rather than rye bread, the Nine to Five Network went into action and brought the secretary's employer before the bar association for unethical behavior.

Politically, women's networks have been more successful in mobilizing women to vote on women's issues and for women candidates (through groups such as the National Organization of Women and the National Women's Political Caucus) than in actually putting women into government leadership positions. As late as the 1950s, surveys by the University of Michigan Center for Political Studies showed a gap of 10 percentage points between male and female voter turnout rates; by the late 1970s, the gap had declined to 1.4 percent.

Though progress for women in assuming public leadership roles is slow, there has been an increase since the early 1970s in the number of women in elective office, especially at state and local levels. In 1969, women were only 4% of America's legislators; today they are 14.7%. Recent surveys show a substantial rise in public support for a woman as President, and perhaps most important, women are now on a par with men in the critical activity of political fund-raising. Unquestionably, women's networks have been responsible for these changes. Women's political networks have been springing up in state capitals, and a powerful network in Washington, D.C., which has been used to recruit women for many political jobs, cuts across party lines to include both Republicans and Democrats.

On the legislative front, women's networking achievements have been formidable. The Ninety-second Congress alone in 1977 passed more women's rights legislation than the sum total of all relevant legislation previously passed in the country's history. In addition to the Equal Employment Opportunity Act and the ERA, Congress put through legislation calling for the prohibition of sex discrimination in federally aided education programs; free day-care for children in low-income families; and a series of antidiscrimination provisions to several federally funded programs including those having to do with health training, revenue sharing, and water pollution. In 1984, Congress passed a revolutionary child support package and significant pension reforms affecting women.

How can we account for this unprecedented congressional response to women's concerns? The most likely answer lies in pressure from the women's networks supporting these issues. According to political organizer and author Jo Freeman, women developed sophisticated lobbying skills during the ERA struggle that made it easier for them to know "whom to approach for information and/or support for other bills." The network provided the women's movement with "easy access to many key points of decision making—a major goal of any interest group."[10]

The grass-roots organizations that make up the women's health movement have also been successful in translating their objectives into political action. The Washington-based National Women's Health Network, representing more than 300 health groups nationwide, is committed to two major goals: education and advocacy. In its advocacy role, it has demonstrated how women can make use of the courts in their campaign for better health care.

Cases brought by the network that have successfully challenged the medical-drug establishment include the following: a suit against the Pharmaceutical Manufacturers Association and the American College of Obstetricians and Gynecologists to make drug companies provide women with printed cancer warnings for estrogen drugs during menopause, resulting in a landmark decision that set a precedent for patient labeling in *all* prescription drugs; and the nation's first class-action lawsuit on behalf of daughters who are at risk for developing cancer because their mothers took the drug DES. Currently, the network is suing the Upjohn Company, manufacturer of the controversial injectable contraceptive Deprovera, on behalf of women who have suffered from the drug's unauthorized use.

By the time the Pregnancy Discrimination Act was passed in 1978 prohibiting sex discrimination in employment on the basis of pregnancy—a legislative breakthrough for working women that resulted from active lobbying by women's groups—there was no longer any doubt that women's networks had come of age. Women had demonstrated that the organizing skills acquired in activities usually associated with the private world can be effectively applied to problem solving in the public world, and even the subsequent defeat of the ERA in the ratification stage did not detract from this accomplishment.

More significant in the long run than the success or failure of network lobbying on particular issues was the public realization that what had begun as a scatteration of small, informal organizations, loose linkages reflecting the egalitarian feminine style, had been transformed into broad-based organizations with the power to bring about significant social change. It was as if Americans had suddenly awakened to, in Daniel Boorstin's phrase, the "little revolution" in their midst and were seeing themselves with new eyes. There was a sense that the country had turned a corner and was heading in a new direction. From here on, the pace of feminization would begin to speed up, and the cultural impact would soon be felt throughout the society.

WOMEN'S NETWORKS IN TRANSITION

Like much of feminine culture, women's networks are in a state of flux, and it is difficult to predict with any certainty which directions they will take in the years ahead. At present, the evolutionary development looks like this: Women in their fifties and older depended on men for their connections. These women, pioneers breaking into the public world, looked to male models, having no others available to them, as they carved out a niche in the system. They relied on their networks primarily for psychological support, regarding any career advantages from their ties with women as fringe benefits.

Women now in their forties connected with other women because the women's movement was just emerging at the time they were moving into business and the professions. This was a heady period of sisterhood and consciousness raising, of women discovering themselves and each other, testing their powers in the public arena and replacing the traditional male models with improvised patterns of their own. Networks like Women in Business and the Women's Media Group were born out of this ferment, and feminine power, or "empowerment," began setting down its roots in the hard-packed soil of the public world.

For younger women, now between twenty and forty, the evolving pattern has been more of a male-female mix. With women's increasing entrance into corporate management and the development by younger women of the "old school tie" with their male classmates, the new male-female networks are beginning to replace the informal clubs or networks of the men in corporate hierarchies. As women become more comfortable and more self-assured in the public world, and as men become more familiar with and more attuned to the feminine style, we are beginning to see more productive working relationships between men and women and a more egalitarian atmosphere in the workplace.

Some of the developing patterns, however, suggest that networking may be susceptible to defeminizing forces that could subvert the process of feminization along with its promise of a saner, safer, more compassionate society. One of these disturbing developments is a growing pattern of stratification in women's networks, as revealed in a recent study of women's corporate networks by anthropologist Terry Odendahl: managerial networks are designed to give individual women a boost up the corporate ladder, while working-class women's networks aim for collective action to improve pay, working conditions, and recognition. Generally, the managerial networks have been more successful in assisting their members to move upward. But upward mobility often presents a woman with a difficult networking dilemma: her prestige isn't necessarily enhanced and may even be diminished by networking with those at the bottom, yet she has developed ties of intimacy and loyalty with these lower-echelon women that pull against the divisiveness of the hierarchical structure.

It is a dilemma familiar to cultural adaptation: how much of one's cultural heritage should be sacrificed on the altar of ''making it'' in the dominant system? Every immigrant group in America has to some extent experienced this conflict of values, which has often forced the more ambitious members into a complex psychological balancing act, a trade-off between deeply inbred values and personal aspirations. As immigrants from the domestic to the public world, women are brought into direct confrontation with this conflict within their networks. The earlier, informal groups were based on trust and goodwill, and leadership was diffused or nonexistent. But successful lobbying efforts often depend upon centralized direction, which leads to hierarchy, which conflicts with feminine perceptions of power and how it should be used. If women in their networks begin using power in the traditional masculine style, to dominate and control, instead of in the more feminine style of mutual ''empowerment,'' would this not be a betrayal of the feminist cause?

There are women who have been involved in networking from the beginning who sense a certain danger to the future course of feminization in the new sexually integrated networks. They question whether these mixed groups will reflect a balance between feminine and masculine culture or—as has happened repeatedly in the past in male-female organizations—if the feminine style, which is more accustomed to compromise and adjustment, will be submerged by the masculine, old-boy mode.

There are other grounds for concern, chief among them the efforts of the new conservatism to rally the forces of God and Mammon in order to discourage women from making further political or economic gains. The antiabortion movement and the Reagan administration's drastic budget cuts in programs assisting women and children are only early symptoms of what may well turn into a serious case of antifeminism supported by a coalition of government, organized religion, and business. An economic recession or another real or perceived threat to national security would very likely set a series of regressive forces into motion to reverse the course of feminization.

But there is some cause for optimism in the egalitarian relationships that are developing among men and women in both their private and public lives. Networking can take a good share of the credit for creating the environment and providing the experience for men and women to organize and accomplish tasks through equal participation. As John Naisbitt notes: "Within the networking structure, information itself is the great equalizer. Networks are not egalitarian just because every member is a peer. On the contrary, because networks are diagonal and three-dimensional, they involve people from every possible level. What occurs in a network is that members treat one another as peers—because what is important is the information, the great equalizer."

Though Naisbitt does not refer specifically to the feminine influence on the networking phenomenon, he uses language that comes directly out of the vocabulary of women's culture: "Networking empowers the individual, and people in networks tend to nurture each other."[11]

It may well be that women's networks are part of a transitional phase and will dwindle away as the public world becomes fully integrated, but even if this should happen, they will have left a considerable legacy of personal and social change. The sense of potency and control that women are deriving from networking is bringing about an explosion of consciousness that some psychologists liken to taking the cap off a steam kettle; it's a release of suppressed energies as women discover that they can pool their resources and expertise without becoming unfeminine.

More effectively than laws, regulations, and court decisions, women's networks have opened routes to power for women and given them leverage into fields that have been traditionally for men only. And this pooling of energy and resources is adding momentum to an evolving trend toward a more open, cooperative style of communication, thus revitalizing stagnating attitudes and institutions and helping them adapt to the social realities of our time.

5. HUMANIZING THE WORKPLACE

As women have been moving in ever-increasing numbers into jobs and professions formerly occupied by men, the working environment in which most people spend the major part of their lives has begun to respond to feminine needs and values. As a result, we are seeing a shift to a more humane, more people-centered workplace, a long overdue development that comes in time to counteract a growing discontent with the conditions of work that has been spreading throughout the occupational spectrum.

The discontents that people are voicing about their work are for the most part connected to a feeling of meaninglessness, a sense of being alienated from what one does during the working day, which afflicts people at all salary levels. Some typical comments from interviews with men and women in the $25,000–$50,000 salary range reflect this:

> I spend most of my time writing ad copy for deodorants and after-shave lotion. Eight to ten hours a day, day after day, year after year, agonizing over stuff I don't give a damn about. When I get home at night after an hour's commute, my kids are in bed and

I'm so strung out, all I want is a couple of good stiff scotches, and maybe I'll watch a little TV before I turn in. (Mark Nevelson, forty-five-year-old advertising executive, Chicago)

I'm just marking time till I get my pension. Twenty years to go, then if I'm not too old, maybe I can do some of the things I've always wanted to do. My job is just a big fat bore, a waste of time. (Helen Jacoby, forty-two-year-old executive secretary to the financial vice-president of a merchandising conglomerate, Dallas)

I go home on Friday evening, lock the door, and don't leave my apartment until Monday morning. It takes me two days and three nights to calm down so that I can go back on Monday and face five more days of it. I hate my life, I hate myself, I hate what this is doing to me. (Susan Ellis, thirty-year-old program coordinator in a federally funded community project, Detroit)

Underlying much of this unhappiness is the divorce of work from the rest of life, an inevitable outcome of the work-home schism. Work takes on meaning only in a context that provides wholeness and balance and that gives us a feeling of belonging to a community. The notion that the activity at which we spend the most productive years of our lives can be divided off from the rest of us—from our character, aspirations, and cultural heritage—the assumption that a human being can be split in two with one-half placed on hold for forty hours a week is a recent and dangerous idea that is damaging to the individual's sense of self-worth.

HOW DID WE GET HERE FROM THERE?

In the preindustrial era, men, women, and children worked together, often side by side. The family was the basic economic unit, and families depended upon each other for subsistence. The tasks were, of course, often gender related: men in the family performed the heavy-duty agricultural work; women were in charge of the kitchen garden, poultry yard, and household, which included manufacturing most of the necessities of life. The preindustrial home was actually a hub of industry in which the woman performed not only the customary tasks of cooking, cleaning, and child care but also made soap and candles, spun cloth, wove lace, and sewed and repaired the family's clothes. A similar system existed in the self-contained world of artisans, shopkeepers, and small entrepreneurs who worked in settings that usually combined workplace and homeplace, with assistance as needed from family members.

The rise of an industrial economy and the urbanization that accompanied it were the beginning and the end of the integrated home-work system. Farmers and small entrepreneurs flocked to the cities, and goods that had formerly been produced at home were now mass produced in factories. The decrease of productive work in the home brought about the segregation of the sexes during the working day, leading ultimately to the development of two very different, polarized environments.

The home, which was transformed into an exclusively feminine domain, came to represent a refuge from the rigors of work, the place where the heart lay, where the spirit was refreshed and the energies renewed. Home became synonymous with warmth, softness, color. It was the "supreme cultural achievement of women," according to sociologist-philosopher Georg Simmel.

The workplace, which for a rising middle-class white-collar work force was usually an office, came to represent the very antithesis of the homeplace. From the beginning, the office or factory was strictly functional—cold, impersonal, colorless. In the pre-Civil War era, it was strictly a male domain. The clerical work was performed by copyists, or scriveners (Melville's Bartleby was one of these), and it consisted mainly of copying out rough drafts of letters or other documents in a fine hand, using a goose quill pen.

The entry of women into clerical work was brought about by

post–Civil War changes in the structure of capitalism, which caused a substantial increase in correspondence and record keeping. Having lost their productive role in the home to the factory system, women who needed to earn a living were attracted to clerical work, which offered them at least a subsistence wage.

But the presence of women in the workplace did not put an end to sexual segregation during working hours. A new form of male-female segregation arose within the workplace itself, facilitated by the growth of hierarchy. A pyramidal structure was designed in response to the growth in size and complexity of commercial enterprises; within this structure, power and responsibility were clearly delineated and ranked from top to bottom. At the bottom of the pyramid were, of course, the clerical workers, who by now were mostly women. Managerial jobs were routinely filled by men, whether or not there were women available with equal or superior qualifications; it was considered a waste of time to train women for managerial positions since it was assumed that they would give up their jobs and return to the home as soon as they were married.

Whereas in 1870 less than 1 percent of women employed outside of agriculture were engaged in clerical work, by 1920 they accounted for nearly 92 percent of the stenographers/typists and nearly 50 percent of the bookkeepers, cashiers, and accountants. Nevertheless, the influx of women into the workplace did not alter the division of labor at home: women continued to be solely responsible for domestic tasks. This meant that, while men's lives had become unidimensional, centering mainly around their work, women were living dual lives: one in the home as the family nurturer and caretaker, the other in the workplace as a performer of routine, repetitive tasks in an impersonal atmosphere. The working environment was alien to the feminine temperament, having been created by and for the men in managerial positions, and it reflected the split between public and private lives that resulted from the separation of work from home, with home life and all that it represented becoming, more than ever before, an exclusive concern of women.

SEPARATE REALITIES

The severing of work from home was like an act of surgery, cutting deeply into the common world of men and women and leaving wounds that only in recent years are beginning to be healed. The idea that "a woman's place is in the home" (except, of course, when she was needed for war work) originated in this separation, as did the man's role as sole breadwinner. The man as producer and the woman as consumer were not, however, two halves neatly fitting together into a whole; women's domestic labor was devalued, while man's labor was viewed as providing the backbone of the nation's economy as well as the family's support. By the 1950s, the flight from the cities added to the work-home schism a geographical separation often involving hours of commuting by car and train.

In the course of this separation, both homeplace and workplace suffered serious losses. The home was deprived of its earlier economic productivity, and work became mainly an endless, repetitive process. With the decline of the extended family and the woman's nearly total preoccupation with child care, the nuclear household, particularly in the suburbs, represented a self-contained nest isolated from the world of action and achievement. (Georg Simmel tempered his effusions by admitting that this "immense cultural achievement" has also proved a prison house.) In this well-appointed dream home, this "haven in a heartless world," the feminine ethic languished and was assailed by a vague, unfocused discontent, a "problem that had no name," which Betty Friedan labeled "the feminine mystique."

Meanwhile, the workplace, having developed during the nation's rapid industrialization as a masculine construct untempered by feminine influence, was experiencing its own form of deprivation—the lack of nurturing and personalism and the sheltering warmth of home. In the modern large-scale bureaucracy, relations are governed by rational procedures. A masculine ethic of rationality and reason, which can be identified in early bureaucratic models of management, elevates traits that are assumed to belong exclusively to men: a tough-minded approach to problems; analytic ability to abstract and plan; a capacity to set aside personal, emotional considerations in the interests of task accomplishment; and a cognitive superiority in problem solving and decision making. The focus is on goals, output, and efficiency, and managers as well as lower-echelon workers are expected to act in their own self-interest.[1]

Living within their separate realities of work and home left both sexes with a sense of being cheated. The bright, energetic woman could hardly help feeling trapped by the limitations of the full-time domestic role, and the upwardly mobile business executive, the obsessed workaholic, the overstressed professional wore out psychiatrists' couches, wondering, Is that all there is?

For a balanced life, human beings need both love and work, claimed Freud, and when these needs are separated and opposed, men and women are condemned to live half-lives.

TRANSFORMING THE WORKPLACE

> Women bring a positive, humanizing quality to the corporate environment.
> —*survey of male CEOs in Fortune 500 companies*

The mass movement of women into the workplace has been hailed by social scientists and historians as a social change of momentous proportions, comparable to the industrial revolution or the waves of immigration in the last century. "It's the single most outstanding phenomenon of this century," says Eli Ginzberg, professor at Columbia University and chairman of the National Commission for Manpower Policy. A *Business Week* article attributes America's rapid economic growth in recent years to one factor: women's entry into the job market as part-time, full-time, lifetime workers in virtually all occupations and at all levels of responsibility.

This transfusion of feminine energy and skill from the private to the public world is, the article continues, "boosting economic growth, and helping to reshape the economy dramatically. Women have seized two-thirds of the jobs created in the last decade. And they have been the linchpin in the shift toward services and away from manufacturing. Because a rapidly expanding labor force is a principal element in propelling an economy onto a fast-growth track, the influx of women into the job market may be the major reason that the U.S. has emerged so much healthier than other countries from the economic shocks of the 1970s.'' Nobel laureate Paul A. Samuelson, professor of economics at M.I.T., adds, "To the degree that women are getting an opportunity that they didn't have in the past, the economy is tapping an important and previously wasted resource."[2]

But the feminization of the workplace is transforming more than just the economy. "Women are neurologically more flexible than men," says Eli Ginzberg, "and they have had cultural permission to be more intuitive, sensitive, feeling. Their natural milieu has been complexity, change, nurturance, affiliation, a more fluid sense of time." As these attributes of feminine culture are brought into the workplace, they are providing a much-needed balance to what has been a predominantly male environment, and slowly but steadily they are eroding some of the obsolete practices and prejudices that have dehumanized work and the work environment.

Much of this change is linked to women's deeply rooted need to integrate love and work. The work-home division grates against the feminine sensibility. "Every woman in America leads a double life," says political scientist Emily Stoper. "She is shaped by a double socialization; she is torn apart by a double pull; often she carries a double burden. One side of her duality turns inward to the world of home, children, 'inner feelings'—femininity, in a word. The other side faces outward to the world of work, achievement, power, money, abstract thought—the 'man's world.' "[3]

Women's efforts to reconcile the two sides of this duality pit them against the structure and rationale of the corporate bureaucracy. As Daniel Boorstin points out in *The End of Ideology*, the contemporary enterprise was set up to obey three "techno-logics": the logic of size, the logic of "metric" time, and the logic of hierarchy. "Each of the three, the product of engineering rationality, has imposed on the worker a set of constraints with which he is forced to wrestle every day.'' These three technologics, which have defined and delimited work in America for the past century, are giving way—inch by inch, moment by moment, step by step—to the forces of change that are in harmony with feminine culture.

The constraint of "metric time" measurement is loosening as the needs of working mothers challenge rigid work schedules and generate more fluid, flexible time arrangements to include part-time, flexi-time and job sharing. These innovative work patterns, offering more flexibility and the opportunity for choice and self-management on the job, make it possible for women to bring their home and working lives into balance.

But it is not only women who are the beneficiaries of more relaxed work schedules; potential all-around benefits abound: the easing of traffic congestion; the weekday access by employees to shopping, education, recreation; an opportunity for both parents to spend more time with their children. (A 1977 Quality of Employment Survey by the Survey Research Center at the University of Michigan found that 51 percent of wives and 42 percent of husbands with children under eighteen preferred to reduce their work time in order to spend more time with their families.) The time clock may, eventually, be consigned to the ash heap of history as the development of technology converges with new, more leisure-oriented lifestyles to bring about a variety of work schedules that can be adapted to individual needs.

The other two technologics in Boorstin's trio of restrictive practices—size and hierarchy—are being challenged by forces of change that are also in accord with the feminine need to reconcile home and work. A service/information economy does not lend itself to massive bureaucratic organization. As John Naisbitt has noted, this hidebound, elephantine structure, with its rigid ladder of separations, slows down the flow of information "just when greater speed and flexibility is needed." He sees mammoth centralized institutions whose very existence relies upon hierarchies being replaced by smaller, decentralized units, linked informally with each other instead of being clumped together. The eventual replacement for hierarchy, according to current management theory, will be networks, a pattern that is already in evidence and which suits the feminine temperament, with its proclivity for connectedness, far better than the divisive pecking order of the hierarchy. (A recent study of female hierarchies concluded that, though women in general do not like hierarchies, they are able, depending on the task to be performed, to work together, defer to authority, and maintain discipline.)[4]

A NEW MANAGERIAL AGENDA

Some of the changes being forged in the crucible of feminization could not have been imagined even a decade ago. Bread-and-butter issues—comparable pay, for example—are forcing managers as well as economic theorists to rethink the basic American concept of equality. The Equal Pay Act of 1963 required that women be paid equally with men for the same job; and women's pay, though still a long way from parity, has risen from 57 percent of men's wages in 1973 to 64 percent in 1980. But the concept of comparable worth asks: What if the jobs are not the same but are equal in levels of skill, effort, and responsibility? Should a secretary, for example, be paid as much as a truck driver? The controversy has been heating up, with employers and union representatives, particularly those representing public employees, positioning themselves for a protracted battle. A judicial or legislative resolution does not appear to be in the offing, but in the meantime, the underlying question of what equality is, once a preoccupation mainly of academic philosophers, will continue to be argued at corporate seminars and meetings of public officials.

Other strange new issues are appearing on the managerial agenda, issues unrelated to production quotas or profit margins that seem, oddly enough, to be closer to the homeplace than the workplace. In the 1970s, babies were not a concern of such enterprises as the Caltech Jet Propulsion Laboratory. At that time, the laboratory was mostly male. But in 1973, when the federally funded lab initiated an affirmative action program, the number of women employees began growing, until today women constitute a quarter of the 5,000-person work force. And a quarter-mile from the lab is the Child Educational Center of the Caltech/JPL community, which serves 150 preschool children of employees and area residents. Women workers drop in to nurse and play with their children; both mothers and fathers are encouraged to visit.[5]

At present, nearly 3,000 corporations nationwide sponsor day-care centers for their employees, or otherwise assist them in finding reliable day care. A recent survey funded by the federal government called employer-supported child care "the fastest growing form of child care today." The survey, conducted for the U.S. Department of Health and Human Services, found that although employer-sponsored programs cover less than 1 percent of children in day care, "the trend is accelerating rapidly."

Obviously, the child-care services currently available are not adequate for the rapidly growing need, but the continuing pressure being placed on officials by working mothers is being felt throughout the economy and is having a significant influence on public policy. The Economic Recovery Tax Act of 1981 offered tax breaks of $2,400 per child to companies that include child care in their benefits package. Several state legislatures are considering similar proposals to encourage local businesses to establish child-care services.

As with any social innovation in its early stages, company-sponsored child care is going through a period of experimentation, during which various child-care systems are being tested. Five Silicon Valley companies make direct contributions to a local service center, which in return ensures employees day care at a discount and priority admission for their children. The Campbell Soup Company operates its own on-site center in Camden, New Jersey. In New York City's Lower East Side, a unique partnership has brought together the International Ladies' Garment Workers Union, a manufacturers' association, and a city agency to establish the Garment Industry Day Care Center of Chinatown. Since most of the parents are recent immigrants from China, the instruction here is bilingual.

So far, the trend seems to favor the Silicon Valley model, in which employers make a corporate contribution to a community-run

center in return for which employees receive certain child-care services. In a variation of this model, companies are instituting referral
programs or reimbursing employees for child care. The system
most advantageous to both parents and children is, of course, the
on-site facility that gives parents and children the oportunity for
close interaction during the day, but since this is the costliest system, it has not as yet attracted many companies.

We may justifiably question the value system of a society that
spends billions on sophisticated weapons yet skimps on care for its
children. But as Eric Nelson, codirector of the Caltech/JPL center
puts it, "It's going to take people of vision at the top and bottom
getting together to solve the day-care problem. In general, management is older and male. Child care is a problem with which they
can't easily identify. Child-care experts have to understand that and
be able to convince hard-headed businessmen that they should be
interested in babies. The fact that women are out of the home is still
a shock to some men, and the thought of babies in the workplace is
the last straw."

But the trend is unstoppable, for it reflects a growing public
consciousness that day care for the children of working parents is a
concern not only of the parents but of the entire society. When
children are not adequately cared for, as many studies show, the
lack is reflected in rising rates of crime, unemployment, and
domestic violence. An argument that is proving more persuasive,
however, especially among "hard-headed businessmen," is that
day care is good for business, reducing absenteeism and boosting
morale. Most companies would be hard hit by the loss of those
female workers who are mothers of small children, and economic
analyses indicate that the economy would go into a severe decline
without the earnings and purchasing power of working mothers.
The facts of economic life make it safe to predict that by the end of
this decade, companies without some form of day care will be regarded as dinosaurs, along with those having no employee benefit
plans.

The economics of feminine employment has also made parental
leave one of the hotter personnel issues of the mid '80s. With the
passage of the federal Pregnancy Discrimination Act referred to in

the previous chapter, pregnancy and childbirth must be treated similarly to any other physical disability, a legislative breakthrough that has forced many companies to change their corporate policies in regard to maternity leave. (It is somewhat ironic that motherhood, to which our public officials regularly pay homage, must be classified as a disability in order for women to be able to have babies and continue working.)

According to a national survey by Catalyst, a New York–based national research organization, companies that had treated maternity differently from other disabilities were required to change their policies after October 1978, with the result that informal, unwritten maternity-leave plans were formalized, and longer-paid leave for maternity was added to company disability plans. Here again, progress has been slow: fewer than half of all working women receive paid maternity leaves of more than six weeks, and the few forward-looking companies that offer paternity leaves find that only a small fraction of eligible fathers apply. But the issue is moving to the top of the corporate agenda as more women return to work after becoming mothers and more fathers are sharing child-care responsibilities from the beginning.

The working mother is also forcing corporations to rethink their policies linking mobility to transferability. Since working wives cannot be moved as easily as the household effects, company personnel divisions are now charged with the responsibility of finding a comparable job for the displaced wife—or for her husband, if she is the one to be transferred. This is not always so simple, and in the case of a professional, a doctor or lawyer with an established practice, it may be virtually impossible. As a result, the mobility-transferability link is no longer a clear-cut either/or choice: either move and climb up the ladder or count yourself out; it has become enmeshed in emotional ties, in friendships and community roots, so that family stability must now be factored into corporate management planning, much to the surprise and, no doubt, chagrin of the more traditional male managers.

This growing interest in the needs of working parents stems less, as we have suggested, from a sudden surge of corporate solicitude for the two-job family than from the new economic realities that business and industry are facing as a result of women entering the work force. The facts and figures are clear and their implications for the workplace are unmistakable: women now constitute one-half of the work force, and of these women, half will become pregnant at some time in their working lives. The majority of these women are no longer leaving their jobs for an extended time to rear their children. According to U.S. census figures for 1982, almost one-third of mothers with infants under six months are working, and a survey of corporations found that the average length of time off work for new mothers is three months. (This coincides with research in infant psychology, which has found that at three months, the infant can be safely separated from the mother for limited time periods.)

These corporate efforts to meet the needs of working mothers, insufficient as they are at present, represent a radical reordering of an institutional mind-set that has been shaped by "the cult of efficiency." Feminization is forcing that mind-set to extend itself to the larger questions of human values and relationships and how these impinge upon people's working lives. For traditional management, confronting such questions has had the effect of shock treatment. To most men in top management, women are "a foreign country," says organizational psychologist Sandra Florstedt. She attributes the slow pace of reform to women's "different heritage" of values, behavior, and style, acquired over the centuries and often baffling to men in the workplace, accustomed as they are to working in an all-male environment. Having started her career as a high school language teacher, she identifies as the most difficult problem in organizations today the development of a common language to span the communication gap between men and women in the workplace.

Florstedt, who has fifteen years of experience in organizational development, believes that though tangible reforms have been slow in coming, attitudinal and atmospheric changes have speeded up as the feminine presence has made itself felt throughout the workplace. To encourage better communication among employees and provide a healthier, pleasanter working environment, many large corporations are moving from private offices to open space, installing cheerfully decorated employee lounges and exercise rooms offering recreation and fitness programs, and, as in the case of the new Levi-Strauss corporate headquarters in downtown San Francisco, including in the building complex small parks in which employees can hold meetings or relax during coffee and lunch breaks.

The most important influence of women on the workplace, according to Florstedt, is that "they're keeping men honest. I know a lot of men who like working with women because it's the women who are calling it the way they see it, at least privately—maybe it's because they're new to the situation, they're seeing it differently, more clearly." At the same time, she recognizes that women's creative energies, which are now being diverted from housework and babies to business and the professions, need to be channeled properly if women are to achieve their full potential for productivity. "They need to feel a sense of connection to the workplace and not think of it as a male world in which they are intruders."

It may well be that the growing presence of women in the workplace holds forth the greatest promise for a humanizing transformation in American working lives: the desegregation of the workplace and the restoration in today's egalitarian terms of a working life shared by men and women, which was disrupted by the industrial revolution. "Men and women are rediscovering each other," said a woman who heads a corporate training program. There is still hostility and resentment, she added, by men who see women taking over jobs that were formerly regarded as strictly male occupational territory, but this is lessening as men become accustomed to women in these jobs. Distance may lend enchantment, but it also leads to stereotyping: as the distance between male and female working lives narrows, the stereotype too is waning, and women are appearing less and less as a "foreign country" to their male colleagues.

Of course, we can hardly expect that a magnetic force as powerful as sexuality will ever entirely vanish from the workplace, nor is this necessarily desirable. Phil Randall, a Chicago management consultant, sees sexual attraction as inevitable in a more humane workplace: "The fact that people who work together can have affairs is something that companies have to allow for. I hope they'll look carefully at teams of men and women whose love—or whatever relationship they have outside the office—makes them more creative at work.'' At the same time, a few men are learning to develop nonsexual relationships with sexually attractive peers, observes Anthony Astrachan, author of *How Men Feel*, ''disentangling competence from sexuality, rather than denying either one. It is neither easy nor traditional, but some men are learning (with some pain) how to do it.''

Those men who succeed in developing nonsexual friendships with their female colleagues—and their number increases daily—are experiencing a gratifying sense of personal growth, an ability to look beyond gender at individual competency and accomplishment. Several men who have made this transition report that it has enriched not only their relationships at work but also their personal lives. ''I'm finding it easier to make friends, with men as well as women,'' said one. ''Women seem to have some sort of special talent for friendship, and it's rubbing off on me.''

The morale-boosting, performance-improving impact of the feminine presence has not escaped the notice of corporate personnel managers. Jane Evans, an executive vice-president of General Mills, reports that corporations are searching for women who know how to help men open up, share their feelings, become comfortable with women. Executive search firms agree, adding that one of the major barriers to the promotion of women is the male executive who does not understand women and can only look on them in such supportive roles as wives, mothers, daughters, and secretaries. This musty attitude is as much a problem for the male executive, whose narrow perspective denies him the productive abilities of qualified women, as it is for the women whose progress he attempts to stall.

As women in so-called traditional male jobs cease to be a novelty, men are beginning to recognize the benefits that women bring to the workplace. A survey of male CEOs in Fortune 500 companies on the effects of women in executive positions yielded a generally positive reaction, with a substantial percentage stating that women bring a humanizing quality to the corporate world and are also improving business. The growth of an information/service economy calls for the kind of skills and problem-solving approaches that are essentially feminine. Information and service are, like women's historic culture, processual; and there is a developing awareness in business and industry of the linkage between productivity and what is usually referred to as "human resources," or the relationships among people at work.

Mary Bradley, a former teacher in adult education and now a corporate training director, has this to say on the subject of the feminine influence on technology: "Formerly, my experience and that of most women has consisted of learning how to function in a male system. But in my present work environment, which combines computer technology with education, the situation is reversed: men have to move into what has always been a female system—education, helping people develop new skills, which is what a high-technology economy is all about—and when it comes to education, men whose training has been exclusively in business and industry are totally lost. They understand equipment, marketing, the good old bottom line, but they don't know what goes into the development of a human being. They've never before paid much attention to human needs in their enterprises—they thought that was for social workers. But now they have to pay attention because it means money and expansion and business opportunities."

In the "improving business" area, women's interpersonal skills receive a consistently high rating among employers. The ability to convey warmth and empathy goes a long way, in everything from selling stocks and bonds to winning cases in court. The once solidly male world of Wall Street acknowledges that female brokers are making a special contribution to the field because of their tendency to pay more attention to a client's needs. Moreover, women are better at selling because of their superior verbal talents. "In this business we sell products that are very ephemeral," says Gail Winslow, who is with a brokerage firm in Washington. "Women have an edge because we tend to paint pictures with our words."[6]

In the tough, combative legal arena, Patricia Bobb, a Chicago attorney, finds an advantage for women in their extra "verbal sensitivity to jurors," a quality that Judge Jerry Pacht of Los Angeles has observed in his courtroom and which he believes gives female attorneys an edge in jury selection. An attorney and professor of

law, Grace Blumberg, describes the process through which a group
of female lawyers developed a brief on a divorce case dealing with
a woman's right to community property as "communitarian and
communicative, full of feeling and interpersonal experience. . . .
They created an atmosphere of social intimacy between relative
strangers." With women approaching 50 percent of law school
graduates as compared with 10 percent twenty to thirty years ago,
legal scholars and other specialists are looking forward to long-
overdue changes in the legal system. Says Derek Bok, president of
Harvard University, "Over the next generation, I predict society's
greatest opportunities will lie in tapping human inclinations toward
collaboration and compromise rather than stirring our proclivities
for competition and rivalry."

For many women in influential positions, changing the workplace is at the heart of their commitment to feminism. For Donna
Shalala, the practice of feminism is not limited to serving as a role
model; it encompasses "thinking of ways in which I can humanize
the institution." She believes that women's issues should be integrated into a larger, humanistic agenda. "My single professional
focus is to make institutions act better than they ever thought they
could act." As assistant secretary at the Department of Housing and
Urban Development during the Carter administration, she called the
department heads together to conduct a "women's impact study,"
as a result of which shelters for battered women became eligible for
community development grants, and housing units to accommodate
large families headed by a woman were included in planning.

Humanizing the institution does not always take the form of
large-scale social advances; it often manifests itself in more subtle
ways, such as the softening of the sterile ambience of the workplace
in an effort to make it more homelike. Sue Bohle, president of her
own public relations firm with offices in Los Angeles and San Francisco, lets her supervisors choose the type of furniture they want.
"I like antique reproductions and lots of plants, and my walls are
done in a rose brocaded print. But if you go next door, you'll see an
office done in contemporary furnishings—teak and beige. Everyone
gets to select her own colors and designs; it's highly individualized." Bohle encourages her staff to develop their social skills and

to consult her about any problems, personal or professional. "It's important for me to feel that they're happy at their work. That may have something to do with me personally, but I think it also has something to do with my being a woman. I'm willing to take the time to listen and talk to them about their problems, even when I'm under great pressure."

The willingness to listen and the quality of caring and comforting that exists in many women comes through in their work, sometimes without their being aware of it, as they go about their daily tasks in the business and professional world. The cumulative effect of such empathic behavior does not show up in organizational blueprints or financial statements; but in building small, often imperceptible bridges between home and work, this aspect of feminization is performing a function essential to the health of the American workplace.

YOU *CAN* GO HOME AGAIN

A trend that reflects most vividly the attempt to bring home and work together is the rise of the home-based business, a form of entrepreneurship that includes among its growing number of adherents many dropouts from the corporate rat-race. Starting a home-based business is a risky venture, and there are numerous failures, recalling the fate of the small entrepreneurs in the late nineteenth century. But the payoffs are attractive enough to lure a growing number of people who prefer a residential work setting and control over their working lives to the security, such as it is, of a nine-to-five job.

Working at home has always been a preferred option for women; for some women, during the early child-care years, it has been the only possible income-producing option available to them. At the turn of the century, women ran boardinghouses, did dressmaking and other types of sewing, and turned out piecework in their homes for sweat shops. Today, an estimated 1 million women in the United States operate businesses from their homes. They work part-time and full-time, earning salaries ranging from pin money to hundreds of thousands of dollars a year, and their businesses cover all kinds of professional services as well as products developed from homemaking skills. They have their own network, a national association that performs educational and informational services for women with home-based businesses.

Today, working at home is attracting men as well as women, in small-town and rural areas as well as in large cities. In Los Angeles, Elaine Carlson baked cookies in her kitchen and sold them out of her home before going into national distribution. In New York, Carlos Echegaray creates painted wooden sculptures of cats and sells them worldwide to galleries and museums. In rural Wisconsin, Jean Ellison hand-looms cloth and sells it as fast as it is woven to neighbors and local shops. Columnist Jim Sanderson quotes a man he identifies as Roger: "Not every man is gung ho about the corporate world. I've always wanted to run my own shop. For three years my wife helped me develop a mail-order business out of our home. Now she's gone to work full-time, which she loves, and I stay home with the kids and still make a modest living. It's terrific; everybody gets what they want."

Other home-based businesses include aerobics exercise, yoga and karate classes, catering services, hairstyling, copy editing, jewelry design, not to mention an ever-expanding variety of consulting services, some of them, like those offered by computer consultants, spawned by high tech. And a number of organizations, among them universities, government agencies, and business corporations, are encouraging some of their employees to work at home by having them plug in the modems of their computers to the organization's computer technology.

The working-at-home trend is being accelerated by several recent developments, especially the growing popularity of mail-order shopping as a time and money saver, and the availability of home computers, which make it possible to run a small business with little or no clerical help. These practical considerations are bolstered by a changing set of personal priorities that are motivating men and women to reexamine such concepts as "success" and "achievement" and to weigh them against the costs of following traditional paths to these goals. Recent studies of masculine and feminine attitudes toward success suggest a growing disenchantment among both sexes with the prevailing standards by which success is defined: the relentless striving, the ruthless competitiveness, the tensions and conflicts endemic to the hyper, all-against-all environment in which the game of success is played.

REEVALUATING SUCCESS

The idea of success has always carried different nuances for women than for men. Traditionally, a woman's success was measured by the achievements of her husband and children. But today's high-salaried women executives or self-made entrepreneurs are still in many cases ambivalent about applying the term *successful* to themselves, unless they are also enjoying a satisfying personal life. Tinka Streibert, who gave up an executive job in television to run a child-care center, defines success as "knowing in your gut that what you're doing is right for you." For Karen Szurek, a New York public relations executive, success is two-sided: one side is material, the other concerns the quality of one's personal life; both are equally important. Younger women starting their own businesses say that they are not interested primarily in making money but rather in doing things they enjoy that fit in with their lives.

As the workplace becomes feminized, the feminine definition of success is being adopted by younger men who, disenchanted by the remorseless pressures of their fathers' lives, are attracted to the feminine model of a balance between work and family. Betty Friedan writes of a man in Rhode Island who quit his job at a bank to take care of the house and kids and to paint at home, while his wife, sick of being a housewife, was happy to get a lesser job at the same bank. "I think you're going to see a great wave of men dropping out," he told Friedan. "All we've been hearing for years now is, What does it mean to be a woman? and How can she fulfill herself? But what does it mean to be a man? What do we have but our jobs? Let her support the family for a while, and let me find myself. . . .''[7] The increasing tendency for these younger men to reject corporate transfers when they conflict with their personal and family life has been reported by Yankelovich, among others. In a recent survey among 400 economics students at Stanford University, both men and women rated a happy marriage as more important than a successful career in attaining the good life.

"We have a large number of students who are turned off on the corporate bullshit," said Dr. Richard Buskirk, director of the Entrepreneur Program at the University of Southern California's School of Business Administration. "They realize that they want control over their own destinies." Social theoretician and futurist Willis Harman adds that work is enhanced when performed in the environment of home and community. "The best solution to having sufficient and satisfactory work roles is found not in some form of job enrichment in the main market economy but in the multitudinous activities involved in a learning and consciously evolving society."[8]

For the majority of working people, who must depend on the mainstream market economy for their economic survival, the good news is that feminization is enriching not only working life but family life as well. Contrary to the conventional wisdom and the gloomy pronouncements of fundamentalists on the subject, it appears that, in families in which both parents work and share breadwinning and caretaking responsibilities, the family bonds and values—human as opposed to material—are strengthened. According to Professor Sheila B. Kamerman of Columbia University, who has studied such families, working mothers and their husbands place more importance and rely more on these bonds, not only with each other and their children but with their parents and other relatives, than do comparable families conforming to the more traditional configuration of housewife-breadwinner.

The feminization of the workplace is making it possible for both sexes to enjoy a greater range of work options, and a more human, more livable working environment; by reintegrating work and home, both men and women can experience these two worlds with a sense of wholeness, "not as tearing their lives apart," says Emily Stoper, "but as weaving them together, as reuniting two halves.'' Combining work and love, Freud's prescription for the good life, is our best hope for avoiding stress and burnout and restoring meaning and purpose to our personal and working lives.

6. RESHAPING THE FAMILY

The feminization of work and the workplace is sending reverberations throughout American society, but nowhere is its impact being felt more profoundly or more extensively than in our basic social unit, the family. We can think of no other social development in recent history that has affected the lives of so many people, regardless of gender, age, or income level. Attitudes, institutions, and relationships long regarded as sacrosanct and eternal are being pulled apart and put together again in new and surprising ways. Motherhood is no longer perceived as a full-time, lifetime occupation. Instead, the idea is gaining ground that a woman whose life is happily balanced between family and work is more likely to bring a positive attitude to the mother-child relationship than a woman who feels trapped in the maternal role. The working mother, who only a few decades ago was denounced as a traitor to womanhood, sacrificing her children on the altar of her selfish ambitions, today is extolled in the media and by psychologists as a model of the contemporary woman who is able to "have it all."

But the transformation of motherhood is only a part of the evolving family story. Because men and women are complementary sexual creatures, any change in motherhood must inevitably produce an adaptive response in fatherhood; indeed, the "new father" may very well turn out to be the most revolutionary as well as the most positive outcome of feminization's reshaping of the family. Even those men with a usually condescending attitude toward all things feminine are beginning to recognize that feminization offers them an opportunity to revitalize the paternal image and put fatherhood and work into balance. The question of whether a man can have a career and a family too is beginning to receive an affirmative response.

The nuclear family, that tight little island with its built-in stresses and strains, is yielding to its inner explosiveness; it is being forced apart by its inability to adapt to a changing world. "Like it or not, the lifetime, male-dominated, two parent, multichild, breadwinner family has ceased to exist," anthropologist Marvin Harris states in his book *America Now*. "While it is true that most children will continue to be born into some kind of family situation, the kind of domestic unit involved and the typical pattern of life experiences with respect to residence, marriage, and child-rearing that Americans can look forward to as they grow up are fundamentally new additions to American culture."[1]

These new additions are bringing about an expanded definition of family, carrying it beyond biological and legal bonds to a more flexible and embracing vision; it is a vision that reflects the emerging realities of our time in which connections based exclusively on kinship and economic dependency are being replaced by wider bondings that supplement and support the central mother-child relationship. The new "feminized family" is, in fact, a social configuration that eases the traditional restraints on both sexes, therefore offering both a greater potential for personal growth.

CLOSING THE IMAGE-REALITY GAP

In revolutionizing the family, feminization has struck a particularly sensitive cultural nerve. The family is a powerful archetypal image that touches deep primal chords in the human psyche. It is our metaphorical security blanket, the repository of our dreams and longings, of our sense of self and place. The family occupies a sacred niche in the American belief system; "family values" is a phrase that is trotted out regularly and reverently by religious leaders and politicians running for office.

Archetypal images are notoriously resistant to change, and an image as potent as the family is particularly tenacious. Even as the reality moves light-years away, the image persists, setting itself up as a standard against which other forms are measured and labeled as deviant. The disparity between the traditional American image of the family and the contemporary reality has become as wide as a chasm; tucked away in our communal memory, wrapped in the glow of nostalgia and wishful thinking is a carefully preserved representation of the family according to Norman Rockwell. The picture is cosy and heartwarming: Dad the breadwinner, Mom the homemaker, and their apple-cheeked children gathered before the fireplace or around a sumptuous dinner table; so strong is the pull of this evocation on the heartstrings that it has managed, aided and abetted by such myth-mongers as Phyllis Schlafly and Jerry Falwell, to defy a growing mountain of contrary evidence.

The preeminent danger in clinging to a false social image is that a gap between image and reality tends to translate itself into a gap between public professions of belief and public action and policy, a disparity clearly evident in America's verbal commitment to "family values" in contrast with social policies that either ignore or erode those very same values.

The realities are clear and inescapable: Women are moving away from historic patterns of early marriage and childbearing to longer periods of singleness. During the decade of the 1970s, the number of women between the ages of twenty-five and thirty-four who had not married increased by 111 percent as compared with the number of women who were married and living with their husbands. The divorce rate has risen from one in six marriages in 1940 to one in two marriages in 1980.

The most disturbing aspect of this transition in women's lives is that women today account for a large and growing proportion of the economically disadvantaged, a situation that has been labeled "the feminization of poverty.'' Over 80 percent of all single-parent households are headed by women, and nearly 50 percent of female-headed families are at the bottom of the economic heap. Children of these families receive inadequate care or none at all while their mothers are at work. In many two-parent families, both parents must work in order to maintain a decent standard of living and provide for their children's education. As the *Wall Street Journal* put it: ''The workingman breadwinner who doesn't have a wife on the payroll just may wind up not having enough bread.''

Yet, until the recent swelling of the tide of feminization, social policies barely reflected these and similar problems. Employer-sponsored quality day-care was proceeding at a snail's pace largely because the corporate sector continued to cherish the antiquated illusion that women were ''temporary workers'' who would eventually return to their true calling as homemakers and mothers. Women's wages were grossly inequitable in relation to men's, again because of a false assumption that it was men who were the economic backbone of the family. Pregnancy usually meant that the expectant mother would lose her job. Professional schools and training programs discriminated against women, and many of the better-paying occupations were for men only. Although there has been substantial improvement in several of these areas, thanks to the feminization of the workplace, public policy is still a long way from matching its words with deeds. Both education and social programs favoring women and children are being scuttled in favor of an obscenely swollen military budget. The United States is still almost alone among Western industrialized nations in having no coherent family policy.

Why has the feminizing trend been unable so far to overcome these remaining barriers to equality between the sexes, barriers that continue to obscure the realities of contemporary American life? ''It almost seems as if we are looking at an effort to deal with a real need by denying that it exists,'' comments Elizabeth Janeway. ''In an individual, we would call that a neurotic reaction. What shall we say about it when we observe it in society at large?''[2]

Of course, changes as sweeping as those occurring in the family invariably meet with resistance, particularly from the more traditional sectors of society, so it was to be expected that the transformation of the family would evoke a certain amount of hand wringing and breast beating. We hear on all sides—from pulpit and press, from authors of self-help books and producers of TV documentaries—that the family today is in crisis. In fact, it would appear from glancing through history that the family is in perennial crisis. "The family in the old sense is disappearing from our land, and not only our free institutions are threatened but the very existence of our society is endangered," warned the *Boston Quarterly* in 1859. For at least a century, observes historian John Demos, the American family has been seen as "beleaguered, endangered and on the edge of extinction. The sense of crisis is hardly new; with some allowance for periodic ebb and flow, it seems an inescapable undercurrent of our modern life and consciousness." Like the theater, that "fabulous invalid," the family appears to be always in the grip of a terminal illness, yet somehow manages always to survive.

The cures and nostrums prescribed for the patient's troubles are numerous and various, ranging from heavier doses of religion and parental discipline to communal, kibbutzim-type living arrangements, but the diagnoses are remarkably similar; they usually involve some reference to women's abdication of their family responsibilities, a charge that grows in volume whenever women enter the workplace in substantial numbers. Thus, each postwar period has been characterized by pressure on women to leave their jobs in factory and office and return to their domestic duties; the preservation of the family, they were assured, depended on it.

Today, however, the "family crisis" has taken on new dimensions. There is no longer any question of women returning to the home; it is generally acknowledged that their skills and energies are essential to a growing economy. And with an ever-rising tide of women in the work force, the old refrain about the downfall of society resulting from women leaving the home is losing some of its persuasiveness. More than two-thirds of the mothers in this country are working women, and child psychologists and other researchers who have been studying this momentous development are coming up with some surprising findings. They are discovering that the working mother, while she has many unresolved problems and anxieties, is not a major threat to marital and family stability. On the contrary, the changes appear to be on the whole beneficial. Although women's economic independence may break up some marriages, it solidifies others, and studies suggest that the children of working mothers tend to be more socially outgoing and adaptable.

As women's changing culture narrows the gap between the image and reality of the family, it is fostering a growing public recognition of the need to replace worn-out perceptions with new concepts and definitions reflecting today's changing family life.

THE FAMILY REDEFINED

> As night falls young boys and girls can be seen in all directions carrying large pots of cooked food. . . . The food is being taken by the children from the houses in which their mothers reside to those in which their fathers live. Thus, one learns that that husband and wife often belong to different domestic groups, the children perhaps sleeping in their mothers' houses and eating with their fathers.
>
> —MEYER FORTES, *"An Ashanti Case Study,"* in *Leibowitz,*
> *Females, Males, Families*

A search through more recent anthropological literature for a definition of the family quickly reveals that there is no such entity as *the* family; rather, there is a large repertoire of adaptive social arrangements, all coming under the heading of family. Only since the 1960s have anthropologists given serious attention to the family, and the resulting cross-cultural studies of non-Western societies have revealed the inadequacy of earlier attempts at definition. The classic definition, offered in G. P. Murdock's pioneering 1949 work, *Social Structure,* proposed three criteria for the family as a social group: common residence, economic cooperation, and repro-

duction. But while these appear to be basic and universal characteristics, recent research has turned up social units lacking one or
more of these identifying marks that are nevertheless still recogniz-
ably "family."

As we see in Meyer Fortes's description of Ashanti domestic
society, an arrangement that bears a certain resemblance to shared
custody in contemporary America, a family need not live together
in order to be considered a family. Another example of families not
sharing a residence nor cooperating in economic activities can be
found among the Catholic Celts of present-day Ireland, where husbands remain with their consanguineal or "blood" relatives after
marriage and their wives stay on with their own parents. On some
kibbutzim in Israel, married couples live in a room together, have
their meals in a communal dining-room, and work in a communal
corporation, while their children sleep, eat, and are educated in
communal nurseries and dormitories. England's famous men's
clubs serve as "incidental or auxiliary residences for upper-class
British husbands, but in a number of societies men's clubhouses are
the regular living places of married men."[3] Today in the United
States, two-career couples whose work requires that they live in
different geographical areas may maintain their family life through
complicated commuting schedules.

In one society alone, the Marquesan Islanders in Polynesia, the
following variations can be found on the family theme: a husband
and wife sharing a household; a wife with several husbands; a married man formally married to an already-married woman who
brings along her former husband; "secondary husbands," or unmarried men who are attached to households but free to leave.
Alongside these sexual combinations and permutations, the shifting
family arrangements in today's Western societies seem almost
staid.

In fact, despite the upheavals and experimentation of recent
years, the independent nuclear family, though fraying at the seams,
remains the prevailing form in modern industrialized societies. As
Philippe Aries points out in his *Centuries of Childhood,* the modern
family in the Western world has moved away from its seventeenth-
century origins in the households of wealthy merchants; there it was

a center of social relations, "the capital of a little complex and graduated society under the command of the paterfamilias. The modern family, on the contrary, cuts itself off from the world and opposes to society the isolated group of parents and children."⁴

But the isolated child-centered family, so admirably suited to an industrial capitalist economy for which it provides a stable supply of disciplined male workers, is today straining against the changing values and needs of a postindustrial global system in which interdependence rather than all-out individualism is the key to survival. In the process of adaptation, family roles and relationships once tightly woven into the social fabric are unravelling, and new patterns are taking their place.

BALANCING MOTHERHOOD

In nonindustrial societies, a woman's role as wife and mother must encompass economic activities as well as child care. "She cannot afford to be exclusively absorbed in her child," anthropologists Hammond and Jablow state in their cross-cultural study of women. "The absence of complete concentration on the child may be reflected in many societies by the ready way in which children are passed from one household to another. A childless couple, an old person living alone, a mother needing a nursemaid—all may be lent a child to live with them for a time to perform needed services."⁵ This kind of mothering—part-time, integrating child-care duties into a multiplex pattern of daily activities—was also the norm, as we noted in our discussion of the workplace, in the premodern West.

How did motherhood in modern Western society develop into an all-consuming professionalized activity? This heart-of-the-matter question leads us back to the home-workplace separation, when the productive economic functions of the home were transferred from the private to the public sector as the nation became industrialized. The vacuum that this left in women's lives was filled by the role of mother, which overshadowed even the role of wife. The clergy, the educational system, and the women's magazines joined in a chorus of praise for woman's maternal function. Motherhood was sanctified, designated as woman's supreme fulfillment, an experience without which she was incomplete, regardless of what other notable achievements she might have to her credit. Let her write the great American novel, climb Everest, discover a cure for a rampaging disease—if she was childless, she was still considered something less than a woman.

Motherhood now became the main source not only of woman's glory but of her power. Like nature, power abhors a vacuum, and the empty space in women's lives would now be filled as would the empty space in their wombs—with children. Here was where women could properly invest their energies and nurturing abilities, fulfill their biological destiny, and make their most valued contribution to society. Through their children, women would gain authority and exercise influence.

Of course, this power has had to be carefully camouflaged so as not to overtly challenge the traditional lines of family authority. Disguising their power is something women have become adept at through long experience in many different cultures. An anthropologist, discussing the power of a Yugoslavian matron he knew in that most patriarchal peasant culture, described her as a "cryptomatriarch," or secret maternal ruler. Her influence had accumulated over time through her control of her sons, her daughters-in-law, the obligations she had created over a lifetime in those around her. But this power always had to be deployed cleverly, with great deference to the social fiction that women were inconsequential and men were in charge.

The cryptomatriarch can be found in various geographical areas and social settings. In America, she has been immortalized by Philip Wylie as the devouring, soul-destroying Mom, whose sins include, among others, emasculating her sons and inducing frigidity in her daughters. With an assist from Philip Roth, she has taken on ethnic trappings, emerging full-blown as that legend in our time, the Jewish mother, whose dominance in the family rests on the twin supports of food and guilt. In Daniel Moynihan's study of the black family, she presides over her fatherless brood with iron fist in velvet glove. She appears again in an Irish variation as the indomitable Juno, subtly ruling a roost officially headed by her pathetic "paycock" of a husband. Wherever and in whatever guise she appears, she is a formidable figure, manipulating, managing, wheeling and dealing, exercising for all it is worth the only power she has been permitted to have.

The price of power is responsibility, and the full-time middle-class mother has been made acutely aware of the heavy responsibility that goes with her maternal power. She has been instilled with the conviction that raising a child is a complex process, requiring a sophisticated level of knowledge and skill. In short, she has become a professional mother, a "super-mom" steeped in the theories of Spock, Fraiberg, Erikson, Winnicott, and Mahler and thoroughly familiar with such concepts in child psychology as "separation trauma," "emotional object constancy," and "core identity." Caring for her children is her career, and she is the family decision-maker where the children are concerned. It follows that she also bears the burden of responsibility for how her children turn out; their achievements are chalked up to her credit; their failures are *her* failure.

This has created a family structure tilted dangerously out of balance, which has become associated with such personality and relationship disorders as the narcissistic child, the displaced father, and in the family's later years, the disoriented, "empty nest" mother, bereft of her raison d'être. It is actually a fragile structure, since it rests on a conflicting image of motherhood, which "has often placed *abstract* woman on a pedestal but has at the same time left *concrete* women at home alone and powerless."[6] The economics of motherhood bears little relation to the ideology. Divorce usually leaves a woman in a drastically reduced financial situation. Only 25 percent of the women awarded child support actually receive it, and 60 percent of these receive less than $1,500 a year. (The flight from commitment that Barbara Ehrenreich details in *The Hearts of Men* includes the evasion by divorced fathers of financial responsibilities.)[7] These are some of the hard realities forcing a reevaluation of motherhood and replacing dangerously outworn myths with more realistic approaches to mothering and its place in contemporary family life.

Foremost among the myths now being reappraised is that of "maternal instinct," which presumably equips all women with the skills, aptitudes, and emotional equipment required for happy, efficient mothering. Relying on this "natural instinct" frequently results in a confused, anxiety-ridden mother who, when the child-rearing experience is not going according to plan, wonders why her instincts are not working properly. Fortunately, this myth is fading into the past as anthropologists, social historians, and other scholars turn up evidence that mothering in the human species is learned behavior, which some women learn better than others and which can also be acquired by men.

An even more stubborn myth, that a child deprived of constant maternal care is susceptible to serious psychological and possibly physical disturbances, is being effectively countered by the experience of working mothers. The earlier view was summed up by the influential child psychiatrist Selma Fraiberg, who maintained that "when a child spends eleven or twelve hours of his waking day in the care of indifferent custodians, no parent and no educator can say that the child's development is being promoted or enhanced."

But as their field of research expands, child specialists are finding that working mothers convey a positive message to their children, both male and female. As a role model for their daughters, they exemplify the rewards of combining work and family and thus encourage their daughters to develop greater self-esteem and independence. The message to their sons stresses egalitarian relationships within the family and greater sensitivity to the needs of women. In "The Working Mother as Role Model," Anita Shreve reports that a nine-year-old boy, asked what mothers can do, responded that mothers can be lawyers, cops, and President—and added as an afterthought that fathers can be lawyers, cops, and presidents, too.[8]

Full-time mothering is not necessarily an advantage for children, says Lois W. Hoffman, a University of Michigan psychology professor, mother of two, and author of several books on working mothers. "A lot of women who stay at home don't feel good about it. They feel that their contribution is not valuable. So they spend their time doing for their children things that the children should probably do for themselves."

Some studies indicate that girls benefit more from working mothers than boys, since girls are more mature and emotionally stable than boys of the same age. Boys whose mothers work occasionally score lower on IQ tests than girls in a comparable situation, but the results so far have been too inconclusive to establish a clear cause-and-effect relationship. There is less doubt on another area of concern, the issue of gender identification. Dr. E. Kirsten Dahl, assistant professor of anthropology at Yale's Child Study Center, says that where such confusion exists, it is more likely related to some deep disturbance in the parent-child relationship and not a result of the mother's career or the domestic division of responsibilities.

A more self-reliant, less narcissistic personality type with a greater appreciation of gender diversity is one of the benefits we can look forward to as a result of more flexible, more realistic attitudes toward the maternal role. It is becoming more widely accepted that the selfless, nourishing love we associate with good mothering has less to do with the measurable quantity of time spent with a child than with the intangible quality of that time. A woman whose life is happily balanced between family and work is more likely to bring a positive attitude to the mother-child relationship than a woman who feels trapped in the maternal role.

BALANCING FATHERHOOD

That some real live men, neither widowers nor grand-fathers, take part in baby and child care was extremely apparent to me in the ethnically mixed neighborhood in which I grew up. . . . Because my experiences told me that there are ethnic and individual differences in both fathering and mothering, the popular American

ideal or image of fatherhood did not strike me as applying to all males everywhere. But when I got to be
an anthropology student my neighborhood and my
experiences began to appear extraordinary, as, over
and over again, the accounts I read of childrearing in
other cultures mentioned men rarely (if at all) and usually only in conjunction with teaching older boys male
skills. Why?

—LILA LEIBOWITZ, *Females, Males, Families*

The father has been the invisible man in social science research, a shadowy figure who when he does make a rare appearance is usually in the background, a footnote to the societal saga of
family relationships. And yet, even in cultures in which child care
is considered woman's work, the father often has important child-
caring obligations. Among the Mbuti Pygmy people in Uganda,
fathers act as "male mothers," sharing some of the experiences of
mothering after the child is two years old; among the Ojibwa
people, the largest tribe of Algonquin Indians in northern Mexico,
the men take on child-caring tasks when their wives are absorbed in
such chores as scraping and curing hides; among the Marquesans,
babies are breastfed briefly and then turned over to be cared for by
their concerned and attentive fathers. Bushmen males care for their
infants or cradle their sleepy or sleeping youngsters while they
chat.[9]

These loving and involved fathers certainly have their counterparts in the industrialized West, particularly in subcultures that en-
courge emotional expressivity in men. "As a parent, I am like my
expansive Italian father," says Joseph Giordano. "He openly
expressed his feelings—in belly laughs, anger, or tears—and I
loved that spontaneity. . . . I too, openly and physically, share my
emotions with my two sons. I need to touch, to feel, to see them.
I can't explain this inner need, but it has always been there."[10]

But like motherhood, fatherhood has developed its own archetypal image, originating in man the hunter, who had to be free of
child-rearing responsibilities in order to provide food for his family;

[109]

the image reappears in the modern world as man the breadwinner-protector, whose financial responsibility occupies him totally, draining him of the time and energy for anything more than a token involvement in the family's affairs. Family problems, according to the conventional scenario, are his wife's department; she is expected to protect him from domestic intrusions upon his scarce and precious moments of relaxation at home.

Like most images, the one of the strong, self-contained male as breadwinner has retained its hold on the popular imagination despite evidence of its growing distance from reality. Barbara Ehrenreich has shown that men began abandoning their family-breadwinner role a good ten years before the 1960s revival of the women's movement, which has served as the standard scapegoat for the "breakdown of the family." Ehrenreich argues that the playboy mentality and the counterculture, conspiring to re-define "responsibility" as "guilt," set off the male revolt against the traditional family structure.

But it seems only fair to suggest that, if men have been reluctant to shoulder the responsibilities of fatherhood, it could well be because they have been cast in such a marginal role in the family drama. Consider the experience of the father in the traditional model of the family. From the beginning, he feels useless, displaced. A typical comment from a father seeing his wife as the center of attention while her focus is turned to the new baby: "I feel like a fifth wheel. What was my role in the whole production, five minutes?"

His problem has been made especially acute in recent years when couples have been taking Lamaze training during the last ten weeks of pregnancy and have become accustomed to working as a team. The husband has been functioning as coach to his wife, has helped her to anticipate every breath, every contraction and suddenly, after the birth he assisted at, he is no longer important. His wife and baby have moved to center stage while he has been left in the wings, ignored and irrelevant.

As his wife becomes totally occupied in caring for the children, he often becomes completely absorbed in his work, and has almost no part in the day-to-day care of the young. The workplace, organized solely for efficiency, has not in the past been concerned with balancing family roles and relationships, and has firmly discouraged personal ties and emotional attachments that conflict with work.

But the work ethic, unleavened by the warm nurturing bonds of family, has begun to seem empty and meaningless. The assumption that all men are comfortable in the workplace, with its rapacious competitiveness and impersonal code of conduct, is as erroneous as the notion that all women are natural-born mothers. The growing number of men going into therapy testifies to the corrosive effect on the male psyche of life in today's business and industrial world. Doubts about intimacy, self-worth, and the work ethic head the list of problems that are sending men to psychotherapists.

"These are men in a state of great personal distress," says Phoenix psychologist Matilda B. Canter. "They may have denied it up to now, but it is finally hitting them. In recent years much attention has gone into heightening awareness and understanding of women's rights, women's issues, and the female experience." Now, she believes, it is time to begin addressing "the many aspects of the evolving male experience."

New York psychologist Herbert J. Freudenberger, whose client load is now 50 percent male, traces the rising tide of male distress partly to myth and role conditioning. Davy Crockett, Kit Carson, Daniel Boone—these legendary heroes of the Old West represented the model for the American male: a man who was in control, who "could do anything he wished; he was all-powerful, courageous." Then came women's liberation, and the increasing number of women entering the work force; this caused "a profound shift in the home, in parenting, and in the previously unquestioned and seemingly predestined male role functioning."[11]

Among men who are questioning previously accepted roles and functions are divorced fathers who see their children only on occasional weekends and who are experiencing an emotional mix of anger and guilt over their loss of day-to-day contact with their children. "I feel betrayed," said one of these men. "I played according to the rules, worked my tail off to give my family a decent standard of living—and then it all fell apart. My kids are growing up without me, and that hurts; I never realized how much it would hurt."

Although many men are experiencing confusion and disorientation, this new questioning and soul-searching can be seen as a sign of health, an indication that masculine culture is being reevaluated and weighed against the values of feminine culture. A working mother takes some of the financial pressure off the man of the family, giving him leeway to pursue more congenial, less demanding employment. When a man is not forced to carry the entire breadwinning burden, he can invest more of his time and energy in fatherhood; he may even discover, as is happening today, that fathering brings him greater satisfaction than his wage-earning activities.

This recent upsurge of male appreciation of the family has been generating new images in literature, the movies, and the press. In the film *Kramer vs. Kramer,* Dustin Hoffman was converted from an indifferent to a tenacious father through day-to-day contact with his son during his wife's absence. In the book *The Duke of Deception,* Geoffrey Woolf writes of the depth and durability of the father-son relationship. John Updike's novels offer poignant portraits of men struggling and surviving, as husbands, fathers, sons. A new newsletter for men, *Nurturing News,* is being published by David Giveans, who is single and childless, and Michael Robinson, who is a househusband and primary care-giver for his two small sons while his wife works full-time as a buyer. The newsletter features topics concerning men and children, grandfathers, stepfathers, and psychological fathers, the latter term referring to those men other than biological fathers who are in some way responsible for a child's development and well-being.

It is becoming apparent, in fact, as working parents negotiate and adjust parental roles, that at times the best mother for a child may be the father. A recent study of the role-reversed family, where the mother works full-time and the father is at home as the full-time parent, has disclosed that the children in these families tend to be more socially active and to perform better on adaptive-skill tests than children in traditional families where the father works and the mother stays home.

Dr. Kyle Pruett, associate clinical professor of psychiatry at Yale, who conducted the study, attributes these differences to the fact that the children of role-reversed families have two "stimulating" parents—the father, who handles the child in a "jostling, stimulating" manner, and the mother, whose comings and goings stimulate the child's curiosity and imagination.

Role-reversed families are still relatively few in number, but the involved father is an increasingly familiar figure on the family scene. A recent national Gallup survey reveals that four out of five fathers are now in the delivery room at the births of their children. Sixty-two percent of prospective fathers attend childbirth classes with their wives, and 58 percent help take care of the babies. Sixty percent change diapers and 67 percent feed their babies. And 24 percent of new mothers who planned to go back to work said their husbands would take care of the child. Men are also increasingly insisting on their rights as fathers by demanding that they be involved in decisions about abortions and access to the children of divorce.

Young fathers are pushing their children in strollers or carrying them strapped to their backs; not-so-young fathers are shepherding their teen-age children to music lessons, movies, sports events— these "new fathers" of the '80s have broken out of the traditional mold and are obviously enjoying it. The future for fathers looks brighter than it has in the past, and this could mean an eventual strengthening of the family as it is reshaped into new adaptive arrangements.

An arrangement that is increasing dramatically as a result of the high divorce and remarriage rate is the "blended" or "reconstituted" family. Families in which the children are a mix of his, hers, and theirs are no longer uncommon. In fact, family therapists predict that by the end of the decade, these families will be the norm. Psychologist Judith Wallerstein, in studying the effects of divorce on children, reports that when stepfamily members are asked to draw a family tree, "dozens of aunts, stepaunts, uncles, stepuncles, stepbrothers and stepsisters, and as many as eight sets of grandparents are sometimes listed."[12]

These shifting combinations and recombinations of family relationships can be, and often are, confusing for the children involved. But parents as well as children in blended families agree that there are positive aspects. As the family tree branches out, the new configuration begins to resemble more and more the extended family of earlier times. Children have a variety of adults to relate to, and through the extension of their family, they develop an expanded view of the universe. Although it will be some years before research on these new family constellations can yield definitive information, some child psychologists and family therapists are making educated guesses that the children growing up in these families, because of their experience with diffuse affectional ties, will have an easier time with personal relationships in their adult lives than the children of nuclear families.

The family today is in an unstable, transitional phase as it struggles in a time of flux to break out of the ancient tribal system of clannish, binding kinship ties, an arrangement based on physical and psychological dependency and a narrowing down of the social group—the "restricted family," as anthropologist Claude Levi-Strauss terms it. But as the rigid and arbitrary forms of the past are rejected in favor of more open, balanced, and creative styles of living together, the family's redefinition and reshaping reflect our changing lives and our everlasting need for nourishing, supportive relationships.

7. FEMINIZING HEALTH CARE

W omen's changing attitude toward their bodies is redefining illness as it has been applied to their normal biological functioning, and this altered perception is affecting not only feminine body consciousness but also the practice of medicine, as well as sexuality, law, sports, politics, and the economy. Health care for women is far more than a feminine concern; it has profound social implications. Women's bodies are the source of reproduction of the species, and it is this power of creation that has endowed the female body with its mystique and its ambivalence.

In the Navaho religion, the ultimate mystery is the power of rejuvenation, which is obtained by identification with Changing Woman, the archetypal symbol of the natural cycle of birth, death, and rebirth. But in Western cultures, the female body, with its potential for bringing forth and nourishing new life, has been through the ages "a field of contradiction," as Adrienne Rich puts it, "a space invested with power and an acute vulnerability; a numinous figure and the incarnation of evil; a hoard of ambivalences, most of which have worked to disqualify women from the collective art of defining culture."[1]

It was this growing sense of exclusion from decisions affecting even their own bodies that fed women's discontent with the male-dominated health-care system. Specifically, their critique of the system cited its emphasis on technology, the depersonalization of the individual, the dominant-subordinate relationship of doctor and patient, the performing of unnecessary surgery (particularly mastectomies, cesareans, and hysterectomies), and the use of intrusive techniques in examination.

The indictment was aimed most directly at two specialties: gynecology and psychiatry. Here, in women's areas of greatest vulnerability, the medical approach to their needs has been most damaging. Gynecologist Herbert Keyser agrees that women are more susceptible to medical abuse. "Women are second-class citizens in medicine, as they have been in all of society. Women are more willing to be told by a man that this is what they have to do."

As women became convinced that the practice of medicine could be hazardous to their health, they began to realize the price they were paying for turning over the responsibility for their bodies to a depersonalized, male-dominated health-care system. The development of a new feminine body consciousness, together with a burgeoning feminist movement in the 1960s and 1970s, coalesced in the women's health movement. Made up of a loose affiliation of groups throughout the country, the movement is community based but has a sophisticated national coordinating effort. This specific social movement emphasizes women's health and body issues and is committed to guiding women toward self-acceptance through understanding how their bodies work. More recently, the movement has expanded to include preventive medicine among its aims.

Through its manifold activities, self-help courses and workshops, lobbying caucuses against cancer-inducing estrogens and hazardous birth control procedures, films, booklets, conferences, the movement has helped women develop a healthy, informed attitude toward their bodies. Many women have experienced this changing attitude as an explosion of consciousness, but the transitional process has actually been a gradual one, marked by signposts that have exposed some of the dangerous misperceptions of the past and at the same time pointed to new directions for the future.

Betty Friedan's *The Feminine Mystique* was one of the early signposts, a basic existential analysis that has remained a dominant influence. The thalidomide scandal, which struck in full force in 1962, had already opened the way for discussions of the appropriate use of abortion and had generated an attitude of extreme skepticism in regard to administering potentially dangerous drugs to women—drugs such as DES and birth control pills which were made available without appropriate pre-testing. Publication of Masters and Johnson's *Human Sexual Response* in 1966 challenged the traditional sexual scenario by offering scientific evidence that women are multiorgasmic and that their sexual pleasure derives from active partnership rather than passive receivership. The formation and spread of consciousness-raising groups in the mid-60s made women aware of their physiological and sexual commonality.

These developments paved the way for the event that became the major rallying point for the women's health movement: The 1969 conference in Boston leading to the formation of the Boston Women's Health Collective, which in turn led to the publication of *Our Bodies, Ourselves* in 1971. The movement now had its bible, notable for having been written collectively as well as for its content, which is essentially a declaration of independence by women, expressing their determination to take more responsibility for their own bodies. Designed as a basic self-help course on female anatomy, the book covered the entire biological life cycle of women, and in addition provided detailed information on self-protection, rape, venereal disease, child-rearing and the American health-care system. (The collective has recently brought out an updated and expanded volume, its third major revision.)

Suddenly, or so it seemed, the barriers of ignorance separating women from their own bodies came tumbling down, and women began repossessing their bodies in many ways, beginning with self-knowledge. The self-examination movement, symbolized by the speculum (an instrument inserted into the vagina which, used with a mirror, makes the internal organs visible), reflected the growing resolve among women to gain a better understanding of their bodily functions, breaking their dependence upon a medical establishment that has traditionally labeled their health problems as weakness, hysteria, or hypochondria. Women began discovering that their "ailments" were in fact normal manifestations of female biology, and that premenstrual syndrome and menopausal symptoms could be alleviated or even eliminated through exercise and improved nutrition. The questioning of technological intervention in childbirth further affirmed women's newly born resolve to participate more actively in their own biological destiny.

As the movement gained momentum, it began tapping new sources of feminine energy, and women's health activities multiplied rapidly. Women's clinics, information and counseling services, and premenstrual and menopausal discussion groups began springing up around the country. Local and national organizations spearheaded action on sterilization abuse, abortion, rape, hazardous drugs and birth control devices, unnecessary surgery, and home births. A small group of women seeking to combat one of the most serious female health threats, cancer of the reproductive organs, initiated what has become the prototype for a new organizing approach that uses access to money and power; their project is committed to raising $1.5 million through corporate contributions to endow a chair in gynecological cancer research at New York's Sloan-Kettering Cancer Center. This represents the first time that funds have been earmarked for research on cancers that afflict women, and it was a small group of women, headed by Rosemarie Sena, senior vice-president of Shearson-American Express, who initiated the project. The fund has been committed to research in the area of gynecologic cancer, focusing on early detection of ovarian cancer in the same way that the Pap smear is used for early detection of cervical cancer.

THE HEALTH-CARE PROBLEM
AND HOW IT GREW

Since the philosopher Descartes separated a transcendent nonmaterial mind from the material and mechanical operations of the body, science has been concerned

with ever more accurately resolving that body into its component parts.
—JAMES S. GORDON, M.D., *Health for the Whole Person*

The women's health-care movement came about as an evolutionary response to a system that had become unbalanced and was losing the compassion and the personalism that make the practice of medicine a healing *art* as well as a science. As medicine became virtually a male monopoly, it began to lose touch with health needs and problems that did not lend themselves to rational-mechanistic approaches. Skewed toward advanced medical technology, gargantuan hospital centers, a high degree of specialization, and miracle drugs, it has become a system generally lacking in the feminine ethic of care and concern for the whole person as a complex unity of mind and spirit. Since health care is literally a matter of life and death, a serious imbalance in this cultural sector must be viewed as a problem of major dimensions. And as the facts and figures show, although the American health-care system is the costliest in the world, Americans are not getting what they are paying for.

Comparing America's health care record with that of other nations, we find that

The United States has one of the highest infant mortality rates in the industrialized world; the United Nations Demographic Yearbook for 1973 placed us fifteenth from the top, and the situation has not altered appreciably since then. Malnutrition and inadequate prenatal services are responsible for this shameful record.

The United States ranks fifth, not first, on low maternal death rates. Again, poor nutrition and prenatal care are the culprits.

Men in fifteen other countries live longer than American men, and American women are outlived by women in five other countries, all of them spending less per person on health care.

The obvious question is Where does all the money go? And the answer comes as no surprise to anyone with even a rudimentary knowledge of our health-care establishment: it goes into costly procedures and technologies designed to repair rather than prevent health problems. We have a system "whose planners seem never to have heard the words *preventive medicine,*" says Claudia Dreifus, editor of *Seizing Our Bodies*. As a result, an inordinate amount of money is spent on unregulated doctors' fees, unnecessary surgery, and high-tech therapies. In 1984, Americans spent $360 billion on health care, double what they spent in 1960. And of the annual increase in personal health-care spending since the 1970s, 30 to 40 percent has been attributed to new technology—drugs, equipment, procedures, and the systems in which they are used. A recent report by Congress's Office of Technology Assessment revealed that Medicare expenses rose an average of 19 percent per year between 1977 and 1982; nearly one-third of that increase was allocated to technology.

Health care is a cultural mirror of the society it serves, and the development of this massive, inefficient system has followed a historical trend that transferred many social functions from the private to the public sector as American society evolved from an agrarian to a corporate capitalist economy. Originally, health care was administered almost entirely at home. Following the ancient tradition of woman as healer, women were responsible for health care in the family, applying what became known as old home remedies often brewed up in the kitchen. Women also doctored each other, sharing information about problems related to menstruation, pregnancy, menopause, and other so-called female complaints. Babies were born at home, usually with the help of midwives. Women's reproductive functions were an integral part of female culture, which offered sympathy and support.

As health care became professionalized, the traditional midwife and woman as healer began to disappear; women were discouraged from entering the increasingly scientific, technological field of medicine, and male doctors took control of health care, including the treatment of women's most intimate physical functions.

At first, during the early years of this century, the doctor was not viewed as an omniscient unchallengeable authority, but rather as a family retainer, the lovable old doc of the magazine covers, a transitional figure between the home-centered health care that was passing into history and the institutionalized system that was looming on the horizon. The family doctor knew the family intimately, and though his knowledge of medicine may have been primitive by today's standards, his familiarity with the patient's life history and his own relationship to the family were often highly effective in bringing about a recovery. And since he relied on the woman of the household to act as his ally and nurse, she retained something of her role as caretaker of the family's health.

With the growing institutionalization of the "helping professions," society, in "the guise of a nurturing mother," to use Christopher Lasch's phrase, began taking over many of the family's private functions just as it had taken over most of its productive functions in the course of the industrial revolution. Health, education, and welfare moved steadily out of the privacy of the home and into the public domain of "experts," trained professionals who became increasingly dependent upon the technology and financial support of huge bureaucracies. Since discrimination against women by medical schools assured that these professionals would be mostly men, the medicalization of society became synonymous with the masculinization of medicine.

The family doctor, who had functioned as a generalist, gave way to the specialist, a product of medical training that stressed science, technology, and efficiency. The age of specialization was an inevitable reaction to the growing complexity of medicine. "To many young doctors, a clearly defined niche of technical competence seemed preferable to the complexity of general practice," writes John McPhee. "To varying extents, specialists could retreat into their specialties. As the medical technocracy grew, it reproduced itself by choosing its own kind from the pool of medical students. In their concentration on a single topic, most doctors seemed more than willing to lose touch with medicine as a whole."[2] The "nurturing mother" was becoming an aloof, impersonal father figure.

This new breed of physician appeared on the health-care scene as a technician whose time is strictly rationed, who has at best a superficial acquaintance with the patient's personal and family life, and who often is familiar with only one component of the patient's physiology. The introduction of Diagnosis-Related Groupings (DRGs), a cost-cutting aspect of medical insurance that classifies and groups illnesses for reimbursement purposes, tends to focus the doctor's and hospital's attention on the illness rather than the patient. The recent development of Health Maintenance Organizations, or HMOs, as they are commonly known, while offering certain cost-cutting advantages, has carried the trend toward impersonality even further: HMO members are treated by a doctor assigned at the time of the visit, which means that they may be treated by a different doctor each time. In such a system, the individual is merely a symptom or mass of symptoms, and the doctor, an authority figure whose relationship to the patient is formal and transitory. In this way, the practice of medicine becomes reduced to that of repairing parts.

In taking health care out of women's hands, the male medical establishment also distanced women from their own bodies. Women with problems relating to their feminine functions now depended not on themselves or other women but on male specialists in obstetrics and gynecology. As women were "helped" more and more, they became more and more dependent on professional help, even in bearing their children. Home births declined steeply—as one critic put it, babies were no longer born, they were *delivered*— and the midwife became, like the family doctor, a relic of the past, her practice limited to poor women who could not afford to go to a hospital.

RECLAIMING THE FEMALE BODY

For thousands of years, a woman's body has belonged to someone other than herself—her husband or his family. Two thousand years ago, the poet Catullus reminded the young girl that "your own maidenhead is not truly your own. One part to your father, one to your mother, only a third to yourself.'' And that third has to be consigned as a "bride gift" to the man she married. Transferring women's reproductive rights ("rights in gentricum"), which gives the male property rights over the progeny, has been a fundamental principle of social organization, society's way of controlling property and group membership.

Now that women can control their own fertility, because of reliable, safe birth control and safe and legal abortion, our social arrangements have been thrown into disarray. Here, where technology intersects with social change, are the gathering forces of a far-reaching revolution in our personal and family lives and beyond. As women reclaim their bodies and take responsibility for their own health and sexuality, the female body is "coming out of the closet," shedding centuries of secrecy and shame.

The embarrassment women have felt about their bodies stems from a long history of having had their physical functions, particularly those related to menstruation, treated as illnesses. Menstruation has been viewed as an ailment, "the curse," a period of fragility and repugnance, set about with taboos and limits. But in some cultures it serves as a socially approved outlet for fatigue and stress: the menstrual hut in which women in many tribal societies are isolated gives them a few days of release from the pressure of daily routines. Men and children are forbidden to enter the huts, and the atmosphere is relaxed and convivial.

Paradoxically, the cessation of menopause is also viewed as an illness, to be treated with hormone injections and surgery. (By contrast, many women in Africa, China, and in native-American societies experience menopause as a time of liberation and privilege. A cultural connection has been noted by Margaret Mead, who reported that menstrual and menopausal symptoms are absent from societies where the female role is less stressful.) In our society, even pregnancy and childbirth are classified as illnesses; as mentioned in our discussion of the changing workplace, the 1978 Federal Disability Act defines pregnancy and maternity as a disability, to be treated by employers as any other non-job-related disability.

Barbara Ehrenreich put it succinctly when she said that the entire female life cycle has been described as "a disease running its course."

FROM SICKNESS TO HEALTH:
The Holistic Alternative

Traditional medicine's critics, a heterogeneous mix of individuals and groups, have been increasing from within as well as outside of the profession, but it was women who first mobilized the multiplying discontents into an effective alternative. James S. Gordon, a physician and advocate of self-help, writes: "Although a variety of individuals of all ages have been active in the movement for self-care, patient's rights, and institutional reform, women have consistently led efforts for change. Ten to fifteen years ago, many women were ignorant about their own bodies and angrily ashamed of the anxieties that overtook them in condescending male physicians' offices. Today women in increasing numbers feel confident and knowledgeable enough to question their doctors' findings and the safety and necessity of the medications and procedures they prescribe."

The strategies and concepts that have emerged from the women's health movement constitute a comprehensive system of health care which, though it encompasses various subsystems, has become identified as "holistic health care." The term *holism* originated in 1926 with the South African statesman-philosopher Jan Christiaan Smuts, whose book *Holism and Revolution* maintained that biological organisms have a tendency toward wholeness, toward righting imbalances, and that these self-healing properties are evidence of a holistic tendency in nature.

Here was a model of health care that expressed the core values of feminine culture, with its commitment to mind-body unity and to the body's natural propensities for health and balance. Holism embodied the feminist challenge to the mechanistic-structural model of traditional Western medicine which, especially since the advances of modern medicine (penicillin, insulin, organ transplants), had come to expect that every disease including mental illness could be traced to specific pathogenic or biochemical abnormalities. The holistic approach instead considers health and healing from the perspective of whole persons in relationship to their total environment.

Where the environment is harmful to the individual, holism believes it should be changed, whereas traditional medicine, observes Stanford historian Barton J. Bernstein, "accepts the world and the environment and seeks to adapt through therapeutic means an individual to that environment." Bernstein, who recently switched his academic focus from the cold war to the study of medicine in relation to social values, asks: "What would happen if, instead of employing dramatic intervention, society looked at whole systems that create the pressures that cause heart disease? Instead of simply encouraging individuals to eat right or exercise, corporations could ask whether they should reduce stress by changing their pressured operations. Society might ask, 'What does it mean to have advertising that encourages people to eat lousy stuff? What does it mean to subsidize the tobacco industry? If the public were more involved in decision making, might it not ask more about the links between poverty and heart disease?' "

Questions like these are central concerns of holism. But though holistic health-care developed in tandem with the mounting criticism of traditional medicine, its practitioners recognize that there are occasions requiring authoritative medical or surgical intervention. The primary emphasis, however, is on education, self-help, and an equal partnership of practitioner and patient. As an alternative health-care model, holism has been strongly influenced by the women's self-help movement, and both share the following characteristics:

A concern with healing the split between mind and body.

Focusing on each individual's biological and cultural uniqueness and custom-tailoring treatments to individual needs.

Viewing health as a positive state rather than an absence of illness.

Encouraging the individual's responsibility and capacity for self-care and self-healing.

Emphasizing nutrition and exercise in promoting and maintaining health.

Nurse-practitioner Mary Ann Comas locates the link between the women's self-help movement and holistic health-care in the sense of empowerment that women feel when they discover they can participate in administering to their own and their family's health needs. Comas, one of the founders of the Los Angeles Childbirth Center, has studied holistic medicine, which she refers to as "the healing arts," and has seen how this approach can overcome the timidity and dependency that many women feel in regard to their bodies. "Women feel that they are reclaiming some of their female power which has been taken away from them." She has seen this happen particularly in pregnancy and childbirth, when women are encouraged to participate actively in the process, and the biological and spiritual come together for them in an intensely personal experience of life creation.

REFORMING CHILDBIRTH

When the pains began on Thursday, I felt that once more there was some meaning to my body. It really belonged to me again.

—EVELYN SCOTT, *in Revelations: Diaries of Women, ed. Mary Jane Moffatt and Charlotte Painter*

The women's health movement, as well as health-care reformers of both sexes, has become increasingly concerned about the overuse of instruments, particularly in childbirth. More than any other aspect of technology, the forceps represents for women their loss of control over the birth of their children. This instrument, which became generally available in the eighteenth century, helped to displace midwives, who were not trained to use this new technology and who took pride in the skillful use of their hands.

The highly sophisticated technologies that have been emerging in recent years—in vitro fertilization, amniocentesis—are an extension of the forceps principle, the application of advanced scientific procedures to childbirth. There are, of course, problem pregnancies for which these procedures are not only helpful but necessary. But when reproductive technology is carried to its logical conclusion— the artificial womb, which some radical feminists advocate as the ultimate freeing of women from "the tyranny of biology"—the result is an Orwellian approach to human reproduction that would reduce women's most highly prized biological function to a mere technological process.

The conflict between the way women feel about pregnancy and childbirth and the training traditional medicine offers is vividly illustrated in the experience of a female medical student who was pregnant with her first baby during her study of reproductive medicine at Harvard Medical School. Perri Klass, listening to the professor discuss ectopic pregnancy, toxemia, spontaneous abortion, and major birth defects, wished that the course would have something to say about normal pregnancy, something to suggest that childbirth could be a joyous event, not just a medical event. She questioned what has come to be known as traditional childbirth, which routinely includes an episiotomy, or a surgical incision to allow the baby's head to emerge without tearing the mother.

"Whose traditions are these?" she asked, "incorporating interventions designed for problem births into each and every birth?" These traditions, Klass observed, developed and perpetuated by doctors trained to define a normal birth as a negative event, exist for the convenience of doctors, not mothers. The emphasis in her medical training on the pathological aspects of pregnancy and birthing overrode other health considerations; little was said about nutrition and nothing about exercise, although "exercise books and classes aimed at pregnant women have proliferated."

Perri Klass's baby was born in a hospital, but without surgical intervention or the use of forceps; hearing the doctor say something about forceps, "I found an extra ounce of strength and pushed my baby out." As she lay back with her newborn son on her stomach, "the birthing room was suddenly transformed into the most beautiful place on earth."[3]

The impetus behind the current drive to restore midwifery and home births has its origins in women's growing resolve to resist this encroachment on their primary role and responsibility for childbirth. Recognizing the difficulty of making substantial changes in hospitals that are controlled by doctors faithful to traditional medicine, health reformers have been pressing for the resurrection of the midwife and of the home-centered birth process with which she is associated.

The midwife of today, who is usually a certified nurse-practitioner, in no way resembles the granny-midwife of the past. Though she does not attend women who cannot deliver their babies vaginally or who suffer from diabetes, toxemia, or other health problems that might complicate their pregnancy, her training has equipped her to provide prenatal care and to deal with normal deliveries, in birth centers or at home.

The return of midwifery and home birthing are part and parcel of the self-help/holistic campaign for more natural, more personalized health care. But at the same time that these alternatives to traditional medicine are becoming better known and more widely accepted, the obstacles to health-care reform remain formidable. One powerful force working against childbirth reform is the fast-growing health industry, whose profits account for more than 10 percent of the gross national product. Manufacturers of obstetrical drugs and equipment clearly have a vested interest in maintaining the status quo, and the connections between the industry and the profession, which have been likened to those between arms manufacturers and the military, have produced an alliance with sufficient clout to influence national health policies. Two strong supporters of the alliance include a medical insurance system that rewards the use of expensive technology and surgical intervention, and also government agencies that bypass the public, relying for information on the medical establishment and the health-care industry.

Nevertheless, there are some bright spots concerning the reform of women's health care, two of the greatest being a changing climate of opinion and women's increasingly sophisticated understanding of their own biological functions and of the health-care system. The latter has made women aware of the risks of passivity and ignorance and of the alternatives available to them. As a result, fewer women today are signing forms blindly before embarking on surgery. More and more women undergoing breast surgery, for example, are considering alternatives to radical mastectomies and are withholding the once-standard permission for a doctor to remove an entire breast.

The soaring costs of health care are another incentive to seek more natural, less expensive methods than those afforded by hospitals. In strictly cost/benefit terms, midwives and other alternative practitioners offer good value. Since economics often takes precedence over other considerations, midwives today are gaining approval, even in some areas of the medical profession itself: nurse midwives have been integrated into the staffs of this country's army and air force hospitals, where they are being acknowledged as colleagues by physicians.

Although most babies in the United States are currently born in hospitals, the home-birth movement has had some success in influencing hospitals to establish alternative birth centers. These are intended to offer a woman in labor the best of both worlds: a homelike atmosphere together with the availability of hospital facilities. They are often designed to resemble a combination bedroom–living room, with soft draperies, easy chairs, pictures on the walls. However, qualifying for admission to a hospital birth center can be on a par with competing for the Olympics, according to one nurse, and the centers are not always faithful to home-and-family ideals.

Independent birth centers operating outside of the hospital are truer to the precepts and principles of natural childbirth. Nearly eighty of these centers were operating in the United States by 1983, and despite strong opposition by the hospital–health insurance alliance, their numbers are expected to grow in the years ahead. One of the most successful of these independent centers is the Childbearing Center in New York City, founded by Ruth Lubic, C.N.M. (certified nurse midwife), who wanted a low-cost facility where nurse midwives could function freely in carrying out the principles and procedures in which they had been trained. The center, which contains two birth rooms, a kitchen, a lab, a family room, and utility and office space, was expressly designed to serve as a model, for according to its founder, freestanding birth centers present an old solution to the present-day problem of where, if a hospital is too expensive or otherwise unacceptable, parents can go for the birth of their children.

These developments, which represent a determined effort on the part of women to become participants in their own health care, are providing a necessary counterbalance to the scientific-technological approach to solving problems associated with the healthcare professions.

HUMANIZING MEDICINE

In recent years, as medical schools have been admitting an increasing number of women, there has been a growing recognition of the need for a more rounded, more humanistic education for doctors. UCLA Medical School has instituted a Medical Humanities program, which includes among its faculty Norman Cousins, formerly editor of the *Saturday Review*. Liberal arts programs have been added to the curricula of such prestigious medical schools as Harvard, Pennsylvania State, Johns Hopkins and Case Western Reserve. Both the American Medical Association and the Rockefeller Foundation have recommended that medical schools admissions committees include criteria for selecting applicants with well-rounded educational backgrounds and interests.

The Women Teaching Associates Program at Cornell University provides its second-year students with a chance to learn breast and pelvic examination procedures from woman instructors. "Our program has made quite a difference," says Dr. Lila Wallace, associate clinical professor of medicine who set up the Cornell program. "Everyone agrees that not only do the students' manual and communication skills improve, but they also show a much better attitude—they are more egalitarian, democratic, and the doctor-patient relationship becomes more a partnership.''[4]

The presence of more women in the profession has also contributed to the development of a warmer and more personal medical environment, through their style of communication as well as their mode of treatment. The difference has been described by several women patients as ''a feeling of empathy . . . as if she understands right away what you're talking about.'' This impression is borne out by linguistic analyses of doctor-patient interaction which reveal that communication between male doctors and female patients tends to be more threatening and less collaborative than between female doctors and female patients.[5]

A difference in examination style was described by a woman who, when attended by male gynecologists, had been put off by the depersonalization of the procedure—the draping with white sheets and probing with cold metal instruments, all surrounded by secrecy and embarrassment. Her current, female gynecologist uses hot-mitts on the stirrups so that the feet are held by something soft and familiar; she does not wear a white coat or uniform; she puts attractive posters on the ceiling for patients to look at while on their backs, serves them tea, and insists that they learn how to examine their own breasts and use the speculum.

Nevertheless, most of the humanizing changes in medicine are coming from women as consumers of health care rather than as doctors, according to Dr. Ruth Crane, a gynecologist on the staff of Kaiser-Permanente in San Francisco. ''Some women doctors are as stodgy as the men,'' she says, ''but women patients today are informed consumers of medical care. As consumers, they are responsible for developments like alternative birth centers, home birthing and a return to breastfeeding.''

Even the traditional male medical establishment is beginning to respond to sociopolitical trends that reflect the feminine emphasis on individual needs. Health research has been expanded to include recognition of possible influences of the patient's family and community on health. In recent years, funds have been made available for social science researchers to evaluate whether health services are providing greater accessibility, more information about the purposes and procedures of medical interviews and examinations, and more consumer involvement in determining costs and methods of delivery.

The results of this research indicate that at least 50 percent of those entering the health-care system are looking for help with problems that are primarily social and emotional rather than medical, and that doctors are, in fact, beginning to respond to this public expectation. As one medical professional said to his colleagues: "We must have a system that does not define quality care in terms of our ability to treat serious disease well, especially when the overwhelming majority of our patients do not have serious diseases." At medical conferences and in medical journals, the theme now coming through clearly is that medicine is a social as well as a scientific enterprise, that the decisions doctors make are often ethical in nature, and that these decisions must therefore be tested against society's ethical principles, which in the American creed are firmly based on egalitarianism and the right of individuals to participate in decisions affecting their lives.

THE NEW DOCTOR

> The practice of medicine is an art, not a trade; a calling, not a business; a calling in which your heart will be exercised equally with your head.
> —DR. WILLIAM OSLER, *Johns Hopkins Medical School*

The humanizing of medical training and practice through the infusion of feminine values is bringing with it a newly minted doctor, who combines within his or her professional persona some qualities of the traditional family doctor together with the more advanced knowledge and technical skill of recent medical research and practice. The doctor as God is being retired. "My friend went to the doctor's office expecting to find God," writes Ellen Goodman. "But what she discovered was that Doctor-God-Sir, the professional keeper of the Temple of the Body, was not available.

Instead, a new doctor sat down before her, opened her chart, met her eyes sincerely and asked her to think of him as her 'junior partner in health care.' '' This "junior partner," who has been educated by the full-disclosure, informed-consent, tell-it-like-it-is school of medicine, does not issue commands, but rather lays out the options. The assumption is that patients are intelligent, competent people capable of taking responsibility for their own health.[6]

This new doctor is often involved with the family-practice movement, which has emerged recently as a reaction against medical overspecialization and which matches in most significant respects the philosophy of the women's health-care movement. It stands for a return to generalism, a concern for the patient as a whole person, a less technological and more humanistic approach to health care, and a commitment to preventive medicine. Family-practice doctors have been described by other doctors as "people people—not in medicine for the technology"; "more conscious of social purpose than other physicians"; "interested in the biology of medicine but equally interested in what people's lives are like, in how people relate to one another in a family." Today, John McPhee reports, "there are about 7,000 family doctors in family-practice residencies around the United States. Family practice as a specialty has become, after internal medicine and surgery, the third most popular choice in specialties among graduating seniors in American medical schools." Moreover, many family practitioners are establishing residencies in rural areas where there is an acute need for quality health care.

The return of the family doctor is regarded by pediatrician Dr. Simon Wile as a positive and corrective trend in medical practice, and one that is particularly important in children's health care. Dr. Wile, who is retired but whose patients still call him for advice, defines family practice as "the screen directing patients to sources where the need is greatest," and he describes the family doctor as a "stalwart counselor" who must be sensitive to the family's needs, emotional as well as physical. In this respect, pediatricians have an advantage, because they are the first professionals to examine the child and are therefore in a favorable position to pick up, at an early stage of the child's development, any distress signals in the family milieu, anything that, as Dr. Wile says, "doesn't look kosher." He believes that the doctor's familiarity with the family together with the willingness to make house calls can alleviate anxiety in the family when a child is ill, as a tense, anxious atmosphere communicates itself to a child, often slowing recovery.

Dr. Wile considers the doctor-patient relationship an important element in the healing process, but its efficacy depends to a great extent on the doctor's ability to pick up on and record symptoms of disorders that may be psychogenic rather than physical in origin. "My female interns were often more sensitive to these subtle factors," he relates, confirming what many have also observed: that women have a significant contribution to make to pediatrics because of their nurturing, empathic, and attentive capacities.

REDEFINING HEALTH

Health, as defined by the World Health Organization, is "not the mere absence of disease but total physical, mental, and social well-being." The feminization of health care is bringing us closer to this concept of wholeness in healing, a perception that blends feminine *and* masculine values and approaches. "The feminine approach in healing *includes* the masculine approach," says Dr. Anne Langford, director of Clinical Holistic Health Education at John F. Kennedy University. It is "an attitude, a way of being. It cooperates with systems, e.g., the medical and allied health professions. . . . It is about creating internal and external environmental conditions so that the natural process of wholeness resurfaces to take its rightful place in our lives." The growth of a health-care system based wholly on masculine culture has led inexorably to a scientific-technological medical mentality that regards illness as a problem to be solved and has ignored such questions as how the problem came about and whether it could have been avoided.

Certainly, medical research, aided by improved housing, nutrition, and sanitation, has made notable progress in overcoming disease, but its unidimensionality has also saddled it with a tunnel vision that has constricted its approach to health care, making it badly in need of the complementary vision-enlarging dimension of the feminine approach to healing.

Health-care reform is currently in a state of suspension—and many feminists are understandably discouraged by the slow, at times almost imperceptible process of change. They point to the trend toward more rather than less intervention by specialists, to the continuing use in childbirth of drugs, technology, cesarian sections, to the pressure on women physicians to conform to the masculine medical establishment.

But as women become effective in the public world, as they develop confidence in their power to bring about change, as they gain control over their bodies and their reproductive function, the transformative effects will come along more rapidly. Already, women's refusal to reproduce on demand means that marriage, the family, relations between the sexes are all subject to redefinition. Even the ponderous legal system is responding to the insistent pressures of feminization by developing new definitions and principles involving maternity leave and health insurance for women, and generating new precedents out of litigation involving harmful birth control devices and drugs.

Women's new pride and confidence in their bodies is being demonstrated in the world of sports, where for the first time, women of various ages and body shapes, women whose only previous form of exercise may have been pushing a vacuum cleaner, are today running, lifting weights, backpacking through wilderness areas. The new feminine body-consciousness was brilliantly displayed in the last Olympics, but more important to the broader issue of health care is women's appreciation of sports—not primarily as competitive activities but as forms of healthful recreation. (The trend has even spawned a new medical specialty, sports gynecology, which is concentrating on the effect of active sports on menstruation and pregnancy.)

The feminine commitment to health care as an integral part of daily life is making its way into the personnel policies of many companies that today are investing heavily in programs designed to improve employees' health. These programs involve both workers and their families, promoting exercise, nutrition, and weight-control classes; the reduction of stress; screening for warning signs of cancer and heart problems; and counseling on alcoholism and drug abuse. Some companies have added the new position of health director to their staffs; Curtis S. Wilbur, who occupies that position at Johnson & Johnson, reports that the company's programs have resulted in "significant improvements in exercise, decrease in smoking, better management of stress and weight."

The feminine redefinition of health in terms of positive attitudes and naturalness is also catching on with a number of businesses. The shift away from packaged, cosmeticized "beauty" toward health and naturalness has been picked up by the ever-alert sensors of the cosmetic industry: Revlon recently identified itself as being in the health products rather than the beauty business. Supermarket shelves are stacked with products whose labels proclaim their ingredients to be "wholesome" and "natural." Holistic health books as well as books and magazines on exercise and nutrition are proliferating, as are health clubs, health food stores, home remedies, health courses and workshops, spas, and "lean cuisine," offering low-calorie frozen and packaged gourmet specialties.

In the area of birth control, women's clinics and other health-care organizations are educating women in the Natural Family Planning and Fertility Method, which monitors natural signs of the female body to control pregnancy. The method has no known side effects, and since it is dependent for its effectiveness on a woman's knowledge of how her body works, it encourages women to become better informed about their bodily functions.

The major limitation on women's reform of health care is its concern with only those areas where women's health care differs from men's. But female health-needs transcend the care of their reproductive systems. The potential of the women's health movement depends not only on the extent to which it provides a more human and less alienating context for women to learn about and control their bodies, but as a model of health care for all of us. Here again, feminism points to humanism—what is good for women is good for society as a whole.

The feminization of health care has made significant progress in raising America's health consciousness and in providing alternatives to an unwieldy and unresponsive health-care system. But it will require the unswerving dedication and cooperation of business, government, the medical establishment, and most of all, the efforts of enlightened health-care consumers, male and female, to reach the ultimate goal of the women's health movement—a more humanistic healing system for all, male and female, young and old, rich and poor.

8. THE THIRD COMING:
In Search of a New Spirituality

What is of epochal importance is this search for a God who is neither male nor female alone, but contains or transcends both. . . . Religious devotion comes from the same part of the human being as all other forms of affection. If the objects of that devotion are only male, one cannot fully experience one's own spirituality.

—PAUL MOORE, *Episcopal bishop*

The new spirituality emerging in America today is actually a replay of a recurring struggle, one that appears throughout history whenever an entrenched belief system is challenged by a rising counterconsciousness. Reacting to the threats the new consciousness poses to its power and prerogatives, the entrenched system (though it may at first essay a few conciliatory measures) eventually hardens its position and attempts through all the means at its disposal to preserve its claim to ideological supremacy. Christian fundamentalism and Jewish orthodoxy in essence follow this pattern today as they attempt to resist the tides of change.

Since the feminine principle is perceived, as it has been in the past, as a subversive force capable of undermining the authority of the religious establishment, male theologians have found cause to reaffirm their position on such issues as abortion and the principle of women being restricted to their biological role, as was recently reiterated by Pope John Paul II. But today's shifting consciousness, which the women's movement has helped to mobilize, has produced a widespread sense of the inability of institutionalized religion to deal with the spiritual needs of both men and women in this nuclear age.

Feminine spirituality constitutes a revolution of consciousness, and women are uniquely qualified to pioneer the newly discovered dimensions of this emerging world view. As creators and protectors of life, women have a vested interest in systems of belief that are unifying and enriching rather than divisive and exploitative. At a profound personal level, women feel cheated of their spiritual heritage and are no longer willing to accept second-class religious citizenship for themselves or their daughters. One woman spoke of this passionately: "As women, we must carry the racial—or perhaps we should say 'gender'—memory about our own powers, our connection to the divine, that has been stolen from us. Women are beginning to get a glimmer of that again, and when they do, they want more. It is a basic question of identity: What does it mean to be a woman?"

The search for a new spirituality is bringing together women of many different faiths who are seeking equal time in their religions for the celebration of the feminine experience. In contrast to the divisiveness of religious sectarianism, the search for this new spirituality is ecumenical in its scope, integrative rather than divisive, crossing over the sectarian boundaries of traditional religions. Virginia Woolf proclaimed, "As a woman I have no country . . . as a woman, my country is the whole world"; so feminine theology takes within its embrace the human spirit in its totality.

This is not to say that there are no differences among women who are seeking spiritual self-definition. Women's spirituality is in a process of transition and growth, and conflicts and disagreements jostle each other here as any developing social movement; but these differences rest upon a broad base of empathy and shared values. Women born into different faiths report that theological differences tend to melt away before the common need to find meaning and purpose for their own lives and the lives of their children in an increasingly chaotic and threatening world. "I found God in myself and I loved her fiercely" is the defiant cry of the black woman in Ntozake Shange's play *For Colored Girls Who Have Considered Suicide When the Rainbow Is Enuf.*

Exclusion from institutionalized religion has provided the impetus for many women to look for God within themselves and to seek communion with other groups who have been ignored or rejected by organized religion. "Exclusion has had some advantages for us," says Carol Edwards, a minister of the Unitarian Universalist Church. "It means being outside of a culture that has its own inherent problems, so that we were not trained to live in a way that has some negative consequences. I consider it valuable that I was trained in a more cooperative model. As outsiders, women are in a position to question authority rather than conform to it."

THE SEARCH FOR A SPIRITUAL LIFE

In our secular society, with its emphasis on the pragmatic and the rational, the movement of women from the warm, nourishing culture of home and family to the public world of action and achievement has been viewed mainly from economic and political perspectives. Women's push toward freedom and independence with its legalistic demands for equal rights and participation has obscured a quieter struggle, one that contains the seeds of a profound and far-reaching personal and social transformation, the struggle for a spiritual life in which woman can be equal partners with men.

A spiritual life. The phrase resonates oddly in our high-tech, space-shuttling age. It seems out of sync with women's true concerns today, with the need to reconcile love and work, with the continuing effort to achieve equality as citizens and wage earners. Some feminists argue that religion has outlived its usefulness, that it encourages passivity and dependence on authoritarian leaders. Their sharpest criticism of the Judeo-Christian tradition, the dominant form in our society today, is that it excludes women. Its language alone resonates with maleness: "God the Father," the "fellowship of man," the "brotherhood of clergy," the "salvation of mankind." Christian doctrine proclaims that "the conception of the Son of God in the womb of the Blessed Virgin Mary is attributed to the power of the Third Person of the Blessed Trinity because the Holy Ghost proceeds from the love of the Father and the Son, and the Incarnation is a work of God's greatest love for mankind." In the Gospel of Thomas, Jesus said: "Let Mary leave us, for women are not worthy of Life. I myself shall lead her, so that she too may become a living spirit, resembling you males. For every woman who will make herself male will enter the Kingdom of Heaven."

The message to women from Genesis is: "In sorrow thou shalt bring forth children; and thy desire shall be to thy husband, and he shall rule over thee." Epistles tells us: "The head of every man is Christ and the head of the woman is man; and the head of Christ is God." Woman came from man, woman was responsible for the Fall.

It is difficult not only for women but for any thinking human being who harbors humanitarian sentiments to accept unquestioningly a religious tradition with as sorry a record as Judeo-Christianity. The God of Israel was a chauvinistic deity who forbade intermingling between his people and those of other faiths; non-Jews were not permitted to enter the temple. Transgressors were severely, at times savagely, punished. Although Christianity in its early stages preached universal love and one God for all, it placed the divine being outside of human and physical nature, a division that has had fateful consequences for the human spirit and the natural world throughout history and into the present day.

Christianity did not oppose slavery. Jesus accepted it and so did Paul, who told Ephesian slaves, "Be obedient to them that are your masters according to the flesh, with fear and trembling, in singleness of your heart, as unto Christ." Saint Leo I wrote in 443 that accepting slaves into holy orders would be a "pollution" and would violate owners' rights.

The Christian persecution of "heresy" is a saga written in blood: the Crusades, the Inquisition, and the witch-burnings are merely three of the better-known landmarks in this record of horrifying cruelty in the name of God. In this century, adherence to the Christian tradition did not move the United States, France, or England to take action on behalf of the Jews in Nazi Germany. Nor do the Islamic and Moslem religions offer a spiritual oasis in this bleak and brutal landscape: the ruthless repression and persecution by the ayatollahs and the internecine slaughter in the Middle East, in India, and in other parts of the Eastern world are perpetrated in the name of one deity or another.

And yet, despite this heinous history and even with the secularization of the modern world, religion today is not only surviving, it is thriving. In America, evangelists thunder their messages of sin and redemption across the airwaves; a Korean self-proclaimed god-figure builds an empire that includes vast tracts of real estate, major newspapers, and other profitable enterprises; cults multiply and subdivide; God is regularly interjected into political campaigns; the President asks for an amendment to the Constitution permitting prayer in schools. "We live in times that are at once soulless and ridden with religion," comments Benjamin R. Barber, professor of political science at Rutgers University. "Catholic bishops pronounce on economic policy and fundamentalist preachers run direct-mail campaigns."

Clearly, Nietzsche's proclamation that God is dead was premature. Yet all of this bustling religious activity leaves many people today feeling as if, despite the feast being offered them, some deep spiritual hunger remains unappeased. The sense of alienation, of being "alone and afraid in a world we never made," has, if anything, worsened in recent years. The level of hatred and violence is rising, and self-interest is replacing the sense of community that existed in preurban, preindustrial eras.

But human beings cannot live with meaninglessness, and recent years have witnessed the emergence of a quest for a spirituality that embraces the female as well as the male, that, as a former nun stated it, contains within it a "reordering of values so that all of humanity has innate worth." This spirituality has little in common with formal, institutionalized religion, but carries a sense of unity between body and spirit, a personal experience that transcends sectarian differences. Even those who have rejected formal religion as irrelevant and archaic and who consider themselves to be completely secular admit that there are moments when the sacred and the secular merge within them, transporting them to another plane of reality where they experience a sense of oneness with nature and all living things. In polls conducted during the past decade, a large percentage of respondents reported interest in "an inner search for meaning."

An eighteen-year-old college student speaks of what religion means to her: "It seems to me that our true humanness manifests itself within two major categories, art and religion. I think that the human potential at its most highly developed stage aspires toward the beauty and mystery of religion. That religion has harmed, destroyed and abused human beings is something that must be expected from such a dangerously potent force. But when I see a Gothic cathedral or listen to a Bach aria or see a painting by Giotto, I *know* what it was that moved these people to create what they created."

This "oceanic feeling," as Freud describes it, has little in common with institutionalized religion, in which women throughout history have been relegated to a secondary role. Accepting their subsidiary status in religion, some women have even justified it as being "appropriate, biologically and sociologically." They have conformed to male expectations by remaining passive, ignorant of liturgy, content to stay in the background while their men enact the rituals and sacerdotal functions of the religious establishment. They identify with the eastern European woman who came to the synagogue early each morning and recited a prayer of her own: "Good morning, God. I haven't much time to spend here; I must go home and feed Abraham, my son, so he will have strength to study your holy Torah. Good day, God."

Denied a primary, public role in religious observance, women have often sought in religion a private refuge, a source of solace for personal loss and disappointment. Simone de Beauvoir draws a poignant portrait of the menopausal woman whose validation comes primarily from men, and who seeks in religion the fulfillment she can find nowhere else. "Denied all human love, even in their dreams, [they] look to God for help. . . . The vague notions of destiny, mystery, and lack of appreciation indulged in by woman as her autumn begins find in religion a rational unification."[1]

Women have also found in institutionalized religion an opportunity through their supporting role to fulfill their need for community service. In church and synagogue, women have been mainly responsible for the good works that the Judeo-Christian creed requires of its adherents: charity to the poor, care of the sick and the elderly. These together with the social and fund-raising activities of the religious establishment—the church suppers, rummage sales, raffles, auxiliaries, and other associations—have given women a sense of serving their religion while remaining in a subordinate role.

RECOVERING GOD THE MOTHER

> Instead of describing a monistic and masculine God, many of these texts speak of God as a dyad who embraces both masculine and feminine elements.
> —ELAINE PAGELS, *The Gnostic Gospels*

The exclusion of women from formal, institutionalized religion has had much the same effect on spirituality as the exclusion of women from medicine has had on health care. Divorced from its early mundane origins, organized religion's seminal vision of spiritual community has been eroded by narrow theological disputation, sectarian divisiveness, and the pursuit of wealth and power. Religious institutions have been deprived of the tempering influence of feminine culture, and the loss has manifested itself in a draining away of the profound, nurturing spiritual sustenance that gives religion its magical potency.

The great significance of religion is that it provides the basic legitimization for social/cultural beliefs and practices. Women in their struggle today for spiritual redefinition are beginning to confront the full import of their exclusion from traditional religion and to recognize that changes in material existence must be linked to spiritual change.

Despite the sexism of the Judeo-Christian establishment, women who have been brought up in these faiths are reluctant to cast aside that heritage entirely. Within this tradition, which has been the dominant influence in America, they believe there are usable principles and precedents that offer opportunities for a redefinition and balancing of religion. Feminist theologians point to the "prophetic principle" of the Bible that denounces all oppressive ideologies in the name of a liberating God, and to various early "counterculture," movements such as the Puritans, Quakers, and Shakers who, like the Gnostics in the dawning of church history, remained outside mainstream religion. There is the early Jesus movement with its concern for the poor, sick, crippled, sinners, prostitutes, all "liminal" people. And there is a rich store of feminine religious imagery in the early Christian movement, as a study of the Gnostic gospels has revealed. The Gnostics, condemned as heretics as early as the first century, rejected priestly authority, believing instead that the divine existed within the human being, that the way to salvation was through self-knowledge, that God was both male and female, and that men and women were spiritual equals. A Gnostic text celebrates the feminine powers of thought, intelligence and foresight. A Gnostic poem contains a revelation spoken by a feminine divinity, Protennoia—literally, "primal thought":

> I am the first and the last. I am the honored one and the scorned one. I am the whore and the holy one. I am the wife and the virgin. I am [the mother] and the daughter. . . . I am she whose wedding is great, and I have not taken a husband. . . . I am knowledge and ignorance. . . . I am shameless; I am ashamed. I am strength, and I am fear. . . . I am foolish and I am wise. . . . I am godless, and I am one whose God is great.[2]

The Gnostic sources—revelations, gospels, mystical teachings —were omitted from the New Testament canonical collection, a rejection which, in view of the openness toward women in the early Christian movement, has been attributed to the social upheavals and cultural cross-currents of that time of transition. As the ancient world was overtaken by the Christian era, contradictory attitudes toward women emerged out of the ferment of change. Whereas women in the Roman Empire had participated in social and religious life, now, as Christianity sought to establish itself, they were accused of being attracted to "heretical groups"; by the year 200 A.D., the majority of Christian communities accepted the antifeminist elements in Paul's views: "Let a woman learn in silence with all submissiveness. I permit no woman to teach or to have authority over men; she is to keep silent."

It would appear that women accepted Paul's dictum, for in the historical record of institutionalized Christianity, women are inaudible and invisible. "The usual model of early Christian communities," Elizabeth Schussler Fiorenza notes, "is that women and men were members, but men were the only leaders." This is a tenet to be challenged, says Fiorenza, a German scholar and Roman Catholic who opposes the Vatican position on women. In her recent book, *In Memory of Her: A Feminist Theological Reconstruction of Christian Origins,* she has been engaged in a rediscovery of women's role in early Christian history. Her search has confirmed that "both men and women were full participants in early Christian history. We just have to conceptualize so the women become visible."

Historical reconstruction has turned up evidence of women's participation in the early Christian missionary movement, in which their work equalled that of men like Apollos, Barnabas, and Paul. A leading figure appears to have been Prisca who, together with her husband, Aquila, established her house in Corinth as a missionary center. Paul refers to the couple as his coworkers and emphasizes that not only he but "all the churches of the Gentiles" were grateful to them.[3]

The cult of the Goddess is a dominant motif in the recovery of women's religious roots. The Great Mother Goddess was for many centuries the chief deity of the ancient world throughout western Asia and Asia Minor. She was worshipped by many different peoples and by many different names: Ishtar by the Babylonians; Asherah and Astarte by the Canaanites, Hebrews, and Phoenicians; Isis by the Egyptians; Cybele by the Phrygians; Anahita by the

Persians. The Goddess, or Great Mother, was considered by all to be virgin, virginity in this sense meaning not chastity but rather an unmarried state. As a virgin she belonged to no one but herself; no husband could impose his will or image upon her. As the goddess of fertility she held in her possession the potent, creative power of the universe. As the embodiment of the archetypal Feminine, she combined within her being both positive and negative aspects.[4] Because of its potency, Goddess worship had to be destroyed, some scholars maintain, in order to make way for the establishment of the Christian church with its male-dominated hierarchical structure.

In a recent study by Barbara Walker, the ancient female religions present a striking contrast to established Christianity: in the female theology, nature is sacred; time is circular; body and spirit are one; original sin is absent; the individual's will is equal to the god's; play, humor, and sexuality have an important place in rituals; and pleasure is a positive force, not a sin. The established church is portrayed as antilife, its energies directed against women, who are seen as the source of evil, sin, and death.[5]

Yet the church, for all its efforts in that direction, was not able to eradicate the female principle. In the Middle Ages, the feminine force, known as the Virgin, the Madonna, or Mary, inspired a spiritual fervor reflected in the design of churches and cathedrals. Mary, holding her Holy Child on her knees, symbolized justice, mercy, and love, thus, according to historian Mary Beard, signifying to the people

> moral, human, or humane power as against the stern mandates of God's law taught and enforced by the Church. As such, her position made trouble for the Church; but the Papacy, if it had been so minded, could scarcely have suppressed the urge of the people to Virgin worship, however successful it was in excluding women from the priesthood and the musical services of its choir. In the popular devotion to Mary was asserted a passionate attachment to the feminine qualities so directive in the long history of the human race.[6]

Within the Jewish tradition, ancient festivals and rituals are now serving as a starting point for a renewal of women's connections with Judaism within the established religion. Go back to the early origins, feminist historians tell us, and you will find that holy observances were held at the rising of the new moon, and that one of the images of the Shekinah, the female aspect of God, is the new moon rising out of her dark phase to illuminate the sky. The ancient connection of the sabbath with the new moon is one of the rituals that women are reviving today in their observance of the sabbath.

Old Testament history, despite its masculine bias, offers ample precedents for extending and strengthening woman's role in Judaism. Female biblical models include Miriam, the prophetess, sister of Moses; Deborah the judge; the learned daughters of Rashi; Queen Esther, whose influence saved her people from the machinations of Haman; as well as Ruth and Naomi, exemplifying the rarely celebrated bond between mother and daughter-in-law. Though these women were exceptions in their day, they can now be seen as lodestars for a reinterpretation of woman's place in Jewish history that could pave the way for equal participation of women in contemporary Judaism.

FEMININE SPIRITUALITY GOES PUBLIC

Organized religion is one of the "hard areas" of culture that resists reform with all the power at its command (and its power is inestimable) issuing as its does from the "word of God" and extending beyond this life into the next. But feminization is making some inroads, and cracks are becoming visible in the once-solid facade of the Judeo-Christian establishment. Two prestigious seminaries, the Princeton Theological Seminary and the Fuller Seminary, have issued formal statements recommending the use of gender-inclusive language. A lectionary of inclusive terminology has been published by the National Council of Churches, which offers specific suggestions for the use of inclusive terms in preaching and scriptural interpretation: "sovereign god" instead of "Lord," "self" instead of "himself," "human beings" instead of "man," for example.

Male resistance to the ordination of women began weakening in the late 1970s as a few women, encouraged by the feminist movement, began entering the seminaries. By the early 1980s, women made up 25 perecent of registrants in seminaries and out-numbered men at Harvard Divinity School. "Seminary growth would be very, very small if it weren't for the women," said Mar-vin Taylor, associate director of the Association of Theological Seminaries, noting that overall, the growth rate for women seminarians is nearly 8 percent higher than for men. In the Jewish religion, since 1972 when Sally Priesand was ordained the first female rabbi at Hebrew Union College, more than ninety women have been ordained, and women are entering rabbinical schools in growing numbers. In fact, equal access is regarded today as a non-issue. "What are we equal *in*?" asks Rabbi Laura Geller. "What is the nature of the religious experience? What would Judaism be like if women's experience had been taken seriously?" These are the questions confronting Jewish women today.

Another question being considered by women of all faiths who are seeking spiritual renewal within established religion: Does the presence of women in the clergy make a difference? Dr. Fiorenza has some doubts, fearing that "there is a lot of co-option" occur-ring, particularly in the Protestant seminaries. There are women clerics, however, who are convinced that they are making a signifi-cant difference by bringing the feminine principle into the liturgy of their faith. Rev. Cynthia Samuel, a dark-haired, vivacious Episco-palian priest, speaks of reviving

> images in our tradition of God as mother, with femi-
> nine attributes. We're only just beginning to hear
> about these. I grew up imaging God as a male; that's
> how our religion presents God. But that's changing for
> me and for the people in my congregation. It limits
> God so much to think of God only in male terms. In
> my preaching, I don't present God as mother or father.
> Instead of saying, "In the name of the Father, the Son,

and the Holy Spirit,'' I say, ''In the name of the Creator, the Redeemer, and the Sustainer.'' Those are the functional roles in which God relates to us, so that it becomes an enriched image which is no longer limited by a narrow sexual definition.

Rev. Samuel, who is of mixed religious parentage—her father is Jewish and her mother Episcopalian—believes that the essential difference between a male and female priesthood is the difference between a linear and cyclical perception. ''A woman's life is cyclical; we have menstrual periods, we have babies. When I had my child, there was a certain sense in which I withdrew from the world into that experience for a period of time.'' This perceptual difference, as she sees it, shapes the way male clerics think about their vocation—as a linear progression up the ladder—whereas women are more oriented toward relationships. She uses personal examples in her sermons, and emphasizes the inclusivity of God.

The liberation of God is the message of Rev. Patricia Budd Kepler, director of ministerial studies at Harvard Divinity School. Rev. Kepler emphasizes the need to free God from the authoritarian, vengeful, nonhuman image that continues to be promulgated by institutionalized religion. She believes that in the unity of the human and the divine, established religion can lead the way to a more human, more humane society.

For Rabbi Patty Carlin, reinterpreting the great myths of Judaism also opens up the possibility of re-imaging the Jewish God, who is generally cast in the role of a stern and vengeful patriarch. Rabbi Carlin points out that although Yahweh has been imbued with maleness, Jews are in fact commanded not to think of God in human terms. In Judaism, God is a divine force transcending gender, and the covenant with God, which is the basis of the Jewish religion, is one of faith with the entire Jewish community.

Rabbi Carlin, who is in her twenties and one of the growing number of women entering the rabbinate, views the haggadic, or story-telling, tradition in Judaism as a source of myth and imagery that women can draw upon in forging or renewing their bonds with the Jewish tradition. The halachic, or legal tradition, is more resistant to change, but even here Rabbi Carlin sees signs of fissures beginning to appear in the age-old barriers against women. She has had male rabbis as mentors and has been encouraged by their profeminist stance. It was a male theologian, she points out, who created the first Freedom Seder, which combines traditional and contemporary liturgy in narrating the ancient story of the freeing of the Jews from Egyptian tyranny as a parallel to the contemporary struggles of oppressed people throughout the world.

An increasing number of male theologians are, in fact, adding their voices to women's demand for a balanced, egalitarian spirituality. A quarter of a century ago, Paul Tillich questioned whether there are elements in Protestant symbolism that transcend the male-female alternative and could be developed to replace "a one-sided, male determined symbolism." At that time, Tillich represented a minority, even heretical, view. But in 1977, Paul Moore, an Episcopal bishop in New York ordaining women for the first time, was overwhelmed by emotion as he spoke from the high altar in the Cathedral of Saint John the Divine. "Let us confess our sins against God and our neighbor, and especially our sinfulness in the oppression of women in the life of the church and the world, and in the wounds inflicted upon one another." To accept women as priests is not only morally right but is also "part of a search for a spiritual reference point beyond gender. If the objects of devotion are only male, one cannot fully experience one's own spirituality. Everyone's prayer life is impoverished if we can only relate to a male God." Bishop Moore emphasizes that the church must become more balanced for men's sake as well as women's. "Ever since women have joined us, I feel more relaxed, more natural."

Mark Gerzon in his chapter "The Lord" in *A Choice of Heroes* describes the search for a spirituality that seeks alternatives to a masculine Lord as a "quest for a new heroism that embraces rather than denies the feminine and that seeks service rather than domination. . . . Spirituality in a man does not require a denial of the feminine. On the contrary, it is an affirmation of femininity as an essential part of ourselves—and of our God."[7]

Presbyterian minister Charles Doak connects a heightened sensitivity among the male clergy to formerly excluded groups—single parents, ethnic minorities—with the feminization of established religion. "Everyone in the church today is more sensitive to gender and the use of language," he says, "and this has centered the attention of the clergy on issues that were formerly peripheral." Two such issues are discrimination against nonmainstream groups and the peace movement. "The church has always been concerned with peace, but women have brought a new power, a new concentration of energy and purpose to this concern."

The concern of women with peace and with humanitarian causes draws its strength from a spirituality in touch with the mundane as well as the divine. Mircea Eliade describes it as a "mystic unity between life, woman, nature, and the divinity."[8] It is this sense of being part of a mystic or cosmic unity that draws women into antiwar and other life-protecting activities. In the turbulence of Central America, in the parched, famine-ridden lands of Africa, wherever human misery and oppression are present, women are on the scene, some of them in the service of religious orders, others as doctors, nurses, or relief workers. The nuns who were murdered in El Salvador have become symbolic figures, tragic reminders of women who have throughout history given their lives as an expression of their deeply personal spiritual unity with all life on earth.

FROM INSTITUTIONALIZED TO PERSONALIZED RELIGION

Most of the great religions have begun with a relatively small group of followers or disciples clustered around a charismatic leader. This individual represents a transcendent body of ideas that respond to the human yearning to make sense out of the universe, to give life order and meaning, and to confront the profound questions that people have always asked: Where do we come from? Where are we going? What will happen to us when we die? Shoring up the theological structure of these established faiths is the assumption that people need integrated belief systems that provide a philosophical focus and coherence for their beliefs.

But social scientists studying religious phenomena are challenging the assumption that people today need central belief systems. At the turn of the century, when it appeared that scientific thought would supplant religion, Emile Durkheim wrote that "the old gods are growing old or are already dead," but that there was no "reason for believing that humanity is incapable of inventing new ones." Durkheim was looking to new individualistic and humanistic philosophies to take the place of the old gods of traditional religion, those "father gods" that Freud held responsible for keeping human beings in a childish state of reliance on external authority. Freud and Durkheim were writing in an age in which Victorian ideas were still part of the bedrock of Western culture, like an alluvial sediment deposited by the tides of modernism. But in a recent issue of the *Journal for the Scientific Study of Religion,* sociologist Reginald W. Bibby speculated that the whole idea that people have to have centralized meaning-systems may be erroneous. He suggested that people might shape their views through "general biographical goals, such as well-being, affluence, and success" rather than interpreting or striving to understand events through a particular meaning-system.

The fixed, centralized beliefs that served people in the past belonged to a static time when the universe and the lives people lived were experienced as closed systems, designed and controlled by external authorities. As our cosmic consciousness has shifted to the perception of a universe that is open-ended, dynamic, and inhabited by self-determining individuals, the old belief systems have been falling into decay. Spiritual yearning today is moving in new directions along the path of solitary searching. Today, well-educated Americans in their thirties and forties are experiencing a quiet, inner awakening. Many of these new adherents have tried psychotherapy and one or more of the Eastern religions but have found that these paths did not lead them to the inner peace they were seeking. In prayer, they say, they have found meaning and direction.[9]

The growing emphasis on individual responsibility and choice does not mesh with adherence to a doctrinal system of received wisdom that lays down universal rules of moral behavior for all time. This dissonance between established religion and an emerging personal morality has filled the air in recent years with the sound and fury of major clashes of belief: a Protestant president endorses the Pope's position on abortion as a crime against human life; a Catholic vice-presidential candidate says she would not impose the view of her church on abortion, which she accepts for herself, upon other women; a proposed constitutional amendment permitting prayer in the schools is entangled in thorny questions of what sort of prayers would be appropriate and who would decide. The pastoral letter of the Roman Catholic bishops, calling for economic democracy in America, is denounced by conservative business and religious groups as "socialism." A group of nuns publicly renounce the position of their church on abortion, comparing the church's threat of expulsion unless they accept its doctrine with a "totalitarian state where you can't speak your mind for fear of sanctions."

This assertion of individual conscience is sending tremors through all religious institutions, even the once unchallengeable Roman Catholic church. "Catholics today are more affluent, better educated, and more willing to question the church than their parents were," writes Elaine Sciolino in a *New York Times Magazine* article. "And their independence of conscience is accepted—or at least tolerated—by growing numbers of parish priests and nuns who feel their primary pastoral mission is to meet the everyday needs of the faithful."[10]

The rift between Catholics and their church erupted into a storm of rebellion in 1968 when Pope Paul VI wrote the encyclical Humanae Vitae, banning all artificial birth control. That was the breakthrough, says Dr. Fiorenza. "For the first time, Catholics realized that there wasn't one answer. It was the first step toward an adult Catholicity, namely taking responsibility for one's own life."

The distinction between institutional and personal religion was defined by William James in his classic *Varieties of Religious Experience* as follows: institutional religion consists of "worship and sacrifice, procedures for working on the dispositions of the deity, theology, ceremony, and ecclesiastical organization." Personal religion takes in feelings, acts, and experiences of individuals "in their solitude so far as they apprehend themselves to stand in relation to whatever they may consider divine."[11]

James's definition of personal religion is a fitting characterization of the feminine spirituality movement, which is diffuse, decentralized, and has been gaining strength without producing a charismatic leader or a body of transcendent doctrine. In the feminine moral ethic, moral obligations attach primarily to human beings and their needs, not to abstract principles and their requirements. In place of leadership there is networking, with women of various denominations coming together to explore and exchange ideas. Instead of transcendence there is immanence—women looking into themselves and building on their own life experience; thus, unity of mind and body, of human beings and nature, replaces dualism and polarization. The theology, if there can be said to be one, is open-ended, a process theology consisting of a responsible search for truth as it unfolds rather than a commitment to absolute truth for all time. There is no formal church or ministry; the "church" may be a woman's home or a retreat in a rural setting where nature serves as the ministry.

Inwardness along with a mythic dimension—both present in feminine spirituality—are features that Carl Jung regarded as intrinsic to a vital, dynamic, personal religion. In his exploration of religious processes within the mind, Jung stressed the significance of myth and ritual that emanate from self-awareness and an enhanced appreciation of one's individuality. Clearly, women's spiritual growth has been linked to a search for greater self-understanding and a more positive identity.

Feminine spirituality is a modern mystical journey, a quest for self-definition and integration with the powers of the universe. In the struggle to shed their identification as the "other," women are generating a sense of connection among people of varying backgrounds and persuasions. This new spiritual consciousness is not a remote mysticism requiring a guru, a Castanedan "man of knowledge" to lead us to its innermost truths; rather, its authority resides within the individual, and since it recognizes no division between body and spirit, it blends sensual, earthy, erotic elements with spiritual reverence and personal mastery.

As a religion of process and synthesis, it is a faith for our time, for this dynamic, pluralistic, interdependent era when people need to find meaning and coherence within the human community rather than in some supernatural, all-powerful father god-figure. As the olds gods die off and the new spirituality replaces them, we can look forward to a "third coming" that will help us achieve more fulfilling personal lives through a spiritual connection with others sharing our common humanity, with the divine mystery of creation, and with the natural world.

9. REVITALIZING THE ARTS

To make prints is not easy. You must think first, and this is hard to do. But I am happy doing the prints. After my husband died, I felt very alone and unwanted; making prints is what made me happiest since he died. I am going to keep on doing them until they tell me to stop. If no one tells me to stop, I shall make them as long as I am well. If I can, I'll make them even after I am dead.
— PITSEOLAK, Eskimo artist

Way beyond my understanding is what goes out through my whole being—a transformational change. After I do a performance, I am asking for change; by the demonstration, I actually instigate desired profound change. It is a prayer, since I have no idea of what will come forth; I say, O God, I am willing. . . .
— BARBARA SMITH, American conceptual artist

An Eskimo woman makes prints to fill an empty space in her life . . . an American woman presents a conceptual performance piece as a prayer for change. Food, childbirth, household tools, boxes, biomorphic shapes appear in paint on canvas, in stitchery on fabric; in theater, music, and dance, unrecognizable forms, sounds, new images explode with the force of bottled up energy suddenly released. In the visual and performing arts, the long-suppressed creativity of women is breaking through traditions and protocol that have governed the arts for centuries.

The feminine influence on the arts is subtle and often imperceptible; as with an atmospheric change, it is difficult to chart its course or measure precisely the extent of its effects. But since art reflects the culture in which it is produced, it was inevitable that the women's movement interacting with other post-'60s social movements would leave an imprint on the arts. Feminine values and concerns, the inward search that is the core of women's spirituality—these cultural attributes can be traced throughout much of contemporary art in the work of both male and female artists. The burgeoning of the women's art movement has accelerated the development of a changing aesthetic consciousness, helping to counter a trend that had set artists and their work apart from ordinary, day-to-day human experience.

ART AS COMMUNICATION

There is something heart-stirring in the thought of art as a medium of communication, in the idea of the artist's personal vision reaching people everywhere in a universal language, an aesthetic esperanto of reciprocal understanding and empathy. For art *can* communicate, art *can* explain. The "vast pleasure of explanation," to borrow Lewis Thomas's phrase, is present in the silhouetted figures and craggly columns of Lita Albuquerque's paintings, which join cosmic concerns to nature. It is present in the openness and candor that portraitist Alice Neel brought to her scrutiny of human beings, herself included, and in the work of Jennifer Bartlett, which affirms the survival of hearth and home.

"Whatever form art takes, it's a language," says Judith Simonian, whose recent work, in mosaic tile, evokes classic and romantic painting. "The pieces are not really completed in the studio, but with the reactions and comments I receive." Her images and materials emanate out of her desire to make an authentic emotional connection with the viewer rather than out of a set of objective aesthetic principles.

Communication between artist and viewer can be set up indirectly, comments John Russell, "as when Alice Aycock builds her cryptic architectures in the open air. It can tremble on the very edge of invisibility, as it does with Agnes Martin, and it can fill the whole room—walls, ceiling, floor, and the spaces in between—with an all-American vivacity, as it does when Judy Pfaff lets fly with one of her environmental pieces. . . . It is in fact as various as communication itself."[1]

Russell speculates that there may be a neurological factor involved in the female artist's steadiness of development and sense of pacing in contrast to the career style of many male artists. His source for this supposition is Lewis Thomas, who writes,

> It is my belief that childhood lasts considerably longer in the males of our species than in the females. There is somewhere a deep center of immaturity built into the male brain, always needing steadying and redirection, designed to be reconstructed and instructed, perhaps analogous to the left-brain center for male birdsong, which goes to pieces seasonally and requires the reassembling of neurones to function properly when spring comes. Women keep changing the upper, outer parts of their minds all the time, like shifting the furniture or changing their handbags, but the center tends to hold as a steadier, more solid place.

Whatever its source, women's art today is providing fresh stimulus for artists to explore the untried, to take the roads not taken. Working often in the interstices of the arts, women are filling the empty spaces between art and everyday life, knitting together loosened strands of the human texture. "Probably more than most artists, women make art to escape, overwhelm, or transform daily realities," comments art historian Barbara Rose.[2] The homely images of daily domestic existence are lifted out of the commonplace in the art of Rosalind Hodgkins, whose paintings could have been inspired by household catalogs. Ellen Lanyon, in a painting titled "Housekeeper's Terror," brings mystery and magic to images of dishes and silverware. Sandra de Sando sculpts plaster birthday cakes decorated with cookies and animal crackers.

Food, not surprisingly, is a recurring image, as are floors, cleaning tools, even dirty laundry. The "Womanhouse" project, created in 1971 by Judy Chicago and Miriam Schapiro working with their students at California Institute of the Arts, is one of the better-known works in this genre. But household art began gaining the respect of the art establishment ten years earlier, when domestic imagery was appropriated by male artists, emerging full-blown in the pop art movement. The fact that the first pop artists were men— the best known being Andy Warhol—rescued household art from being dismissed by critics as "another woman's genre." The feminine influence was temporarily submerged, but it was working away below the surface, a force to be reckoned with in the not-too-distant future, when the public would become disenchanted with art that appeared to be deliberately distancing itself from human experience.

DEMYSTIFYING THE ARTS

> It is true of women painters as it is true of women in all walks of life that human relationships are more important to them than ambition for personal success. The artistic ego is to most women repulsive for themselves, and compelling in men.
> —GERMAINE GREER, *The Obstacle Race*

The dominant image of the creative artist—painter, writer, composer—is that of a solitary figure immured within the walls of his genius, towering above and reaching beyond the visions of those who people the quotidian world of getting and spending, an Olympian archetype removed from the mundane concerns of ordinary men and women. The prevailing image of the performing artist is more mixed, a composite of shaman, trickster, clown. But creator and performer have this in common: both are shrouded in the cult of personality, which draws forth an ambivalent response from the general public. On the one hand, there is awe for the mystique of artists and their work, which exist in a rarefied element outside of ordinary society; on the other, there is an attitude of condescension toward those whose life work is lacking in utilitarian value and is therefore out of place in a producing-consuming economy. These attitudes, together with the aid of professional image makers and the cooperation of the media, have combined to separate art and the artist from the common life of men and women, prompting statements such as this by author and humanities scholar Joseph Meeker: "Great works of art are not devices for communication between an artist and his public."[3]

There are of course other, more complex, evolutionary factors involved in the distancing of art from life. As religion was removed from daily life through its clerical hierarchy and elaborate mystifications, the arts in the Western world have also become remote from ordinary human concerns; the process of separation in the arts has followed the broad cultural development of our civilization—a three-stage evolution from religiosity to humanism to abstraction.

In an age of moral and political absolutism, Bach added to each composition the signature *Grazia Deo*. For Bach as well as for his contemporaries and predecessors in musical composition, for the master painters—da Vinci, Giotto, Caravaggio—art was a celebration of God. By the late Renaissance and through the Age of Enlightenment, as absolutism in state and church was being challenged by thinkers like Locke, Hobbes, and Luther, the arts were moving from piety to humanism; now it was not just God being celebrated, but humankind. Rousseau and Voltaire elevated reason above faith, and held out the hope that humanity could achieve salvation on earth by freeing itself from the trappings of a corrupt social order. In the arts, this new vitality and sense of human possibility were given image and voice by painters like Rembrandt and Bosch, composers like Mendelssohn and Mozart.

Today, in our age of secularism and individualism—this "darkest of all dark ages," to use Heidegger's words—art has become a celebration neither of God nor humankind but of itself. Art for art's sake has become the aesthetic principle of the twentieth century. It is art retreating into itself, into an aesthetic solipsism, the worship of pure technique.

Piet Mondrian, Max Ernst, Jackson Pollock, Mark Rothko have achieved magnificent effects through experimentation with design and texture. Ernst experimented with random techniques such as "frottage"—rubbing a pencil against a grained texture and using the resulting impression as the basis for an image; he is said to have invented a machine for randomly spotting the canvas with paint. The extreme which this level of abstraction has reached is an art that, as art historian Barbara Rose puts it, is "so absolute and demanding that it requires a state of focused consciousness different from our mundane way of seeing to be perceived at all."

A reaction against formlessness and anticontent was inevitable, and when it burst forth in America in the late 1950s, it appeared in the indigenous form of pop art. With their antecedents in the abstract expressionists (Willem de Kooning, Charles Demuth, Arshile Gorky) and in an aesthetic environment that owed much to the influence of composer John Cage ("All noise is music"), pop artists such as Andy Warhol, with their commonplace images of rusty nails, rags, scraps of newspaper, set about attempting to close the gap between art and life. In doing so, they were, perhaps unconsciously, expressing the feminine impulse toward the integration of the arts with everyday human experience.

Through the '70s and the '80s, American artists have continued to experiment with new images as well as with imagelessness toward the goal of effacing the boundary between the arts and human experience, spiritual and material. Abstract illusionism, minimalism, automatism, conceptual art, photorealism are some of the innovations that emerged from artists' studios as art strove to capture and become a part of the flux and dynamism of American life. But some of these experiments, such as Robert Ryman's all-white canvases or Jackson Pollock's drip paintings, while they produced striking painterly effects, were too obsessed with texture and technique to achieve their aim of unifying art with ordinary human life experience.

With the ripening and recognition of women's art, this vision of an integrated aesthetic experience is being translated into a multidimensional reality. The flow of dammed-up feminine creativity is releasing currents of experimentation in the visual and performing arts that are shaking up the art world and forcing it to confront from a new perspective the question What is art? Female artists, unfettered by centuries of the very artistic tradition that ignored them, are exercising their freedom to strike out in new directions, to integrate tradition with innovation, to draw upon their feminine experience in developing their own aesthetic style.

The communication of women's experience through art transforms daily life into an aesthetic experience. Throughout the ages, women's lives have unfolded within houses—in kitchens, bedrooms, nurseries. Woman's total immersion in the process of creating and sustaining life has predisposed her toward the immanent rather than the transcendent. As an artist, she is usually in the midst of life when she puts paint to canvas or words to paper (few women artists have the luxury of complete isolation while they work), and her art reflects the inseparability of her life and work.

A pioneer in the women's art movement, Judy Chicago discovered in her study of women artists that their attitude toward their work was very different from that of men artists; for women, there was "an interpenetration between their life and their art that made it hard to distinguish where one left off and the other began. Objects, toiletries, children's toys, pets, old postcards and curios, paintings and drawings all intermingled in a rich, womanly environment." She saw how the fragmentation of women's lives, the blurring of boundaries between the roles of wife, mother, and artist emerged as a lifestyle common to many women who managed to "fit their artmaking into a multiplicity of activities that included making breakfast, getting the children off to school, doing the laundry, painting; then, while waiting for the paint to dry, doing the dishes, after which it was back into the studio until the children came home."[4]

The question of whether there is a "women's art" or just "good art" pops up in almost any discussion of the subject and evokes heated arguments on both sides. It is a question with a contemporary resonance, since it is only in the modern age that female artists in Western societies have begun to gain acceptance and to be taken seriously. In certain other cultures—with the Navajo and Hopi Indians, the Bedouin, the nomads of Central Asia, for example—art has always been created by women. But in Europe and America, women's relationship to the arts has been essentially that of consumers and supporters. Female artists, working within a male culture and forced to do battle with monumental restrictions and prejudices, have been caught up in a struggle with their identity as women and as artists, uncertain where the two converge and where they separate. "Why are we all still so afraid of being *other* than men?" art critic Lucy Lippard asks. "Women are still in hiding. We still find it difficult, even the young ones, to express ourselves freely in large groups of men. Since the art world is still dominated by men, this attitude pervades the art that is being made. In the process, feelings and forms are neutralized."[5]

Since Lippard wrote these words in the mid '70s, the surge of women into the arts has somewhat mooted the issue of women artists in a male-dominated culture. "The creativity of women in the 1980s is one of the great incontrovertible facts of life," states art critic John Russell, and a survey of the work of women artists today reveals that the qualities generally identified as feminine—the communal impulse, orientation to process, centeredness, emotionality—appear all across the spectrum of women's creative work. As life givers and nurturers, women are attuned to meaning and substance, to unity of form and content. Lucy Lippard makes the point that "the formal anti-content tradition that has been prevalent in the last fifteen years of abstract art militates against comprehension of a feminist art with different values."

A unique opportunity to compare the values and self-perception of female artists with those of male artists was presented recently when two separate exhibits, appearing simultaneously in Los Angeles, featured the self-portraits of women in one and of men in the other. Critics reviewing the showings and struck by the marked differences between the two pointed to the contrast between "male severity and dominance" and "feminine exclusivity and abandon." The neat regularity of the paintings in the male artists' exhibit was replaced in the female showing by unstretched canvases, montages, and tiny pencil drawings. The women's self-portraits were described as "more introspective," having less to do with external appearance than with "representing feelings and psychological conditions."

The redefining of familiar forms, which is often brought about by the special feminine perspective, was one of the outcomes of the women's exhibit. "We had to think about what a self-portrait really is at present," said Tressa Miller, director of cultural affairs for the Security Pacific Bank, which sponsored the women's exhibit. As an example of extending the definition, she points to Phyllis Bramson's canvas, "Splitting," in which the subject appears twice: once as a half-beast, along with a male counterpart in the lower portion of the canvas, and again above, with only one arm and part of her head visible, tentatively gripping the top of a wall. Another self-portrait is a painting by Anita Stekel, in which the artist is flying through the Sistine Chapel. In "Waterborne," by Ruth Weisberg, the artist is revealed sitting sidewise in the nude, immersed in a shimmer of watery tendrils. Mary Beth Edelson presents herself in "Woman Rising," painting her body with ancient ritual signs, symbolizing woman's ascent from the earth and the sea.

Even abstraction, usually associated with masculine rather than feminine culture, is approached differently by women artists. Male abstract expressionists—Arshile Gorky and Piet Mondrian, for example—attempted to detach art from personalism and from its cultural roots, so that it would transcend tradition; Mondrian's stark, geometric designs represent this principle of aesthetic reductionism. By contrast, women's abstract art tends toward a merging of the personal with the form and style of abstraction. Abstract painter Joan Snyder identifies the feminine sensibility in art as a "kind of softness, layering, a certain color sensibility, a more expressive work than any man is going to do right now. . . ." She finds that women's art is "more autobiographical. . . . My work is an open diary. That's what I often miss in men's work—an autobiographical or narrative aspect. . . . When I look at women's art, I look for ideas and images that not only move me visually but tell me something about who the artist is, what she is, what she's trying to say. I'm not interested in art so mysterious that it doesn't tell me a thing."

COLLECTIVE ART

> This "gatherer" style, which makes a tightly woven
> texture of independent and equal parts (in essence
> counterpoint), I take to be symbolic . . . of a feminine
> preference for egalitarian interaction.
>
> —ALAN LOMAX, *"A Note on a Feminine Factor in Cultural*
> *History," in Raphael, ed., Being Female*

From primitive gathering groups to suburban car-pools, the collaborative impulse has been one of women's most reliable survival strategies, and as we would expect, it is becoming an important aspect of women's art. The needleworkers in Judy Chicago's "Dinner Party" and "Birth Project" are a type of collective, although its structure is closer to the master-artisan arrangement of the preindustrial world than to the more egalitarian art collectives that have been emerging within the past decade.

The governing principle of the true art collective is group participation, an opportunity for all participants to use their creative energies to the fullest through techniques that aid communication and awaken dormant abilities. Of course, the collective form did not originate with women artists; chamber music ensembles and repertory groups have a long and honorable history in the performing arts, and many great artists of the past—Raphael, Tintoretto, da Vinci—worked so closely with apprentices that art historians sometimes have difficulty distinguishing the masters' works from those of their novices (they circumvent the problem by referring to "the school of . . .").

But women have taken to collective art as if it were their natural creative element. In fact, there is some anthropological evidence that collaborative creativity is an important part of feminine culture in societies as far-flung as central Asia, northern Europe, Amerindia, Malaysia, and Australia. Anthropologist Alan Lomax in studying these cultures has found that feminine performance style leans in the direction of rapport and cooperation:

The tenderness of this performance profile suits the role of mother, of nurturer; the slower, softer, refrain-filled, rhythmically regular, relatively unembellished and melodically repetitious style of women presents the profile of the lulling song and thus may be its source. . . . Indeed, feminine performance symbolizes and reinforces a choral, integrated style; women sing in better vocal blend than do men and their dances are marked by more cohesiveness, especially in the rhythmic sense.

A notable exception are those societies, such as that of aboriginal Australia, where women's roles are "slave and drone-like."

TRANSCENDING THE BOUNDARIES

The contemporary collectives that are emerging out of women's art are blurring the boundaries between the various art forms and complicating the perennial question What is art? The visual arts in particular have always been associated with the creation of a tangible product: a painting, a fresco, a piece of sculpture, a tapestry, a vase. "The western European art tradition," muralist Judy Baca says, "is based on the creation of an object that is valued because it can be sold, traded, and owned." As such, it is art as a commodity, subject to the fluctuations of the art market and, like other luxury goods, available to a small, wealthy elite.

But what about "conceptual art," in which the product is incidental to the process or may even be nonexistent? Can the definition of art be expanded to accommodate forms of expression such as these? The feminine tendency to transcend traditional boundaries and divisions has added fuel to the heat of controversy that has beset the visual arts community in recent years. West Coast artists and art purveyors have been confronting such questions as Was the Muppets exhibit an art show or a crafts show? Was the cowboy exhibition at the San Diego Museum of Art an art show or a cultural show? Was the Italian industrial design show at the La Jolla Museum of Contemporary Art an art show or a trade show? The central question for painting today is how it can distinguish itself, not from the other arts, but from other objects and events in the world, a question that has been accentuated as women artists have expanded the scope and definition of aesthetic expression.

The question is simpler to deal with in the performing arts, which are process-oriented by nature. Some women's theater groups have been experimenting with nontraditional modes, using repetition and symbolism to break through ordinary consciousness and move beyond familiar conceptions. Other groups, in dance and music as well as theater, are seeking to preserve traditional forms by transfusing them with new themes, techniques, and creative energies. Informality and making a special connection with the audience are characteristics of feminine culture that appear to be indigenous to women's art collectives. A recent work by conceptual artist Suzanne Lacy, "Whisper, the Waves, the Wind," features white-clad older women sitting on a beach discussing their experience of aging. Lacy describes the production as a "tapping into a cultural memory that honors and deifies the wisdom and experience of older women as well as the special relationship that older women have with each other. I'm trying to create an archetypal image, trying to bring forth an image of older women that has been robbed of power. In some cultures, they're seen as goddesses, great forces that carry you from life to death. In this culture, not so." Lacy brings the audience into the act by inviting them onto the beach to mingle with the performers and then take their places in the chairs as the performers leave.

Ultimately, bridging the space between artist and art consumer in art collectives leads to merging creator and consumer into a creative unity. The proposition that anyone can participate in an art experience is now restated to affirm that anyone can *be* an artist, since creativity resides within and needs only to be stimulated and encouraged in collaboration with others in order to find its full expression.

Contemporary artists who have been exploring aspects of audience participation in the arts, recalling the "happenings" of the '70s, include composers John Cage and Pauline Oliveras (whose technique consists of activating sounds through audience actions), as well as many dance and theater ensembles that involve the audience using ritual and improvisation.

But by taking the process a step further, groups of people who have had little or no contact with the arts are discovering their own inner springs of latent creativity. Susan Hill, an artist and art educator who has made a career of working with community groups, is a fervent believer in the "everyone is an artist" doctrine. Allowing for the fact that genius or exceptional talent are not granted to all of us, she is nevertheless convinced that every human being possesses a store of creative energy, and that in a group environment these dormant potencies can be activated and guided toward a gratifying aesthetic result. With a background in art photography and as a volunteer in Judy Chicago's "Dinner Party" project, Susan Hill brings her vision to women who are institutionalized or who lead shut-in lives because of age or illness. She has supervised the design and execution of quilts with women in prison and is currently developing a quilt project with women in senior-citizen homes. "I ask people to think of an image that means a great deal to them, and then we develop a context in which to place their images." Hill sees the complex and interlocked design of quilting as a "metaphor for how women manage their lives." Recurring themes in these group projects are feasts, rituals, birth, death, loneliness—"the intrinsic feminine themes that women relate to so readily and therefore are encouraged to try to express."

CHALLENGING THE MAINSTREAM

The new images, sounds, textures, combinations, and configurations erupting out of the unconfined energies of female artists have not been received with unalloyed enthusiasm by the art establishment. Some of the more nontraditional productions, particularly those with social content, have been dismissed by critics as being neither good art nor good social criticism. It is a valid concern

,nether the concept that everything and everyone can *be* art stretches "art" so thin that it ceases to have any meaning. And when Rachel Rosenthal declares that performance art requires no audience, are we not confronted once again with the familiar conundrum of whether the tree falling in an empty forest makes a sound?

Whatever the future of these works, art history offers ample precedents of breakthrough movements that have made a major contribution to the arts as catalysts, stimulating a flow of fresh creativity and the clearing away of cultural deadwood (dadaism is one example). These challenges to tradition perform an important function above and beyond their inherent aesthetic value: they prepare the soil out of which great and lasting art can grow, and along with it the social criticism that is often embodied in great works of art.

As women's art is absorbed into the mainstream, it is being judged solely as good or bad art without reference to its gender. But it continues to serve as a catalyst, motivating artists toward a more human-centered creativity. It would be premature to attempt at this time an exact assessment of the cause-and-effect relationship between feminine culture and the visual and performing arts; we leave that to the art historians of the future. But we can state unequivocally that, since women's art has become a vital part of the American cultural scene, the lively arts have never looked livelier. A recent Harris poll revealed that attendance at performing arts events, which began booming in the '70s, is continuing its upward trend in the '80s. "This poll shows that the arts in this country have been vastly underestimated by the Establishment, both political and economic, in terms of the role they play in people's lives," Louis Harris commented. "Given more leisure time and proper choices, people are still opting for live art presentations as an uplifting source in troubled times."

Community art, dance, and theater groups are springing up around the country, partly as a grass-roots response to the less-than-equal acceptance of women's art by the art establishment in metropolitan areas. Hardly a town of any size in the United States today does not have at least one amateur theater group and a community center that serves, among other things, as a showplace for local and other artists. Art classes for the general public are among the most popular offerings in adult education, second only to business and professional courses. Corporate support for the arts is increasing—witness Security Pacific Bank's establishment of a cultural affairs department, which sponsored the women's self-portrait exhibit; corporate funding is supporting such avant-garde projects as the Social and Public Resource Center, founded in Los Angeles in 1976 by muralist Judy Baca, painter Christina Schlesinger, and film maker Donna Deitch as an interdisciplinary arts forum for nontraditional artists; and corporate support is the lifeblood of the arts conferences and programs that are mushrooming throughout the country.

In the professional and performing arts, women's jazz and rock groups, though still few and far between, are beginning to find their own style and tone in what has been a solidly male bastion. All-woman jazz groups have been forming since the early '70s, among them the Jazz Sisters in New York, Airhart in Missouri, Second Hand Rose in Ithaca, Thornebird in Boston, Maiden Voyage in Los Angeles, Sojourner out of Chicago and Detroit, and the Aerial Quintet, featured in the 1979 Women's Jazz Festival and the first all-female group to appear at the Newport Jazz Festival that same year. Alive! is a West Coast–based group that includes women trained in classical music as well as jazz; the group, which is leaderless, communicates to audiences what it describes as its "feminist-humanist philosophy" by performing in a warm, relaxed, and informal style. Drawing upon original compositions and eclectic sources, its repertoire includes musical pieces that express the abrasive, fast-paced reality of urban life, a liberated woman's rallying cry, and an exhortation to find spiritual strength within oneself.

How much of this feminized jazz style is rubbing off on male performers is still an open question. Carol Comer and Dianne Gregg, organizers of the Women's Jazz Festival, view women in jazz today primarily as audience builders and role models. In Comer's words to aspiring jazzwomen: "A trombone player who once said, 'I want to play like Bill Watrous' now can say 'Janice Robinson' or 'Melba Liston' . . . and that's important." Equally important, she believes, is the setting up of female images to counteract the prototype of the "macho, hairy-chested male with his open shirt and his saxophone."[6]

New images are also turning up in the theater, where female playwrights are working with themes, characters, and techniques that expose private, hidden places in the human psyche. "It's a time of great exploration, of secret worlds," says Marsha Norman, whose Pulitzer Prize–winning play 'night, Mother is a heart-rending treatment of a failed mother-daughter relationship. Playwrights like Mary Gallagher, Lavonne Mueller, Kathleen Tolan, Beth Henley, and Wendy Wasserstein are moving beyond feminist issues to concentrate on identity and evolving relationships between women and men and women and women. It is the intensity of this concern that, according to New York Times drama critic Mel Gussow, makes the characters in their plays seem "more emotionally affecting to the audience than characters men have been writing about. While men are dissecting characters and detecting flaws, women are creating characters you can love. That says something about women's new, positive sense of self. They are finding a kind of support system for each other."[7]

By offering alternatives to the well-made mainstream drama, women's theater is also providing a support system for dramatists, male and female, who are seeking new directions. Typically, the well-made play presents recognizable characters whose story is told in linear narrative style, with fixed stage sets and a curtain dividing the scenes and acts. This neat and tidy form has served the theater well, but it cannot accommodate the disregarding of conventional unities of time and place, as in Caryl Churchill's Cloud Nine and Top Girls, or the mixing of images and media, as in Myrna Lamb's multimedia dramatic pieces.

Here again, female dramatists' historic position on the threshold of theatrical art has made it easier for them to explore unconventional dramatic terrain. Non-narrative theater—Ntozake Shange's For Colored Girls Who Have Considered Suicide When the Rainbow is Enuf is an early (1976) example—has been adopted by female playwrights for its fluidity and openendedness, more compatible with women's experience. The form is also being taken up by mainstream theatre where it has been successfully applied in several productions including *Dead End Kids,* the 1980 mixed-media performance by the Mabou Mines theatre collective, a history of nuclear power in theatrical collage form. The performance weaves together scientific history with satirical sketches of American consumer culture, dramatizing without preaching our inability to confront the reality of the dangerous forces we face. A 1984 production by the Wooster Group, titled *L.S.D.* features a collage of readings from the works of such counterculture gurus as Timothy Leary, Allen Ginsberg, and Kerouac mixed with rock songs, fragments from plays, and a debate between Leary and G. Gordon Liddy, all of this presented in a spirit of self-questioning which suggests that the answers to human problems lie within ourselves. Although the non-narrative form springs from various sources aside from feminist theatre, among them Dadaism and Surrealism, the self-questioning of the form is especially suited to the inward quest of women's spirituality and creativity.

The feminine approach to dramatic content as well as form has strongly influenced the work of John Ford Noonan, one of Off-Broadway's better-known comedy playwrights. Noonan, a 240-pound ex-prizefighter, ex-basketball coach, ex-construction worker finds women more interesting to write about than men, explaining it this way: "I feel more female than male. I identify more with women than men. I find women with their intuitions much more interesting." In his recent play, *A Coupla White Chicks Sitting Around Talking,* the male characters are shadowy off-stage figures, the women the center of attention as they struggle for their own self-definition. "My whole sympathy goes to them," says Noonan. "They're redefining the rules they live by."

In redefining the rules of musical composition, women composers of "serious music," as it is generally known, are producing new sounds and combinations of sounds. Mel Powell, composer and teacher of composition at California Institute of the Arts, points to Kathleen St. John as an exemplar of the feminine sensibility in new music; he describes her multimedia work as a "strange amalgam of pop and rock music fused into a serious statement . . . an uninhibited, roaring sound." Anna Rubin, a former student of

Powell's, defines the feminization of music as "interpreting the human side of life into music." Her electronic pieces combine language structure with the human voice as a carrier of meaning and emotion.

In the dance, which has always been considered a feminine art form, a new generation of dancers and choreographers are counteracting the overstylization of the dance and the idealization of the female body. Following in the footsteps of Isadora Duncan and Martha Graham, who liberated the body of the female dancer, the new language of the dance is based on natural body motions and realistic gestures in place of the distortions and exaggerations of classical ballet. The modernist revolution of the '30s and '40s is being revived as women weave social comment and emotion into their dance pieces. Anna Sokolow, who has enlivened choreography in her fifty-year career, has used social themes in many of her most successful works. "It's humanity's struggle that has touched me," she says, and in her dance performances she has explored such contemporary issues as the plight of political prisoners and social dissidents, juvenile delinquency, labor abuses, personal and social alienation. "I don't believe in ivory towers," she states firmly, adding that artists should belong to society without feeling that they must conform to it.

Sokolow has influenced several generations of dancers, among them Alvin Ailey, Paul Taylor, Jeff Duncan, Susan Thomasson. "For me, coming out of abstract dance," Thomasson says, "Anna provided a totally different kind of motivation, filled with emotional imagery and emotional intent. There is less focus on exact placement and more on where it comes from internally."

Among the popular arts, film and television are somewhat belatedly catching up with the feminizing trend, having put up a strong resistance until the mid '70s when the women's movement was rapidly gaining momentum. In the prewar years roles for women in Hollywood movies and in television dramas were for the most part a variation on one of the following: the dumb blonde sexpot, as epitomized by Marilyn Monroe and more recently by Goldie Hawn; the harlot with a heart of gold, typified by Marlene Dietrich in *Destry Rides Again*; and the prim schoolmarm type, as portrayed by Grace Kelly and recycled endlessly in westerns and gangster films. Strong, courageous, intelligent women were rarities; female friendship was practically nonexistent. When two women did appear in leading roles it was usually as competitors for the male protagonist, and at some point they would invariably engage in a hair-pulling fracas, a scene dear to many a movie director's heart.

From the forties onward, the evolution of women's roles in films followed a zigzag course, from the independent, courageous woman of the war years portrayed by a powerful female star to the woman-as-victim prevalent in the films of the 1960s to an opposite trend in the 1970s. Film historian Molly Haskell interprets the victimization of women in the violent films of the 1960s as a backlash against the growing women's movement.

"The closer women come to claiming their rights and achieving independence in real life," says Haskell, "the more loudly and stridently films tell us it's a man's world."

But by the mid '70s, the backlash was retreating before the irresistible tide of feminization, and Hollywood began making a number of films centering on the process of a women's self-discovery and independence. The genre (which includes *Alice Doesn't Live Here Anymore, Starting Over, An Unmarried Woman, Girl Friends, Julia, Testament,* and *Places in the Heart)* focuses on women who are not necessarily glamorous in the conventional sense and who are usually engaged in a struggle from which they emerge, in one way or another, as triumphant. Even in the painfully poignant final scene of Lynne Littmann's *Testament,* Jane Alexander as the mother of the doomed family determines to survive the nuclear holocaust and bear witness to future generations. As intended by the producers, these "new women" films, as they are sometimes called, give women in the audience a chance to identify with positive female images and to feel as if they, too, can be winners.

This is not to suggest that the male-controlled film industry, in which money and power have always played larger roles than talent or creative energy, is devoting itself exclusively to socially redeeming works that celebrate feminine values and purposes. Violence, pornography, and all-around mindlessness continue to be ground out by movie mills that aim mainly at the teenage audience who, as the movie moguls appear to believe, are devoid of both taste and intelligence.

But violence and sleaze are no longer the only games in town. When an actor-director like Clint Eastwood takes a U-turn from brutal, sadistic productions like his Dirty Harry films to a funny, ironic, politically prescient fantasy like *Honky Tonk Man* (which has been compared to *The Grapes of Wrath),* when this actor-director who has been reviled as a lowbrow, a "lunkhead," a "cinematic caveman" is now being hailed as a feminist film director, something important must be happening in mainstream film making. What is happening, of course, is that even in Hollywood, perhaps the hardest of the soft areas of popular culture, new men are becoming involved with and affected by new women, and these personal transformations are revitalizing and humanizing the movies.

Similarly, the process of feminization is providing a few oases in the wasteland of television. Within the past few years, the dreary sitcom/cops-and-robbers TV scene has been enlivened with programs like "Kate and Allie," a series about two single mothers sharing a household and the problems that are common to women in their situation, and "Cagney and Lacey," featuring two policewomen buddies who, through all their adventures and crises, remain real, recognizable human beings who personify the values and concerns of many women today.

The latter show is one of those occasional breakthroughs that acts as a beacon illuminating the field around it; a creation of Barbara Avedon and Barbara Corday (several years prior to Corday's appointment to the top job at Columbia Pictures Television), it would not have made it to prime time without the persistence of executive producer Barney Rosenzweig, who became feminized in the process. As Rosenzweig tells it, when he first became aware of the Avedon-Corday project in 1975, "I didn't know an awful lot about feminism and so decided it was important to have my consciousness raised. . . . One of the things that struck me was the fact that never in the history of Hollywood films had two women had a relationship like Robert Redford and Paul Newman in *Butch Cas-*

sidy or Elliott Gould and Donald Sutherland in *M*A*S*H**. . . .
The Hollywood establishment had totally refused women those
friendships.'' Rosenzweig convinced Ed Feldman of Filmways Productions to put up the seed money, and TV's first feminist film
series was on its way.

Since success tends to breed more of its own kind—and nowhere more than in film and television—there are, not surprisingly,
other plans on several Hollywood drawing boards for more productions featuring real women with real human problems and interests.
In fact, a report issued in December 1984 by the National Commission on Working Women states that ''there are more female characters, more minorities, new family structures, job diversity, new
roles for men and a focus on issues of concern to women.'' The
report noted also that on NBC 51 percent of the new characters are
women, adding that, though there is still too much stereotyping of
female characters, most of them being young, white and single, the
1984 season is ''a step in the right direction.'' There is at least
some basis for the hope that a new Golden Age may be dawning in
feature films and television.

RECHARGING THE ARTS

The vitality and dynamism that women are bringing to the arts
are contributing to an upsurge of spirit, a sense of regeneration that
is being felt not only in the professional art community but throughout mainstream culture. With it comes a growing recognition of the
human potential for creativity, and of the diversity of shapes and
forms this need for self-expression can assume. Today, while
women artists are still underexhibited, a museumgoer can find
quilts hanging on walls not far from those displaying offerings of
the Old Masters, as well as exhibits of china painting, needlework,
jewelry, costume design—genres that have never before been permitted within the sacred portals of Art. A few male artists are de-
signing quilts, and Julian Schnabel, the current wunderkind of neo-
expressionism, paints on velvet surfaces, broken dinner plates, and

linoleum, and points to emblems in his paintings that refer to physical states, such as his wife's pregnancy.

Art as communication is winning acceptance in the art establishment. "I am sick and tired of art for the pleasure of the artist," says Tony Duquette, the first and only American artist to have had a one-man show in the Louvre. "I want the spectator to be the star." In a recent exhibit of contemporary art at the Hirshhorn Museum in Washington, D.C., titled "Content: A Contemporary Focus, 1974–84," the main theme was the reemergence of content as the prime motif of art. Content, form, meaning, connection—all expressions of feminine culture—are providing a healthy alternative to abstraction and solipsism in the arts.

In challenging the arid dictum of art for art's sake, women are giving the arts a human face, and in the process more realistic, recognizable images of women and of men are emerging in painting and sculpture, theater and dance, film and television. Strong, confident women are featured in contemporary works by both male and female artists, replacing the idealized, objectified female images of the past; and the outsize heroic male figures that once dominated the arts have been scaled down to human size. The feminine influence is bridging the gap between men and women in the arts as it bridges the gap between art and human life.

10. PROTECTING LIFE

*A grim specter has crept upon us almost unno-
ticed, and this imagined tragedy may easily
become a stark reality we all shall know.*
            —RACHEL CARSON, *Silent Spring*

*Peace without freedom is unthinkable; freedom
without peace is impossible. This is one proposition on which conservatives and liberals can
agree. Therefore, the making of an enforceable
peace that serves the conditions of freedom is at
the top of the human agenda.*
            —NORMAN COUSINS, *Human Options*

Women's historic commitment to the nurturing and protection of life is moving public sentiment closer to feminine
values and goals and away from the traditional and once
widely accepted masculine creed of guns before butter and profits
before people. Current polls show that more than 80 percent of
Americans want an immediate halt to the arms race. According to a
recent report from the Center for Defense Information in Washington, there has never in American history been such an outpouring of
citizen activism in the cause of peace. This clear expression of a
growing public antiwar position, which is directly contrary to the
continuing U.S.–Soviet arms buildup, testifies to the mounting impact on mainstream culture of the feminine concern for the preservation of that most endangered species, the human race.

Women's activism in the peace movement is a logical extension of their historic role as creators and protectors of life. The

ethic of responsibility for human life is a thread that runs throughout the complex weave of women's culture. Carol Gilligan,
Harvard professor of education, calls it a "moral imperative" and
distinguishes the feminine insistence on caring for others in an active, positive way from the masculine perception of a negative obli-
gation of noninterference with others' rights.

Most women accept without question their responsibility for
protecting life, and since the feminine role throughout history has
been to nurture and heal, women have acquired a highly developed
set of responses to anything that appears to be life-threatening to
themselves or to others, whether it takes the form of toxic wastes,
handguns, drunk drivers, or military hardware. And since women
are constantly on the alert for such dangers, their inner detectors
often flash a warning before the mainstream has become aware of
the threat. Biologist Rachel Carson's *Silent Spring,* published in
1962, sent out such a warning, alerting us to the destructive potential of pesticides on the balance of nature.

But efforts to preserve the planet and its teeming, diverse forms
of life can succeed only if they are supported by both masculine and
feminine perspectives and energies, and one of the most encouraging developments of our time has been the joining of men and
women in life-protecting endeavors. Changing standards of masculinity and new attitudes toward fatherhood, which are bringing
with them a deepening concern among men for their children's
future, appear to be the prime motivators for men's increasing antiwar activities. It is a healthy and hopeful balancing act; women's
fine-tuning to the personal and men's longer experience with political power can merge to form an irresistible political force.

Achieving this new masculine-feminine balance in the cause of
world peace is bringing about a historic reversal: in nearly all public
world activities, women have had to adapt to male models, these
being the only ones available to them. But since traditionally men
have been involved in planning and fighting wars while women
were seeking and working for peace, it is women's experience as
peace activists that is currently providing the stimulus and example
for men who want to participate in the drive for world peace.

WAR AND PEACE:
Closing the Gender Gap

Because of women's historic exclusion from decision-making roles in military and foreign affairs, war making has been an exclusively male preoccupation and one identified with the highest form of citizenship. "Historically, the emerging concept of a citizen was tied to soldiering," says Jean Elshtain, professor of political science at the University of Massachusetts. "This separates women from citizenship in a large way." But in feminine culture, citizenship extends beyond national interests to human interests. It is this sense of connection, extending from family, community, and nation that women have been bringing with them into the peace movement.

Working for peace is for women today what the suffrage movement was in the late nineteenth and early twentieth centuries—a chance to pull together for a cause that can transcend personal and partisan differences and obliterate long-standing boundaries and barriers, be they ethnic, generational, regional, or even national. But while the suffrage movement was supported entirely by women working for a woman's cause, the peace movement, in becoming sexually integrated, has been attracting a broader constituency and cutting more deeply into mainstream culture.

It is tempting to suggest that the desire for peace is so deeply embedded in women that it provides a universal definition of feminity. But this would require that we amass the supporting data selectively, omitting such countervailing evidence as the women who guarded the concentration camps as cold-bloodedly as the men; the women who have throughout history cheered their men on to war and glorified their military exploits, who have shared in warfare, according to historical accounts, with no less ferocity than men.

Simone de Beauvoir writes of those women who exalt male prowess in hunting and war, who fashion the weapons and roll the bandages, accepting tributes in return for the lives of their men.

Although women do not usually take part in active duty, they can be assigned a certain number of "reactive duties." According to political scientist Judith Stiehm, such women can include

> sympathetic nurses like Florence Nightingale or seductive spies like Mata Hari, or cheerleaders, running along the sides of trains and waving good-bye to the departing men in uniform; they can be "castrating bitches" who belittle and berate men for refusing to become macho murderers. . . . They can be miracle mothers who give birth with exceptional prolificity if a charismatic leader needs babies for cannon fodder; they can be wistful wives holding up these babies (especially male babies) in posters inciting men to join the fray; they can be treacherous tramps who are aroused by the sight of flashy uniforms and therefore tempted to find the invading army sexier than their own; and finally, they can be cooperative citizens, developing quasi-masculine stamina for field and factory work which will just as suddenly evaporate when war is over.[1]

But if it is difficult to establish an airtight case that women are by nature more peace-loving than men, there is no denying the fact that the organized antiwar activities that have captured the public imagination have been mainly the result of women's efforts. Although men and women are in full agreement on the very clear and present danger of nuclear war, their perceptions often part company in the debate on how to deal with this cataclysmic possibility. Long before the phrase *gender gap* was coined, there was a general recognition that men and women differed on various political issues, and particularly about war and peace. Over the long course of human history, women have learned that war brings them more losses than medals, more suffering than glory.

But why are men drawn to warfare? This age-old question, which has a special urgency for us in today's nuclear world, is enmeshed in a tangle of nature-nurture argument and speculation.

The arguments for nurture are offered as "rational" explanations, reducible to culture. It has been suggested, for example, that men engage in war to maintain an economic balance, to hold down population growth or land pressure. Nonetheless, in many warring societies economic motives are absent, and the conflict is a profound expression of ceremonial behavior. New Guinean tribesmen who do not take captives or gain land and who return from the battlefields on rainy days so as not to spoil their body paint and feathers, as well as modern armies that observe courtesies of cessation for religious holidays are engaging in conflict behavior as ritualized as an American football game.

Those arguing for nature hold that males are innately aggressive, as though a genetic element prone to killing could be found on the Y chromosome. This school of thought argues that men are biologically predisposed to a "territorial imperative," having been endowed by nature with traits selected in the course of human evolution that equip men to protect and feed their women and children. But those on the nurture side of the debate can turn the argument to their advantage by pointing to the historical and anthropological societies where men and women, socialized in nonviolent behavior, show no "biological" predisposition to violence.

Hunting and warfare are not universal; they are cultural, based on customs, they are options. Childbearing, however, is more than merely customary; women must produce life or life ceases. In nearly all known societies, women are exempted from activities that involve the taking of life. (Some societies make an exception for the killing of birds and small animals for food. And when it is a matter of survival—to save the lives of other children, usually those in the nursing stage—or when subsistence compels it, women may even kill their own infants.)

In hunting-and-gathering societies, no matter how egalitarian the division of labor, women are not permitted to participate in the hunt or even be associated with animal blood. Women who imitate men in killing or hunting are considered anomalies. An Amazon must amputate one breast to be a successful archer and thus becomes half a woman in order to be able to shoot and kill. When women of the African Ndembu tribe dress as hunters, they are thought to be sterile. Anthropologists have suggested that there seems to be a nearly universal association of woman as life giver versus man as life taker. *Female* is associated with the magical, awesome blood of menstruation, highly taboo and dangerous to men; *male* is associated with the blood of warfare and the hunt.

Western societies have also been tenacious in maintaining this line of separation, steadfastly resisting the drafting of women for combat. In our own society, this hard-line attitude toward women in the military has dominated recent congressional debates. It is as if procreating and killing must be segregated or else our bedrock belief in the structure of the universe will begin to crumble. A negative consequence of this form of segregation is that it not only places women at a distance from war but in addition assures that they will be poorly informed about it. It also reinforces women's passivity and impotence in the war-making process.

Women's aversion to war is generally ascribed to their biologically determined mothering role. But as recent studies have affirmed, the mother-infant bond develops not during pregnancy or at birth but with the nurturing of the child. The mother's protectiveness grows over time with her investment of care and love in her child, and this protectiveness expands from a specific child to children in general. When a woman is nursing, the cry of any child will stimulate lactation. Childless women, too, speak of feeling this pull toward children and other forms of life, this sense that all women share of being attuned to the rhythms of their bodies.

The theme of coming together through a common bond of womanhood, a sense of connection to all women and their children, is poignantly evoked in Helen Kazantzakis's account of a visit to a Greek village after the Second World War. The Germans had passed through there. "I had five sons," said one woman, no longer of any determinable age. "I have none left."

"Why were they killed?"

"Because I hid some Englishmen."

"And why did you hide them?"

"Because I was thinking of their mothers."[2]

This act of courage by a simple Greek woman on behalf of other women's children is a true expression of female community which, when fully realized, expands boundaries and gives rise to a vision of an enlarged humanity.

Women have also been linked to peace-keeping by a system that traditionally associates war with such "manly" virtues as heroism and courage. Conversely, as psychiatrist Judd Marmor has noted, "The avoidance of war or the pursuit of peace are generally regarded as 'effeminate,' passive, weak, dishonorable, or subversive." Associating peace with these disdained "feminine" characteristics and values has often placed the peace movement not only outside the mainstream but often in confrontation with it. Women who have always considered themselves to be solid citizens with conservative views on most issues are shocked to discover that they are suddenly transformed into radicals and deviants when they join an organization that supports disarmament.

As long as the peace movement was associated primarily with women, it was tolerated by mainstream society as another expression of women's "otherness." But the growing support of the peace movement by men and by mainstream groups has been causing concern in the ranks of the vast, interlocking military-industrial establishment, which has reacted by stepping up its efforts to discredit antiwar activities. "Peacenik," a familiar term of opprobrium, during the 1960s was often used for peace activists, especially males, for whom it was supposed to carry connotations of wimpishness (there has never been a comparable, opposite epithet, such as "war-nik"). "Hawk," referring to those favoring the military, symbolizes such male-associated attributes as strength and clear-sightedness; "dove," the symbol of peace, suggests instead such stereotypical female traits as weakness and timidity.

As military budgets continue to grow at the expense of social programs, peace activists are frequently labeled unpatriotic and their motives called into question. "Commie sympathizer" is only one of many strident epithets hurled at antiwar protesters by diehard believers in the military solution to all problems. Still, antiwar groups continue to multiply, an increasing number of them organized and run by men who have been drawn into the peace movement as a result of women's determined effort to mobilize public support for survival rather than extinction.

PEACE ACTIVISM, FEMININE STYLE

Women organizing and acting together for peace is not in itself new. The first Women's Peace League was formed in Europe in 1854 by Frederika Bremer. An antiwar novel, *Lay Down Your Arms*, was written in 1889 by Bertha von Suttner; it became a runaway best-seller and was translated into twenty-seven languages. In 1915, while war was raging, and in the face of many problems and difficulties, over 2,000 women from all over Europe, the United States, and Canada met in The Hague to protest against the war and form the International Commission for Lasting Peace, later to become the Women's International League for Peace and Freedom. Their resolutions were used by President Wilson in drawing up his fourteen-point plan for peace in Europe.

The decades of the '50s and '60s, in response to the cold war and nuclear testing, spawned other new organizations in America and Europe, such as the Voice of Women and Women Strike for Peace. Women mailed their babies' teeth to congressmen and came to Washington en masse to protest against strontium 90 in milk and other damaging effects of radioactive fallout. The campaign succeeded in leading the United States and the Soviet Union to sign the Atmospheric Test Ban Treaty, which has kept both nations from testing above ground since 1963.

Today, with the proliferation of nuclear weapons, the women's peace movement has become worldwide: West Germany and Holland have Women for Peace, England has Women for Life on Earth, among others; Japan has its Shibokusa Mothers' Committee, and women's peace groups have been springing up in Norway, France, Crete; even Russia has its "Group for Trust."

The sense of mutual empowerment that women experience when they pool their energies in a compelling cause is evident in the style of their organized peace activities. Two landmark events, the Women's Pentagon Action and the Romulus Peace Encampment, offer revealing glimpses of feminine culture at work in orchestrated peace actions; these two protests have been particularly successful in capturing public attention through the artful use of feminine ritual and symbolism. Both are modeled on England's Greenham Common demonstration, in which 30,000 women formed a human chain around the RAF Greenham Common Base, an intended site for ninety-six cruise missiles.

The Pentagon event began on an early spring day in 1980 with the arrival of 700 women in Northampton, Massachusetts, to attend a conference titled Women and Life on Earth. The women came from all over the northeast, and they were there to talk about what kind of action would embody their vision and their fear for life on earth. For many of them this was a new experience; some were there against the wishes of husbands and boyfriends and were edgy, sensing it was something new, possibly a turning point in their lives.

The women agreed that what they wanted to do was to send a message to women around the world that would convey their awareness of and opposition to the growing militarization of the United States. The message took the form of 2,000 women gathering in Washington on November 16 and 17, 1981. They came with sleeping bags and backpacks, bearing signs that read WE ARE MOURNING, and the TV crews were waiting for them. Holding aloft a black mourning puppet twenty feet high, the women walked rhythmically to a slow drum-beat toward the river entrance of the Pentagon. Chanting "No more war" and "Take the toys away from the boys," they began circling the Pentagon, hand in hand, using scarfs as extenders. Pentagon workers crowded the windows. A few women inside the building were seen giving signs of solidarity. The TV cameras whirred busily.

Ynestra King continues:

> We first wove a braid around the Pentagon as we cir-
> cled, and then wove all the entrances shut with yarn.
> We retied and started new weavings with help from
> women who were not blocking entrances. There were
> cheers, chants, and whistles, and women sang as we
> wove. . .'. At the end, there was a braid around the

Pentagon, and beautiful weavings at all the entrances.
Women who were not arrested held a closing ritual
circle.

The Romulus encampment, which occurred three years after
the Pentagon action, also made effective use of rituals and symbols,
beginning with its starting date, July 4, 1983. On that day, 600
women began camping out on a fifty-two-acre farm in the town of
Romulus, population 1,600, in the Finger Lakes region of New
York State. They were protesting the storage of nuclear weapons at
the nearby Seneca Army Depot. The women were mostly white,
middle class, and well educated. They came from many states and
countries, and they called themselves the Women's Encampment
for a Future of Peace and Justice.

Representing about twenty peace organizations, the women had
bought the farm for $37,000 in the name of Seneca Encampment,
Inc., a nonprofit corporation formed at the Conference on Global
Feminism and Disarmament held in June 1982. The farm is a collection of run-down buildings including a ramshackle farmhouse.
The rear of the property abuts the Seneca Army Depot, which the
women claim is a "transshipment" storage area for nuclear weapons destined for deployment in Europe.

Certainly, this quiet, conservative rural area, which includes
seventy-two Mennonite families among its population, was an un-
likely locality to choose for any cause that could be interpreted as
antiestablishment. But even a more liberal community might have
been put off by an influx of women marching through the streets,
waving banners, shouting slogans, scaling the barbed-wire fences
of the depot, and refusing to fly the American flag on July 4th. And
the townspeople were not appeased by the fact that the site was
chosen in commemoration of a landmark event in American history, the first women's rights convention in 1848 in nearby Seneca
Falls, which gave birth to the women's movement, resulting
seventy-two years later in women's right to vote.

The hostility of the community was expressed in terms of economics as well as morality. The county supervisor estimated that
the women's encampment cost the federal government "well over a

million,'' including such items as fence wire and guard towers and not including housing and transportation for extra personnel brought in to beef up the army depot staff. ''The county's tab so far is a quarter of a million,'' he said; ''the county cannot absorb another expenditure of this sort.'' (The astronomical cost of war in lives as well as cash, multiplying many times the cost of peace-promoting efforts, had no place in the supervisor's calculations.)

But despite such voices of disapproval and a few ugly incidents, like the tossing of lighted gas cartridges into the encampment by teenagers and the arrests of fifty-three women during a demonstration, there was some support from the community. While a Pentecostal minister was denouncing the peace camp as ''Sodom and Gomorrah inspired by the devil,'' a Roman Catholic priest was offering praise and assistance from the pulpit, and a group of women on a candlelight march from nearby Yates County brought home-baked foods to the encampment and also joined the campers in twining grape leaves through the wire fence at the army base. Trudy Nicastro, who runs a family restaurant in the neighboring town of Waterloo, opened her café for a series of dialogues with the peace campers. ''During a couple of power failures, they came over with candles for every one of my tables,'' she said, ''and they helped wash the dishes. That was real nice. I think I've learned a lot.''

Alison Lynch-Miller, a premed student at the University of California, Santa Cruz, sums it up this way: ''The whole community has had to deal with the issue of nuclear arms in their backyard. We may not have stopped them from deploying the bombs, but we've done a lot of educating, both of them and ourselves. That's what building a better world is to me.''

PEACE ACTIVISM, MASCULINE STYLE

The feminine organizing style as exemplified in the Pentagon and Romulus actions—leaderless, egalitarian, loosely structured, appealing strongly to the emotions—was especially effective during the earlier stages of the contemporary antiwar movement; at that time, the most urgent need was to dramatize and heighten public awareness of the growing threat of nuclear weapons. But as the peace movement has become sexually integrated, the pattern of organization has been shifting to a fusion of feminine and masculine styles, retaining the emotional appeal and egalitarian relationships but with the addition of structure and formal leadership.

The masculine style of peace activism comes out of an evolving psychological orientation shaped by a complex interaction between the changing nature of war and new standards of masculinity. Since men have invested less of themselves in the creation and nurturing of life than women, they have in the past been more readily reached by appeals to such traditional masculine ideals as bravery in the face of danger and protection of the homeland. In war men have found comradeship and the adventure that is often missing in civilian life; and when they return from the battlefields, they have been welcomed back as heroes.

But nuclear conflict offers no opportunities for personal heroism or comradeship, and its potential for the destruction of all life on earth nullifies the distinction between soldier and civilian, or between men, women, and children, or between human beings and other forms of life. The masculine war-glorifying ideals of the past have been rendered obsolete by nuclear technology, but they were beginning to be questioned in any case with the development of a nuclear age antiwar consciousness. The men who have been reaching military age since the '60s have been raised by, loved by, and influenced by women who saw in motherhood the opportunity to realize through their children the postwar dream of a peaceful and humane world, and they instilled in their sons a profound regard for human and natural life.

These are the men, says Tillie Olsen, "who in other times were raised to carry patriotic fever into battle to be slaughtered like cattle." Instead, having grown up in child-centered families during the rise of the women's movement, they have been raised to feel that "their lives were meant for something greater."[3] For these men, heroism has been redefined, consisting not of acts of derring-do in far-off battlefields but in those "daily small acts of self-denial" common to the feminine experience which de Tocqueville identified as the American principle of enlightened self-interest, and which a growing number of men are carrying out in work, family, and community activities.

The peace movement includes men like these who have never served in the military and who have developed a feminine perspective toward issues of war and peace; it also includes a sizeable number of Vietnam veterans who emerged from that tragic conflict with a sense of futility and waste, and the determination never to let it happen again. The veterans entered the war as patriots, many of them say, believing in the war and in the essential goodness of their leaders and convinced that their country could do no evil in the world. They emerged bitterly disillusioned with both the political and the military leaders who, they felt, had not been honest with them; further, they were now bearing within them the painful knowledge that America, like other nations, has the capacity to do evil in the world. But along with the pain and the bitterness has come a deeper understanding and a keener appreciation of human commonality. As a former officer in the air force who is now active in the nuclear freeze movement expressed it: "The Vietnam experience made a big change in me. I have become much more aware of human suffering. I want my children to grow up in a world where people live and let live."

The personal growth that brings men into the peace movement is usually translated into purposeful, clearly defined economic and political action. In male-directed organizations, there is likely to be more formal structure than in all-female groups, and the emphasis is on grass-roots organizing, fund raising, public relations, and lobbying. A model of this approach is the Washington-based Committee for a Sane Nuclear Policy (SANE), which is committed to arms reduction. The organization has a professional staff, headed by executive-director David Cortright, and a board of governors. To publicize its activities, SANE uses extensive radio advertising, audiovisual resources, and publications, plus a computer network developed with seven participating peace movement groups. A legislative database with detailed information on members has been entered into the system, as well as an activist database, which merges the grass-roots activists lists of the participating organizations. The system has been designed to provide the peace movement with an unprecedented degree of cooperation and technical sophistication.

SANE's infrastructure is bolstered by a communications system that provides its chapters in many parts of the country with films and other educational materials, while the publications department produces and distributes fact sheets on such subjects as the U.S.-Soviet military balance, the MX, Euromissiles, arms contractors, and intervention in Central America. As a means of taking its message to the mainstream, SANE established an organization called Athletes United for Peace. Directed by sports agent Robert Swan of Lawrence, Kansas, the AUP's initial effort brought a Soviet track-and-field team to the Kansas relays in April 1983. Through similar athletic exchanges with the Soviet Union, the group is seeking to improve understanding and communication between the people of the two countries.

The SANE organizing approach demonstrates how the strategies of marketing, public relations, and computer technology commonly used in the selling of goods and services can be effectively applied to promoting ideas that have been generally regarded as antiestablishment. Co-opting mainstream marketing methods has helped to give the peace movement a more sophisticated, more respectable image; and as both masculine and feminine skills and approaches have been invested in its aims, it has begun attracting support from such pillars of the establishment as the business community, religious institutions, the educational system, and the medical profession.

BREAKING INTO THE MAINSTREAM

> As influential stockholders in our national enterprise, business leaders must mandate our management—our employees in government—to stop and reverse the arms race. We must tell them: Find a way. Come up with a plan. It can be done. It must be done.
>
> —HAROLD WILLENS, *Business Executive and*
> *Antiwar Spokesperson*

The merging of feminine and masculine cultures in the peace movement has produced a healthy hybridized approach to war and peace issues that complements emotional appeal with a dollars-and-sense pragmatism. Where arguments from the emotions would have at best a limited impact on big business, practical considerations have been highly influential in the development of a propeace stance among corporate executives. The business community has become increasingly aware of the long-term economic dislocation caused by excessive military spending. The consumption of human and natural resources by the huge and insatiable maw of the military machine is blunting America's competitive edge with Japan and other countries in the consumer goods sector. Business executive Harold Willens has pointed out that business leaders who succeed are those who know that when the survival of their enterprise is at stake, they must change course. In Willens's book, *The Trimtab Factor* (trimtabs are small flaps that assist in balancing and stabilizing aircraft), he argues that business leadership can be the "trimtab" to balance and guide U.S. policy toward a safer course.

In seeking this safer course, business exectives have set up a variety of organizations that focus mainly on pragmatic objectives:

Business Executives for National Security involves business leaders in research and legislation on national and security issues. Their concern is that increasing levels of military spending will weaken the investment climate and hinder capital formation by keeping interest rates artificially high and increasing pressure for higher taxes.

High Technology Professionals for Peace helps professionals find employment outside of weapons-related work. The group provides speakers and publishes a newsletter, *Technology and Responsibility*.

General Electric Stockholders Alliance also publishes a newsletter updating their work to influence management in the direction of more enlightened socially responsible policy-making plus a packet on forming other shareholder alliances.

The Calvert Social Investment Fund offers portfolios in nonnuclear, socially responsible companies.

The Interfaith Center on Corporate Responsibility provides information and serves as a clearinghouse for corporate-responsibility challenges by a wide range of religious and other groups.

Nuclear Free America offers a "nuclear free investment packet" with a list of defense contractors, which serves as a research guide to determine if an investor's portfolio includes companies that build nuclear weapons; the packet includes a directory of alternative investment firms.

These and similar efforts by big business are being augmented by organized labor, which has come to recognize that, whatever its differences with management, both are threatened by increased military spending. The International Association of Machinists and Aerospace Workers has found that, contrary to the argument frequently offered by the military establishment, increased military spending does not increase employment; in fact, due to the high-technology, capital-intensive nature of today's military, it has the opposite effect. Research makes it clear that money spent on construction, transportation, education, and other peaceful, life-enriching activities would create more jobs than spending an equivalent amount on the military. Labor is promulgating this message through such groups as the Jobs for Peace Campaign and the Trade Union Committee for the Transfer Amendment and Economic Conversion.

Religious institutions are also transcending differences in their common resolve to preserve the planet from a nuclear holocaust. The Interfaith Center, based in Pasadena, California, typifies the increasingly ecumenical nature of the religious community's anti-war effort. The organization is nondenominational, and its board of directors is made up of rabbis, priests, and ministers as well as secular community leaders. Established as an educational and information-disseminating organization, the center has demonstrated a flair for staging events that dramatize the antiwar cause, bringing it to the attention of the media and a broad public. One such event was the August 1984 memorializing of the Hiroshima bombing forty years before, which featured art exhibits, film festivals, plays, special religious services, Stevie Wonder playing "Creation" and "Symphony for the Future," Nicolette Larson singing "It's Gonna Take a Lotta Love (to change the way things are)," and the Pointer Sisters performing the "Neutron Dance."

Similar religious groups have been forming around the country, among them the Center for Peace Studies, Interhelp, Pastoral Counselors for Social Responsibility, and Mobilization for Survival.

The educational system is making a few tentative beginnings in curriculum development at pre- and postsecondary levels. Educators for Social Responsibility is an umbrella organization of teachers, parents, and administrators that provides curricular guidance (from kindergarten through adult education), bibliographies, speakers, and teacher education on bringing nuclear issues into the classroom. The Ground Zero Pairing Project makes available elementary school materials on Russian language, geography, and literature in the form of stories and exercises for the purpose of bridging the yawning gap of ignorance separating the American people from their Soviet counterparts.

In the federal government, a U.S. Institute of Peace was established by Congress in September 1984. The institute's mandate is to promote and conduct research, education, and training in conflict resolution and peace studies. Though the scale of this new activity is in no way comparable to the magnitude of the war effort—the initial funding of $16 million would hardly cover the cost of a single fighter plane—the precedent it establishes is a significant one.

In academia, peace research pioneer David J. Singer, a political scientist at the University of Michigan, has written a number of books on arms control and disarmament in which he proposes a systems approach to war and peace, adapted from the general systems theory of biologist Ludwig von Bertalanffy. Instead of focusing on the transgressions of individual nations and leaders, Singer suggests that we concentrate on reforming the international system through promoting pro-peace policies based on the interactive interests of nations. Robert North, a Stanford University political scientist, and Richard Kent Ashley of Arizona State University are among the growing number of scholars who have become involved in peace studies.

Even the military has not been wholly immune to this burgeoning of propeace activity. Admiral Hyman Rickover is one of the more audible voices among the military higher-ups on the subject of arms reduction. Retired Admiral Gene La Rocque is director of the Center for Defense Information which, in addition to providing information on defense-related matters, acts as both a guide and a goad to citizens wishing to end the arms race. Admiral La Rocque has devoted his retirement years to promoting the peace movement. "Peace is patriotic," he says. Also, "There is no defense against nuclear missiles. There's nowhere to hide. When people begin to recognize that, then I think they will begin to write to Congress and to the newspapers and say, 'Look, we want to survive on this planet, so knock off trying to build all these new, sophisticated, expensive weapons systems.' "[4]

Would these life-protecting developments have taken root so deeply and extensively in the mainstream if women had not spearheaded the peace movement in the prenuclear era? Any answer to this question would have to be speculative since, as in so many areas of cultural change, it is risky to attribute a single causation to such a complex phenomenon. But we can offer through the example of one individual's experience a striking instance of feminine influence advancing the cause of peace in that most conservative mainstream sector, the medical profession.

Dr. Richard Saxon, an orthopedic surgeon who heads the Los Angeles branch of Physicians for Social Responsibility, a national network dedicated to abolishing nuclear weapons, credits his involvement with the organization to two women: his wife, Pauline, a longtime peace activist who persuaded him to take on the responsibility (in his words, "She pushed me into it") and Dr. Helen Caldicott, a pediatrician who rejuvenated the organization and has become its leading advocate. Physicians for Social Responsibility had been launched in 1961 by a group of Harvard physicians who wrote an article for the *New England Journal of Medicine* predicting the effects of a nuclear attack on Boston. The shock effect of the article convinced the doctors that it was time to put words into collective action. But after the partial Test Ban Treaty and the diversion of the Vietnam War, the organization had languished until Caldicott became involved. She is an Australian pediatrician who had settled in Boston with her family, and was practicing at Harvard Medical School.

By this time, the late 1970s, Helen Caldicott was just beginning to be known in this country for her antinuclear activities. In Australia, she had had some modest successes in petitioning the government to ban atmospheric testing, and in America she was continuing to maintain a heavy schedule of speaking engagements, traveling constantly and, like a modern-day Cassandra, uttering apocalyptic warnings, intent on alerting a world bent on global suicide.

The meeting between the two physicians was kinetic, both believing fervently that their work as healers was meaningless with the threat of nuclear extinction hanging over the human species. Soon afterward, Helen Caldicott, traveling the country as a missionary for peace, resurrected Physicians for Social Responsibility in many cities. In Los Angeles, starting with a meeting of ten doctors in the Caldicott living room, the organization today has a membership of over 20,000 doctors, dentists, and medical students who educate members of their own profession and the public through a wide range of books, studies, films, symposiums, speeches, consultations, and TV/radio broadcasts.

A highlight of the PSR's recent history was a meeting in the USSR in June 1984 with fifty Soviet physicians who are members of the International Physicians for the Prevention of Nuclear War. The purpose of the visit was to start a movement on a person-to-person level that would encourage the participating American physicians, when they returned home, to report to their peers about the meeting and discuss with them the urgency of banning nuclear war.

"The Soviet doctors could talk freely up to a point," says Dr. Saxon. "But if, for example, the conversation touched on the issue of pressuring the government to discontinue the manufacture of nuclear weapons, they would say, 'Sorry, that's a political subject; we can't discuss that.' " Nevertheless, Dr. Saxon believes that the dialogue was a useful one, and that it advances mutual understanding in place of the fear and distrust that has been fostered by the cold war.

TOWARD A NEW PATRIOTISM

My country is the world and my religion is to do good.
—THOMAS PAINE, *Rights of Man*

Therefore, if you insist on fighting to protect me, or "our country," let it be understood soberly and rationally between us, that you are fighting to gratify a sex instinct which I cannot share; to procure benefits which I have not shared and probably will not share; but not to gratify my instinct, or to protect either myself or my country. As a woman, I want no country. As a woman, my country is the whole world.
—VIRGINIA WOOLF, *Three Guineas*

Helen Caldicott and Richard Saxon exemplify an emerging consciousness, a global vision of a nonviolent world whose geopolitics reflects the growing interdependence of nations. The idea of an interrelated world strikes a deep and resonant chord in the female psyche. Because women's culture places such a high value on connectedness, women are preconditioned toward thinking globally, envisioniong a world system in which negotiation and compromise would govern relationships among nations as it does among our families and friends. No sensible person believes that this will be easy to achieve, but in a nuclear age there is clearly no alternative.

The women we interviewed, regardless of age, religion, income level, or political beliefs, spoke almost with one voice in their insistence that nationalism and patriotism must be reevaluated, particularly when an increasing number of nations are developing weapons with the capacity to destroy all life on earth. Nationalism has never, in fact, evoked the kind of passion among women that through the ages has set men to killing each other. In the feminine value system, loyalty goes to the individual rather than the abstract institution; "I feel patriotic toward people," is the way one woman put it. And another woman said, "I would kill to save my own life or the lives of my family, but for no other reason."

Also, as Virginia Woolf reminds us, women have not, until very recently, procured the benefits of their native land that have been available to men. When people are denied education as well as participation in the economic and political affairs of their country, they are not likely to feel a strong link to that entity. The experience of "outsiderness" has become part of the feminine collective unconscious, and even as women gain access to full citizenship in their countries, they carry with them a certain suspicion of the symbols and slogans of nationalism that perpetuate hatred and violence and are as obsolete in today's interdependent world as the notion that the Earth is the center of the Universe.

But as women's and men's lives become more balanced, as they share more equally in the work of the world and the responsibility for life, the developing global consciousness is no longer confined to the female psyche. Throughout history, there have been a few men of exceptional foresight and vision whose thinking transcended narrow xenophobic nationalism. Plutarch writes in "On Banishment" that Socrates claimed to be not an Athenian or a Greek, but a citizen of the world. Thomas Paine also spoke of himself as a world citizen, as did abolitionist William Lloyd Garrison.

Today, this sense of belonging to a fragile and endangered planet is becoming part of male consciousness. We find it in the work of poet Robert Bly, author Jonathan Schell, sociologist Morris Janowitz, astrophysicist Carl Sagan. "There are no national boundaries visible when you look at the earth from space," says

Sagan. "It's a planet—all one place. All the beings on it are mutually dependent, like living on a lifeboat. Whatever the causes that divide us, the earth will be here a thousand—a million—years from now. The question is, will we?"

In an age of missile weaponry, in which there are no secure borders anywhere on earth, the nation-state can no longer offer its citizens even the illusion of security. But Morris Janowitz, professor of sociology at the University of Chicago, believes that global consciousness is not incompatible with the nation-state. In his recent book, *The Reconstruction of Patriotism: Education for Civic Consciousness*, Janowitz urges a "wholly new kind of patriotism" that resembles the feeling we have for our families. He makes the point that people have been able to love their families without disparaging everyone else, whereas tribal, racial, religious, or national loyalties have usually devalued other groups.[5]

Today, not only the visionaries but men in all walks of life are finding the connection and community that has been common to women's experience in working toward the goal of world peace. This sense of community, anthropologist Victor Turner reminds us, is not only that which finally mitigates our ultimate human experience of loneliness. It also has quasi-mystical attributes. It represents unity, the mending of human separations, and comes to stand for the original human condition, in religious as well as psychosocial terms, of being part of an undivided totality—an original vision of Paradise.

This new form of patriotism is felt as a quiet, nonchauvinistic love of country, compatible with empathy for and a sense of connection with people living in other parts of the world. It is sometimes referred to as "horizontal nationalism," a linking together of people across national boundaries through some common interest—science or the arts, for example, or professional concerns, as in the meeting between the American and Russian physicians. This is the type of patriotism that is giving people the impetus to reach out to each other over national boundaries and formidable barriers of fear and distrust in order to support each other in furthering the cause of peace.

These signs of a redefinition of nationalism and patriotism, emerging among men as well as women, offer us our first real hope for the evolution of a peaceful, problem-solving world community. Today, in our nuclear age, protecting life on earth is a human, not just a feminine, concern, and the pursuit of peace is the responsibility of everyone, everywhere.

11. NEW MEN, NEW WOMEN

T he changes we have been tracing in American culture reflect
the struggle of both sexes to free themselves from the socially
prescribed roles of the past. As feminine culture has threaded
its way through the once solidly male social texture, masculine
culture has been challenged, at times forced, to respond with adaptive, complementary patterns. Out of the ferment and confusion that
are inevitable side effects of such profound and sweeping cultural
change, new women and new men are emerging whose self-images
have been shaped by changing definitions of femininity and masculinity.

Who are these new women and new men, these protagonists of
the contemporary drama of American cultural transformation? Despite the attention they have been receiving from the media, they
remain elusive. And yet they have been appearing on the American
scene ever since the founding of the republic. De Tocqueville gave
credit for the nineteenth-century emergence of a new specimen of
humanity, the American, to the "general equality of condition
among the people." (Since this "equality of condition" could
hardly apply to the slaves in the South or to women, who had few
political or legal rights, de Tocqueville's American would have to
have been a white male.)

Since then, the "new man" has come along at regular intervals in history as an archetype of America's changing national consciousness, his various guises having included the frontiersman, the hunter, the cowboy, the soldier, the tycoon, the breadwinner. These changing images, however, have been mainly external, mere window dressing for an underlying steady state of masculinity that embodied toughness, coolness, and control.

THE MAKING OF A NEW MAN

> It's not easy being a man today . . . there has to be something between macho and wimp.
> —ART BUCHWALD, *"What Are You—a Man or a Wimp?"*

The new man has appeared earlier in this book: as the humanistic business executive, the nurturing father, the doctor as holistic healer, the artist as communicator, the clergyman sensitized to feminine spirituality, the peace activist. And in each case, he has been the harbinger of a dawning age striving for wholeness and balance. In the human as in all species, male and female are complementary sexual systems, so that a change in the one must in time bring on a corresponding change in the other.

As women have been shedding the feminine stereotypes of the past, men have begun following suit, discarding the masculine images that are beginning to seem outworn and burdensome. Barbara Ehrenreich in "A Feminist's View of the New Man" quotes Sheldon Kotel, a Long Island accountant in his early forties, who says that from the 1970s "you could see what was happening to women, and we had to get our act together, too. They didn't want to be in their traditional role anymore, and I didn't want to go on being a meal ticket for some woman."[1]

In relinquishing the role of sole breadwinner, the new man is enlarging his sphere of choice. "I feel as though I have some options now," says a thirty-four-year-old man who left his bank teller

[203]

position the day after his wife took a job that would cover the family's basic expenses. "While she supports the family, I'm going to take the time to find myself."

For the new man, family and personal interests are as important as his career, and at times the career takes second place. If he chooses the corporate path, he moves along a horizontal plane, eschewing the fast, steep ascent up the ladder. He turns down a promotion that would mean longer hours and a heavy schedule of travel. His wife is having a baby, he tells his boss, and she's attending law school at night, so he'll have to keep his work in line with his added domestic responsibilities. "My family is very important to me," he says. It is not that he lacks ambition. Rather, in his unwillingness to subordinate all other interests to the corporation, "he may be defining another type of ambition," suggests D. Quinn Mills, teacher at the Harvard Business School and author of *The New Competitors,* "to advance in the company but also to balance other responsibilities." His boss, however, a traditional man in his fifties who has a heart condition and was recently divorced from his third wife wonders, "What sort of man is it who'd turn down an opportunity to get to the top so that he can babysit?"

The fact is, this sort of man is becoming more prevalent. He may not be receiving as much media attention as the yuppies, those indefatigable seekers of upward mobility, but at the beginning of this decade, a Yankelovich survey reported that an increasing number of men were refusing corporate transfers in order to have more time for themselves and their families. And a recent *New York Times* poll, which asked men and women whether, given the choice, they would prefer to go out to a job or stay home and take care of their families, turned up this thought-provoking result: The women divided equally, with those who were younger and in the work force opting for the job. Of the men, 21 percent said they would choose to stay home, and this percentage held for managers and professionals as well as those in less-skilled occupations.

These shifts in masculine life-choices stem from two inter-related sources: a changing economy and the influence of the women's movement. Since the workplace is no longer a masculine domain operating solely on male values, the work-home separation is becoming blurred, and the attractions of home are beginning to outweigh those of the workplace, particularly for men whose jobs are unsatisfying. Women's entry into the work force, coinciding with the spread of modern technology, has feminized job categories that were once regarded as male preserves. Political scientist Andrew Hacker points to the insurance industry as a prime example of this type of displacement. "The positions of adjusters and examiners were once largely held by men, who went out and inspected dented fenders. Today, the work consists mainly of sitting at a computer terminal, entering insurance claims. Women now hold 65 percent of these jobs, up 27 percent from 1970." In the meatpacking industry, the introduction of machinery to take over much of the heaving and hoisting has increased the proportion of women in that occupation by one-third. Lower-level jobs in offices and the expanding service industries are being filled mainly by women.[2]

At the higher levels, the trend is much the same. The proportion of women receiving higher academic degrees has been steadily rising; in 1984, for the first time in history the number of women exceeded the number of men receiving doctorates in education; a similar shift in male-female student ratios in law, medical, and engineering schools is being mirrored in the declining proportion of men to women in those professions.

Feminism meshed neatly with this changing economic environment by challenging the old style of male-female conformity to roles. Feminist leaders like Betty Friedan and Gloria Steinem hammered away at the theme of potential male gains from the liberation of women, envisioning a world in which neither sex would be dependent on the other: "You have nothing to lose but your coronaries," said Steinem.

These changes are part of a gradual and complex process of psychological development out of which evolved a new man, resembling in certain respects the new woman; but his development has proceeded in counterpoint to hers. Whereas her transformation grew out of her struggle for the opportunities and rewards that were formerly his simply by virtue of his gender, his self-definition incorporates his desire to relinquish some of those opportunities and rewards in return for some of the privileges and prerogatives that have in the past been exclusively hers. He would like, for example, to have her access to emotional expressiveness and to warm, intimate relationships; to the social approval that is bestowed on her predilection for the sensual delights of food, color, texture; and to the permission that is hers, as if by natural right, to concern herself first and foremost with human behavior and relationships.

Interviews with men twenty-five to thirty-five years old as well as recent studies of this new man reveal that feminine values and tastes entered into his early development through his mother, who was the dominant influence on his formative years. In fact, as Tillie Olsen has suggested, that middle-class woman of the 1950s and 1960s, overeducated for full-time domesticity, chafing at the restraints of her role, may have had a larger share in the counterculture revolution than she has been given credit—or blame—for. As Robert Duncan writes in *The Noise,* a history of rock and roll,

> it shouldn't have been so surprising that with those women as our primary image of adulthood we should grow up to demonstrate suspicion, even contempt, for the conventional "work ethic"—not to mention the "real" world in which it operated . . . that we should manifest an exceptional interest as well in the arts . . . and in crafts . . . that this generation of boys, in other words, should grow up to be a generation of men, *real* real men, man enough, human enough, afraid and uncertain enough, to live and work alongside a generation of women who are woman enough—like Mom, in one sense—to live and work alone.[3]

Many of these new men who grew up in a traditional family with the father in the dominant role have opted for less rigid, more egalitarian arrangements in their own marriages and family relationships. The new man's lifestyle has changed. He tends to prefer tennis, skiing, jogging, and swimming to the traditional team sports. He is independent politically, voting selectively on issues and candidates, but his leanings are liberal, and he wholeheartedly supports environmental and antiwar causes. His religious beliefs are, like his politics, ecumenical and derive from his personal moral and ethical system.

Physical fitness has a high priority for him—he is a firm believer in mind-body unity—and in addition to his morning run, he belongs to a health club and works out several times a week. He watches his weight, and long ago gave up the meat-and-potatoes diet that he grew up on for low-calorie, low-cholesterol foods. Food is more than mere nourishment—it ranks high in his scale of values and he prides himself on his cooking, which he considers a form of creative expression. Conversations with his friends, male or female, often center on exotic recipes and newly discovered restaurants.

He takes a creative interest not only in his choice of food but in his clothes, home furnishings and other aesthetic elements.

On the surface, the image of the new man is in keeping with his urban, affluent lifestyle but it is also the outward mirror of a profound inward transformation. Adopting a more feminine style is a strategy in the campaign of heterosexual males, as Leslie Fiedler has observed, "to establish a new relationship not only with women but with their own masculinity." Mark Gerzon, who is in his mid thirties, speaks for this generation of men when he says, "To heal, nurture, or mediate is neither a masculine nor a feminine role. To be a companion or a colleague is not the monopoly of one sex or the other. These traits are based on values; they are not sexual, but ethical. . . . Unlike the old archetypes, which were for men only, the emerging masculinities are not. They are, in fact, emerging humanities." Gerzon quotes John Lennon, who said shortly before his death that he did not want to be "looked upon as a sex object, a male, macho rock 'n' roll singer. I got over that a long time ago. . . . I'd like it to be known that yes, I looked after the baby and I made bread and I was a househusband and I am proud of it."[4]

The "emerging humanities" of the new man can be summed up this way: he believes that the needs of the poor, the ill, and the elderly should be a national priority; he considers shrill chauvinistic patriotism not the last refuge of the scoundrel, as Samuel Johnson defined it, but the first.

He is well represented by Thomas Flanagan, author of the

prize-winning novel *Year of the French,* who describes himself as "what the self-proclaimed moral majority calls a humanist. My college reading in Erasmus and Montaigne long ago instructed me to regard that word as an honorable one, but then, I was also instructed by Thucydides that words lose their meanings in times of cultural crisis. In religious matters, however, I am indeed what the moral majority intends by that term—I am an agnostic, and assume that whatever value human life possesses is that with which human beings are able to endow it." Flanagan redefines "wimp," rescuing it from its pejorative connotations and using it to describe true courage and manliness—the "sinewy and muscular strength of spirit" that are required "to live within uncertainties and complexities."

As this profile suggests, the new man is in the process of a not-always-easy but necessary adaptation to the changing realities of the 1980s. He has been able to integrate his feminine and masculine selves as part of his normal process of development, and he is guided not by codes or creeds but by his own individually-arrived-at system of ethics, values, manners, and tastes. The national traumas of the 1960s and 1970s, especially Vietnam and Watergate, have instilled in him a deep distrust of the traditional uses of power and of the masculine values that underlie these tragedies.

Is the new man's transformation really working? And equally to the point, is this new man the man the new woman really wants? Dr. Nancy L. Good puts it this way: "As a psychotherapist and a woman, I know of many men who are achieving great success not only in their careers but in satisfying and emotionally open monogamous relationships. Both areas of life require tremendous outputs of energy." But this emerging group of new men, says Dr. Good, is somehow "doing both. They are, with great courage, braving ancient emotional barriers by making a commitment not only to the relationship but to accepting and expressing all the difficult feelings that occur between two people in love."

The new man, it appears, is a fit companion for the new woman who, as his mother, lover, wife, coworker, has helped him become the expressive, open-minded, vulnerable, empathetic man he is today.

THE MAKING OF A NEW WOMAN

In seeking the origins of today's "new woman," we find that she made her debut earlier than the "new man," emerging as a public figure during the suffragist movement. Satirized by Henry James, idealized by George Bernard Shaw, denounced by press and pulpit as a menace to home and family and to all that society holds sacred, she was resurrected during the First World War in the image of Florence Nightingale and in the Second World War as Rosie the Riveter. During the 1950s, she lapsed into the obscurity of civic-minded domesticity, only to be born again in the wake of the second feminist revolution as the liberated woman.

The difficulty with putting these new women and new men into clear focus is their volatility. This is especially so for today's new woman whose former identities, whatever shape they took, were understood to be temporary stopgaps on the way to her true role as wife and mother. But today, having broken from her traditional moorings, the new roles and responsibilities are no longer temporary, they are lifelong. As an agent for change who is changing herself, she is moving beyond survival toward self-respect and growth. Her voting habits and other forms of social behavior indicate that she is not easily categorized; her range extends from the woman who has been pulled out of her traditional role, often by the force of circumstance, all the way to the militant feminist who continues to fight on all fronts in her determination that the past shall not be prologue.

Out of this diversity of transitional women, we can trace three stages in the development of women's gender identity, having differing impacts on the feminization process: the new feminine woman, the masculinized woman, and the hybridized woman. Each of these is, like the new man, a composite, pieced together out of interviews and surveys; within each category, there are fine shadings, and the boundaries between them are fluid and overlapping as women move in and out of them at developmental transitions in their lives. But for all their differences, on certain issues, such as environmental protection, peace, and child care, the three groups of women come together in one unified, indissoluble entity. Like branches growing in different directions out of a single stem, the three categories have their roots in the common process of female socialization that unfolds throughout a woman's life cycle as a saga of adaptation to social change.

Observing these models of women in cultural transition provides us with some insights on the personal-social interaction of feminization and where this process may be taking us in the future.

THE NEW FEMININE WOMAN

> As the masculine forms of discipline sit ill on most women, it is possible that we will have to find a way to live in large groups that has more of graciousness and less of discipline.
> —FLORIDA SCOTT MAXWELL, *Women and Sometimes Men*

The new feminine woman is in transition from the mind-set of the traditional system of male-female roles to a consciousness of women's new opportunities and responsibilities, but because of her background and the fact that she usually arrives at this stage of development in her middle years, she rarely moves beyond this point on the cultural spectrum. This woman comes from a family in which the roles were strictly defined. She identified with her strong, competent mother, who invested herself totally in her home and children; her father took pride in providing his family with a comfortable standard of living and was satisfied to leave most of the decisions regarding home and family to his wife. Their ambitions for their daughter were simple and straightforward; they wanted her to have a good education and to work for a few years before marrying and settling down to raise a family.

In college, she majored in a liberal arts subject, joined a sorority, and had some vague ideas about teaching or social work after graduation. But along the way, she married and dropped out of college, planning to go back someday; she worked full-time while her husband attended law school, medical school, or the university's graduate school of business and management. Soon after he graduated and launched his career, she became pregnant and had three children in quick succession.

At this stage, she was playing out her parents' scenario and would have probably continued doing so except for events that neither she nor her parents could have anticipated. Her husband was killed in Vietnam or Korea, or else the marriage ended in divorce and after she had put her emotional pieces together, she realized that she was for the first time in her life entirely on her own. Or perhaps the needs of a growing family were outstripping her husband's income and it became obvious that she would have to find a job to make up the difference.

Having grown up in a warm, supportive home, she is committed to marriage and motherhood as a woman's deepest source of fulfillment. But she is not a throwback to the values or perspectives of her mother's generation. She is acutely aware of the changes in the world around her and of the need for a woman today to develop resources outside her home and family if she is to survive.

She has strong leanings toward the religion in which she was brought up, but as the years go by she attends formal services less and less frequently. When she is being entirely honest with herself about her spirituality, she admits that she finds more comfort and inspiration in solitary walks in the woods or in personal relationships than in institutionalized observances.

The new feminine woman finds herself agreeing at times with Adrienne Rich's "nonfeminist woman" who, repelled by the sterile competitiveness and narrow self-aggrandizement of the masculine public world, concludes, "There's something wrong here. Better to stay at home where at least some semblance of emotional life remains, than go out there and become another emotionless flunky."[5] But this option is not as readily available to her as it was in the past, nor is she certain she would choose it if it were, for she discovers when she enters the public world that, despite its problems and frustrations, it is more absorbing and mind stretching than the private domestic world.

At work, she remains faithful to her feminine style, carrying out her not very demanding duties conscientiously, and doing what she can to give the office a more homelike atmosphere. She waters the plants, keeps in her desk a supply of Band-Aids, aspirin, and eau de cologne that she makes freely available to her coworkers, is in charge of the office coffee pot, and organizes the office parties. In fact, without being aware of it, she does exactly what women in the workplace have always been expected to do: the office housework.

The metaphor of the family having been deeply imprinted upon her, she infuses it into her work relationships, mothering and being mothered, as the occasion requires, by her female coworkers. She sees her male boss as a paternal figure or alternately a husband figure, and she readily admits that she prefers working for a man. (In a study of women in organizations, Rosabeth Moss Kanter tells of a former executive secretary who was promoted into management and found that leaving her former boss was like getting a divorce. For the first four months on her new job, she stopped in to see him every day and hung her coat in her old office.) Her boss often responds in kind, seeing her as his "office wife," or if there is a considerable age difference his "office daughter," to be petted and indulged but certainly not entrusted with managerial responsibility.

She believes in equal opportunities for women but has little sympathy for such practices as married women refusing to take their husbands' names after marriage. She has a wide circle of women friends, some going back to her college and even high school days. She relies on her women friends, as they do on her, for emotional support and as an outlet for tensions and anxieties. "I'm closer with women than with men," she says. She has no male friends, "probably due to sexuality."

She enjoys romance novels, dislikes movies or TV shows that feature violence, and has little or no interest in spectator sports. She worries about her children's future and about the limited time she has to spend with them, but realizes that full-time motherhood is no longer a satisfactory answer for her. When it is economically feasible, she compromises by working part-time. (The new feminine woman is the mainstay of part-time employment.)

The new feminine woman prides herself on being noncompetitive and on forming warm relationships at work as well as in her personal life. If she enters the professions, it is usually in traditional women's fields—teaching, nursing, and more recently marriage and family counseling, a field with obvious attractions for women moving from the home into the public world.

Her psychological transition takes her from the traditional full-time wife-and-mother role, in which she tended to accept her husband's opinions on public issues, to a more independent appraisal of the world outside her home and family. Usually this inner shift is a gradual adjustment accompanying the realization that economic and political issues affect her more directly now that she is in the work force, but it may be a more jolting experience that shakes her out of her customary acceptance of the way things are. At work, it may start with something like the promotion of a younger, less experienced man whom she helped train for his job and who then becomes her supervisor. (A class-action suit brought by female middle managers against the Bank of America some years ago cited this as a major grievance.)

A woman who worked for the Ford Foundation recalls that for her the shift in awareness clicked into place when she learned that the Ford pension plan was inequitable: women paid more into the plan and got less out of it. She joined the company's women's committee and worked on the pension project; her reward was seeing "that our efforts helped to bring this issue to the attention of Congress."

At the community level, a woman who is a full-time homemaker can be transformed into a social activist by issues that affect her family, such as the location of a nuclear or chemical plant, an unsafe traffic crossing, a landlord-tenant dispute. Whatever it is that serves as the trigger, it leads her through a changing self-image to a reordering of her time and energies, and sometimes to a completely new life. As she begins studying, reading, questioning, she feels as though she has been roused from a long sleep, as though her dormant energies are demanding to be released and rechanneled. She begins to make connections with groups, committees, organizations at her place of work and in her community. When sufficiently motivated, she can draw upon previously unsuspected strengths within herself and significantly alter her working or community environment.

It happened to Candy Lightner when her eleven-year-old daughter, Cari, was struck and killed by a hit-and-run drunk driver. She began asking questions and learned that nothing effective had ever been done to keep the drunk driver off the roads. Beginning as a one-woman crusade for personal justice, she formed Mothers Against Drunk Drivers (MADD). It has burgeoned into a broad-based grass-roots movement with ninety-five chapters in more than thirty states, and it has succeeded in accomplishing what had never been done before—stiffening the jail sentences for drunk driving and persuading President Reagan to appoint a presidential commission on drunk driving.

In the case of Mary Sinclair of Midland, Michigan, wife of an attorney and mother of five children, who thought of herself as "just a housewife," the transformational process was sparked by a projected plan of the Consumers Power Company to build a nuclear power plant in Midland, a proposal she saw as a threat to her family and community. Her one-woman campaign turned the community against her, but she has carried her convictions all the way to the United Nations, where she served as a U.S. delegate to a conference in Nairobi on renewable energy development in the Third World; moreover, she has succeeded in moving the issue of nuclear-power-plant safety higher up on the agenda of the U.S. Congress.

In the corporate bureaucracy, one of the "hard areas" of American culture, the new feminine woman, despite a few notable achievements, has been generally less effective as an agent of change than in the community. She does not really understand the masculine power games or style of communication, and her lack of sophistication in these areas comes through in the image she projects, which reflects her modest career expectations. She admires but has no wish to emulate women who achieve top management positions. "I have no need to prove myself," she says, while secretly fearing that she might not be able to handle responsibility and power.

As with most women in the work force, her job does not exempt her from the running of the household and the care of her children. If she is married, she resents this at times, but reminds herself that after all, her husband does provide a larger proportion of the family's income. When his job requires it, she will act as hostess for his company activities, and she offers the emotional support that he and the children require of her. If she is divorced or widowed, she hopes to marry again, but is confident that she will never return to full-time domesticity and financial dependency. She feels connected now to a wider world, and she wants to extend those connections as far as they will go.

THE MASCULINIZED WOMAN

I ask myself whether many of today's women, in their struggle to free themselves from male domination, are not making the mistake of denying their own female natures. . . . Are they not being caught unwittingly by collective male prejudices, which in turn tend to be constellated and reinforced by women's own downgrading of female values?
—JANE H. WHEELWRIGHT, *Women and Men*

As women make their way into the the male system, the pressure to adapt to the masculine style is constant and inescapable, an insistent drum-beat on the feminine consciousness. "Why wouldn't a woman want to become masculinized?" asks Patrice French, professor of psychology and communications. "In the marketplace, a woman is worth 64 percent of a man. Most women who are anywhere near the top have had to be more male than the men."
As a recent study of women at work concluded,

The high-profile women executives in their $300 dressed-for-success suits and silk blouses are hardly representative of women in the work force. Women's

[215]

yearly earnings still average only about three-fifths of men's earnings, about the same as in the 1950s. The wage gap—wider than in most European countries—exists across the board, in almost every occupation and every industry, in entry-level jobs as well as on the assembly line. . . . The growing economic power of women has done little for women at the bottom.[6]

This frustrating lag in women's economic progress may be a significant factor in the development of the masculinized woman, who comes to the conclusion that the system's rewards go either to men or to women who emulate them. She is a generation or two younger than the new feminine woman (many in this group are daughters of new feminine women), and her profile is etched against a background in which both parents worked. But her mother started working only after the children were in school, which is why, both mother and daughter believe, she was never able to make much progress in her job. Identifying with her father, who repeatedly urged her to "make something of yourself," she was primarily motivated during her growing-up years by the desire to please him and win his approval.

By the time she enrolled in college, she had a firm grasp on what she wanted her future to look like. First, a career—law, medicine, business management—something that promised substantial financial rewards and an expansion of personal power. Throughout her undergraduate years, she concentrated on her studies and achieved the grade-point average she needed for admission to graduate school. When she completed her studies, she found an entry-level position in her chosen field, and almost from the start began making herself over in the image of the men at the top.

Since the masculinized woman wants to be identified with winners, the men she chooses to emulate are not the androgynous type but those who present an image of extreme masculinity. This prototypical male, identified in a study of 250 managers as "the new corporate leader," wants above all "to be known as a winner, and his deepest fear is to be known as a loser." He wants to maintain "an illusion of limitless options," has little capacity for "personal intimacy and social commitment,'' depends instead in all his personal relations on the admiration or fear he inspires in others, and sees the external world as a mirror-image of himself.

In adapting to this macho model, the ambitious, upwardly mobile woman becomes a surrogate male and in this guise is admitted to if not entirely accepted by the upper reaches of the organization. Lulled by the blandishments of being "different," more rational, more intelligent, more dependable than other women, flattered by being told she "thinks like a man," she begins to see herself as differentiated from "typical" emotional, irrational women. She begins to believe it is her special qualities, modeled on those of the men at the top, that are conferring upon her the glittering prizes that come with recognition and approval from the masculine power structure.

This is all so heady that she does not notice, or else chooses not to notice, how neatly she has been separated from feminine culture. She has nothing but scorn for "fluffy, clinging females," for the kind of woman who wants nothing from life but a husband and babies. She is discriminating in her choice of women friends, preferring those who share her interest in business, politics, and sports. She has no difficulty finding such women since she belongs to at least one network that follows the old-boys model to which masculinized women tend to gravitate. When she meets her friends at lunch or a dinner party, the focus of their conversation is their careers.

She may be unsuccessful in her first marriage—and even in her second or third; how well she can sustain a relationship with a man depends upon whether he is secure enough not to be the center of her life. She is an accomplished role-player and can shift from the masculine style at work to the feminine style in a sexual relationship with a man when she senses that her masculine persona would be a turnoff for him. But it is conscious play-acting, and requires effort and concentration.

She expects to have children someday, and if by then her biological clock has run out she may adopt—either way, she will insist that the man in her life take at least equal responsibility for the household and children. She has little sympathy for the child-versus-career lament that fills the pages of magazine articles and women's fiction. "Children are remarkably adaptable," she says, "and they grow up quickly and are on their way out the door." The critical problem, she maintains, is functioning in a man-made world on men's terms.

Her politics tilt toward moderate conservatism. She believes in a strong defense, but otherwise favors as little government intervention as possible. She considers formal religion important, mainly as a social regulator, but she has not attended services in a church or synagogue for many years. She considers herself too rational for religious observance, and her spirituality is rooted in the material world.

In shedding her feminine "otherness," she has succeeded in becoming one of the boys, a woman who is more like a man—even down to her speech, peppered with sports lingo and scatological terms and scorn for displays of emotion and other "typically feminine" behaviors. But the switchover is not accomplished without cost. Adrienne Rich warns that "if in trying to join the common world of men . . . we split ourselves off from the common life of women and deny our female heritage and identity in our work, we lose touch with our real powers and with the essential condition for all fully realized work: community."

The loss can be especially damaging to feminine creativity. The female artist who adopts the masculine model in order to be perceived as sexless and universal may succeed in becoming an "honorary man," but, as Germaine Greer concludes in her history of women in the arts, it is "an immensely costly proceeding in terms of psychic energy."[7]

When Cynthia Ozick, in her 1966 novel *Trust*, stripped her female protagonist of feminine qualities, "wiped the woman out of her," she also wiped something out of herself as a writer. "By censoring and unnaming herself as a woman," comments Elaine Showalter, professor of English at Princeton University, "by internalizing the contempt for 'women's writing' . . . by attempting to placate the gods of high art, Miss Ozick sacrificed her authentic voice and at least half of her literary heritage." And, ironically, the book was reviewed and dismissed as a novel about the female predicament.[8]

THE HYBRIDIZED WOMAN

> Hybrid: an interbreeding between a male and female of a species; hybrids may show various combinations of the characters of the two parents, or exhibit new characters or reversion to ancestral ones.
>
> —*Webster's New International Dictionary*

> She's the kind of female executive who dresses for success without ignoring sensuality, who easily makes the transition from talking bucks and contract terms to assuaging 16-year-old daughter Evie's fears about having her wisdom teeth pulled.
>
> —JUDITH MICHAELSON, *"TV's Front Office Feminist,"*
> *interview with Barbara Corday, President,*
> *Columbia Pictures Television*

Fortunately, the feminine sensibility often manages to break through the facade of masculinization. A case in point is geneticist Barbara McClintock, who has lived entirely for her work, neither seeking nor requiring human intimacy, insisting on being regarded simply as a scientist, not a female scientist, and displaying none of the qualities or interests usually identified as feminine. Yet the attributes that McClintock credits for her Pulitzer Prize–winning discovery of the dynamism of genetic organization are those associated with feminine culture—the ability to integrate, a "feeling for the entire organism," and for the differences of each individual plant.[9] Biologist Evelyn Shaw suggests that perhaps, because McClintock was not in the mainstream, "she was able to avoid au courant research and let her intuition guide her as she unfolded the order within the genetic system."

These distinctively feminine qualities are beginning to be welcomed where not long ago they were either disdained or ignored. Executive search firms report that corporations today are seeking women who, in addition to being fully qualified for the job, also know how to help men open up, express their feelings, and become comfortable with women. One of the major barriers to the promotion of women is the male executive who does not understand women and can only look on them in such supportive roles as wives, mothers, daughters, and secretaries. For this reason, corporations with an eye to the future are seeking the kind of female executive who has a sense of personal style and the ability to develop not only herself but also the men in the organization.

Patricia Mearns, president of a large executive search firm in Los Angeles, has been finding that feminine aptitudes are particularly valuable in personnel work. "When a woman is conducting an interview, the person being interviewed, whether it's a man or a woman, will usually be more open with her than with a man. Women tend to ask more direct questions, which invite more direct responses. They also seem to have a more highly developed listening faculty."

The sought-after and successful female executive in today's corporate world, according to Mearns, is able to keep her feminine qualities in proportion with the exigencies of her position. She occupies a middle ground between the extremes of emotional indulgence and emotional control, sensing when it is and is not appropriate to inject her personal life into her work. She is adept at "thinking with her feelings" and "feeling with her mind." She is a new breed of woman, a hybrid whose values and behavioral style skillfully blend the masculine and feminine.

The hybridized woman identifies herself with feminism, but having missed out on the earlier struggles and battles of the women's movement, she takes for granted the gains women have achieved and believes that they can best serve their cause today by proving themselves and working productively with men.

By merging her feminine and masculine orientations, she is able to blend action and community, achievement and cooperation, vulnerability and independence. She has no problem retaining her feminine world-view, her objective stance from her position on the threshold while at the same time giving full reign to her energies and aspirations in the business or professional world.

In college, she majored in the social or physical sciences but took as many courses as possible in other fields. She refused to join a sorority, considering the sorority-fraternity system elitist and discriminatory. She began working soon after graduating and eventually, after a series of meaningless jobs, found her way, at times by accident, into the kind of work that offered some satisfactions and the possibility of personal and career growth.

Unlike the new feminine woman, she thrives on responsibility and does not consider power a dirty word, for she believes it can be used nonmanipulatively. However, she is not entirely comfortable with the hierarchy and frequently crosses the lines—for example, by inviting a lower-echelon employee to a meeting intended for those in the higher ranks when she has reason to believe the employee would have something of value to contribute.

Politically, she has no party affiliation and, like her masculine counterpart, the new man, votes for issues and candidates. She is in favor of the ERA although she feels it does not apply to her—"I don't need any crutches, I can earn my way." She is generally anti-ideological, feeling no need for a set of doctrines to be guided by. Pragmatic to the core and eminently flexible, she is self-guided and self-motiviated, skeptical, eclectic in her tastes and opinions, as well as in her spiritual inclinations.

She may be single or married; when she marries, it is usually after a living-together arrangement that has gone on for several years. She would like to have children someday, but not until she is sure she can combine her career successfully with motherhood.

Her profile, drawn from a recent study of 300 successful women executives, looks like this:

She grew up in an urban setting, typically a city of less than 100,000, was the first-born child in her family and was closer to her father as she was growing up. (Psychologists of motivation are discovering that it is the father-identified girl who tends to become a successful achiever; their fathers nurtured their talent and made them feel attractive and loved at an early age.) Her father was a business executive or a professional; her mother did not work outside the home.

If she is married, her husband is employed in a professional/technical/managerial position, earning 44 percent of their household income. Of her peers who are divorced, most cite their career as a factor in the breakup of their marriage.

She works fifty-three hours a week, about the same as her male counterparts, and spends about thirty-three days a year traveling for her company. She had a male mentor and now serves as mentor to lower-level men and women.

Her career has not only progressed better than her husband's but has also been financially more rewarding as well as more rewarding in other ways. She takes primary responsibility for her children's care and supervises the running of the household. Although she believes she has adequate time to spend with her husband and children, she is never entirely free from the thought that her worktime and on-the-job travel time may be having a negative effect on her family life as well as her social life.[10]

The woman who emerges from this study is engaged in a complex balancing act, but is on the whole successful in reconciling her working life with her personal life. She is, in fact, a triumph of hybridization: her blazer/skirt uniform conceals sexy lingerie. She discusses sports and cost control with the men in the executive dining-room, and at lunch with a woman friend has an animated conversation about the children's grades at school, the remarriage of a mutual acquaintance, the latest news about her nuclear-freeze group, a recipe for ratatouille. Her office is an equally artful mix—Barbara Corday, president of Columbia Pictures Television, who exemplifies the hybridized woman in the corporate world, occupies an office that combines floral chintz with the kind of large, clean-lined furniture that in the symbolic vocabulary of the corporation spells power.

The hybridized woman can be competitive or cooperative, depending on which stance will yield the greater payoffs in the circumstances. Bank president Linda Fluent describes herself as "very competitive, with a strong drive to win, but it's softened by the cooperative side of me."

A cautious risk-taker, the hybridized woman readily accepts

responsibility, views power as a positive force and uses it judiciously. Above all, she is a skilled compromiser and negotiator. She adjusts, she fits in, straddling her two worlds with a commendable degree of poise and equilibrium. If there are occasional moments of discomfort, she swallows hard and reminds herself that she has a fiscal and business responsibility that must somehow be reconciled with her feminist principles.

The hybridized woman glides smoothly, unlike the self-conscious role switching of the masculinized woman, from the efficient, no-nonsense executive during the working day to the playful, sensual, nurturing wife, mother, lover during nonworking hours. In this respect, she has much in common with women in very different cultures who are engaged today in a similar balancing act. In India, a woman with a career manages her life by compartmentalizing her modern role from her traditional one: a female physician, for example, may behave in her clinic very much like her counterpart in the United States—crisp, controlled, self-assured—and swing back to her role as a "feminine wife" or a daughter-in-law at home, changing from work clothes to her domestic sari.[11]

The hybridized woman may occasionally experience twinges of doubt as she juggles her roles and commitments, especially when, in her darker moments, she feels she is sacrificing her children to her selfish needs and interests. This is the most painful issue she faces, and one she never really resolves. "At work, you think of the children you've left at home," the late Israeli Prime Minister Golda Meir once confessed, "at home, you think of the work you've left unfinished. Such a struggle is unleashed within yourself. Your heart is rent."

In the modern corporation, the hybridized woman serves as an effective builder of bridges between feminine and masculine culture. She is a centering force; her femininity puts her male colleagues at ease and links her to the other women in the organization. Thus, she is in a particularly felicitous position for initiating and implementing such innovations as pregnancy and paternal leave, company child-care centers, and increased employee participation in company policy-making. "Only such a woman is able to mediate between the public and the private, the social and the personal," says anthropologist Marshall Sahlins.

Of the three groups we have profiled, it is the hybridized woman who is in the vanguard of the feminizing trend in America today. The significant shifts and stirrings, the rooting out of obsolete practices and prejudices, the development of new models and alternatives—this transformative task can be performed most effectively by those women who can negotiate comfortably between feminine and masculine culture. These are the women who are best equipped to humanize the environment in which they live and work; they may accomplish this in small, almost imperceptible ways—or, like Helen Caldicott, they may take giant leaps for humankind.

The woman at this stage of development is not androgynous—there is no blurring over, no neutralizing of her femininity; rather, her sexuality is accentuated by her firm sense of personal identity. She is a connecting link between two worlds—to paraphrase Matthew Arnold, one dying, one struggling to be born—a new species embodying an evolving concept of human equality. And like her partner, the new man, she is overcoming ancient emotional barriers and behavioral patterns so that she can share with him equally the responsibilities of these complex and challenging times.

Which is not to say that there are no anxieties, doubts, confusions, conflicts in these new men–new women pairings. From the 1970s into this decade, the decibel level of male-female anger has risen at the inevitable misunderstandings and confusions that have accompanied the rapid role changes of this era. In Leonard Michaels' 1981 novel, *The Men's Club,* one of the male characters defines male liberation as "not feeling anything." The 1980 musical play "I'm Getting My Act Together and Taking It on the Road" includes a character identified as the Stage Manager who rails against the "hostility of women" which he says is driving men to homosexuality. And author Anne Roiphe, in a 1973 review of the television series "An American Family," has said, "I feel often as if I have been set too free. Culture, if it means anything, must mean the binding of the individual into the social fabric. My threads are all undone."

The two strongest threads—sex and economics—which have historically bound men and women into the social fabric through marriage, have come undone. In the past, marriage afforded men the sexual and emotional sustenance and the domestic comforts they could not find in the single life; in return, women received financial support for themselves and their children. This mutual dependency was hardly utopian; it put men on a treadmill and kept women in a state of economic and sexual subjection. But while it lasted, it served as an undergirding for the structure of male-female relationships.

The structure began breaking down when women left the domestic world to seek financial independence. Meanwhile, men were learning how to cook their own meals (or fall back on takeout foods), sew on their own buttons, and decorate their apartments. At about the same time, with the development of the Pill and the "new morality," sex became readily available outside of marriage on a short-order, uncommitted basis.

With the erosion of mutual dependency for survival needs, men and women, in becoming sexually and financially liberated, are confronting each other for the first time in history stripped of the connections that held them together in the past. Bereft of these old, reliable dependencies, they are searching for new connections, new threads to knit together the social fabric that has been torn apart in so many places.

And here is the crux of the dilemma: As independent, autonomous beings, men and women today can rely on no other binding forces except those that exist within themselves. It is no simple matter, history tells us, to make the transition from dependency to independence and equality; the "escape from freedom," as Erich Fromm has shown, is an all-too-familiar chapter in the human saga.

The future unfolding before us contains a critical question: can men and women build lives together as free, equal, and self-reliant human beings? Here is the basic challenge for new women and new men in the years ahead. How well they meet this challenge will determine the kind of world all of us will be living in and that our children will inherit.

12. BEYOND FEMINISM

*The values that have been labeled feminine—
compassion, cooperation, patience—are very
badly needed in giving birth to and nurturing a
new era.*

—ROLLO MAY

W omen's resolve to make the changes necessary for a peaceful, livable world has been fortified by their growing awareness of how feminine culture has always served as a humanizing force, capable of enriching the cultures of both sexes, of society, and of the individual. In their everyday lives, women have throughout the ages quietly carried out their responsibility as the creators and protectors of life, but it was the agenda of the women's movement that welded them into a political force. Whatever their social, religious, or political orientation, few women today remain untouched by the ideas and ideals of the women's movement. Consciously or subliminally, the vision of a nonsexist, nonracist, nonexploitative human family is irresistible to the feminine sensibility.

As an ideology, the women's movement has done its work well, galvanizing women into action in an attempt to end centuries of discrimination and achieve full participation in the public world. It has been a profound educational and personally transformative force, deepening women's understanding of themselves and their history and helping them to develop pride in their self-defined femininity; it has presented a social and psychological challenge to our sense of what it means to be male and female, thus stimulating new ways of thinking and behaving as family members, workers, citizens.

The women's movement has brought women together on behalf of principles they hold to with a passion. We are seeing women from a variety of backgrounds joining in collective action to protect the environment, protest against the madness of the arms race, and make the world a safer and healthier place for themselves and their children. Women are developing into an antiestablishment force and are building a new political agenda that, as political analyst William Greider comments, "turns away from the mindless masculine reflexes of the cold war and pursues more egalitarian, life-preserving objectives."

But feminism is moving beyond the transformation and mobilization of women; we have seen how its educational, psychological, and social impact is being felt throughout our society. Feminism in its essence offers an enlarged vision of the human experience, and it is not surprising that this expanded vision should have been generated by women rather than men. The perspective of the outsider is precisely what is necessary to give rise to an original approach, which is why women are able to interpret the world in fresh, even revolutionary ways. As "mysterious" and "unpredictable" creatures, existing outside the established order, they have not been programmed to operate within rigid, mechanistic structures.

Because of their "otherness," women have been associated with marginality, with nonbelonging, the very qualities that offer opportunities for questioning the givens, the conviction that one is in possession of the only truth. The feminine experience of outsiderhood has been the critical ingredient in the innate perspective of woman as a change agent. The "yeastiness" of women's influence was acknowledged even by Karl Marx, not exactly a feminist, who said that "anyone who knows anything of history knows that great social changes are not possible without the feminine ferment."

CREATING A COUNTERUNIVERSE

Because women did not create the public world, they do not experience the same torment and interior conflict that men do when they disagree with its rules. De Beauvoir makes this point when she comments on women's ability to see the absurdity in "the imposing structure built by males," in women's discomfort with "ready-made cliches and forms." As challengers, as questioners, women have always posed a threat to the well-ordered machines of money and influence that grind on endlessly to enlarge the power and dominion of men over, in Francis Bacon's phrase, "the universe of things."

The same point is made in a different context by Thomas Kuhn, who argues that accepted scientific paradigms are severely culture-bound, blinding us to any but our own assumptions. Scientific revolutions, or alterations in our conceptions concerning the workings of nature, are most often mounted from outside the discipline responsible for amassing expertise on the subject. The outsider, in other words, can conceive of that which is unimaginable when viewed only from the inside. It is frequently the gifted amateur—the Darwin, Einstein, McClintock—who questions the taken-for-granted assumptions and provides the unexpected insight to demonstrate once again that "facts" are usually interpretations buttressing what has been accepted as incontrovertible truth.

Outsiders act as innovators, quite unconsciously at times, by simply attempting to gain access to resources that society denies them. Adult education, for example, began in England in 1867 when a group of women in Cambridge invited James Stuart, a fellow at Trinity College, to deliver a series of lectures. Since women were not permitted to attend the university, the off-campus lectures provided the only opportunity for them to gather a few gleanings from the intellectual harvest of higher education. The lectures were a success, and within a few years, the formation of the London Society for the Extension of University Teaching grew out of the founding of London University. Oxford followed suit, and by 1889 over 45,000 students were attending extension courses in England.

In America, adult education owes its rise to another group of outsiders, the eastern European immigrants who crowded into night schools to learn English. Indomitable women like Henrietta Szold and Julia Richman helped to transform this "teeming refuse" into productive American citizens; their efforts, among others, were a seedbed for today's flourishing field of adult and continuing education, the one branch of education that has enjoyed healthy and sustained growth in recent years, and which serves "re-entry women," minorities, and others whose special learning needs cannot be met by formal educational institutions.

The outsider, in other words, often creates out of sheer necessity a counteruniverse that becomes a source of innovation and renewal for the traditional system. Today, the feminization of the mainstream is acting as a healthy stimulus to the system, and new ways of thinking and doing are breaking through the hard-packed soil of habit and tradition in many areas of the American cultural landscape. The signs point to a new synthesis, a convergence of opinion and action coming from many directions, some of them antithetical in their origins. Science and religion, conservative and liberal, artist and technician, female and male—all are moving closer together in this convergence that reflects a spreading uneasiness, a sense that the world as we have known it is not working, and that it has become too dangerous to allow the future to repeat the past. The looming threat of nuclear conflict makes it clear that we are all in this together and that we can no longer afford the divisiveness of the past if we are to survive and flourish as a species.

WHOLENESS AND DIVISION

This inner fragmentation . . . mirrors [a] view of the world "outside" which is seen as a multitude of separate objects and events. The natural environment is treated as if it consisted of separate parts to be exploited by different interest groups. This fragmented view is further extended to society which is split into different nations, races, religions and political groups. The belief that all these fragments—in ourselves, in our environment and in our society—are really separate can be seen as the essential reason for the present series of social, ecological and cultural crises.

—FRITJOF CAPRA, *The Tao of Physics*

The male principle, having had the field virtually to itself, has conducted the affairs of the world primarily on the basis of competition, confrontation, and conflict. Not only have human beings been separated from each other and from nature, their source of life and nourishment; but within the individual, mind has been separated from body, and the body has been separated into its component parts in the cause of healing. The very texture of life has been pulled apart—sex from intimacy, individual from community, work from the satisfaction of personal achievement.

Dualism and polarization have marked much of our history, replacing the natural wholeness and unity of life and humankind with separate, disconnected entities, alien to each other and to themselves. The principle of rational analysis and cognitive absolutism that has dominated Western culture perceives the world in terms of opposites that exist in a state of mutual suspicion and hostility: East versus West, north versus south, Jew versus Christian, Christian versus Muslim, proletariat versus bourgeoisie, scientist versus humanist, masculine versus feminine (or yang versus yin). The sensibility that divides the world into oppositions inevitably ranks them after dividing them, then sets itself up as superior —in value judgments, clarity, order. It is a sensibility that, as Fritjof Capra puts it, "banishes all shadows, all shadings before the bright analytic light of conscious critical thought." This either/or mentality, Czech author Milan Kundera comments, "encapsulates an inability to bear the essential relativity of human affairs, an inability to come face to face with the absence of a supreme arbiter."

Evelyn Fox Keller, professor of mathematics and humanities at Northeastern University, in speaking of the "genderization of science," argues that male scientists are most comfortable from a stance in which the subject is cut off from the object. When the scientific object is placed at a distance from everyday life, from the world of emotion and relationships, the scientist is convinced that he has achieved the proper detachment and "objectivity."

"We can see why men would be drawn to this construction of science" adds M.I.T. professor Sherry Turkle. "Men are highly invested in objective relationships with the world. Their earliest experiences have left them with a sense of the fusional as taboo, as something to be defended against. Science, which represents itself as revealing a reality in which subject and object are radically separated, is reassuring. We can also see why women might experience a conflict between this construction of science and what feels like *their* way of dealing with the world, a way that leaves more room for continuous relationships between self and other."[1]

Barbara McClintock, for example, describes her work in genetics as an ongoing "conversation" with her materials, and she speaks of her frustration with the objectification of scientific research. "If you'd only just let the materials speak to you . . . " Fusing subject with object makes her feel that she is part of the cellular system; in this way, the microscopic chromosomes she was working with during her research in genetic biology became visible and personalized. "I actually felt as if I were down there and these were my friends." She has always, she says, had an "exceedingly strong feeling" for the oneness of things: "Basically, everything is one. There is no way in which you draw a line between things. What we [normally] do is to make these subdivisions, but they're not real. Our educational system is full of subdivisions that are artificial, that shouldn't be there."[2]

McClintock's dynamic, integrated approach to science is emerging as today's "new paradigm" in the sciences, replacing the linear, reductionist thinking of the past. Lewis Thomas tells us that cooperation is a law of survival in the natural world, that the fittest to survive are the forms that exist in symbiosis with their environment, enhancing rather than overpowering the environment's ability to sustain them. The advantage of cooperation, or synergy, which Buckminster Fuller defined as "the behavior of whole systems unpredicted by the separate behavior of any of the system's parts," is that it focuses attention on comprehensive thinking, whereas specialization, with its devotion to narrow expertise, has resulted in corporate exploitation of natural resources and technological gains, frequently for the short-range power and profit of the few rather than the long-term benefit of the many. General Systems Theory, which is associated with biologist Ludwig von Bertalanffy, was formulated in the sciences prior to the growth of specialization, and its current resurgence can be credited to increasing public concern with the devastating effects of undimensional preoccupations with technology.

The synergistic perspective is evident in the growing awareness of ecology, of the earth as an ecosystem. The relationship between women and nature, with its roots in ancient myths, is assuming new forms as women today endeavor to politicize their life-protecting responsibility and extend it into the public sphere. "Human ecology," which expresses a commitment to the interrelatedness of human beings and to the connections between all living things, is a feminine value that is being taken up in some areas of masculine culture as a reaction against the impersonality and aridity of hierarchical bureaucracies and the threat of a deteriorating environment. We see evidence of increasing concern with these problems in the growing attention that the public sector is giving to more flexible styles of management and to such issues as toxic waste disposal and the effects of pesticides.

Business and industry are, in fact, beginning to give serious attention to the development of a more humanistic working environment. A new breed of managers is being trained to encourage common goals, employee participation, cooperation. This new manager is expected to exhibit qualities of sensitivity, compassion, caring for others. (Ironically, these are the qualities that women have been expected to repress in their public activities, since these typically feminine traits were regarded as out of place in the hard-headed world of commerce.) The new manager will be working in a corporate environment that treats people, according to Eric Flamholtz, professor of management, as "valuable organizational resources. Corporations must begin to emphasize that management implies a stewardship of human resources. People should not be managed as though they are a replaceable commodity."[3]

Rosabeth Kanter refers to these new managers as "change masters" and offers the following example of how they put the new style to work: "At a staff meeting, a manager of General Foods recently drew a pyramid upside down on the board and told the group, 'I am here at the bottom to hold you up, to support you.' "

The high-innovation companies, says Kanter, reward people for being collaborative, and building social relationships both within the company and with its clients is becoming an important priority.

MOTHERISMS AND MOTHERHOODS:
Developing a Human Ecology

For women, this "new humanism" is hardly new; it is the way they have conducted themselves within their families and communities from time immemorial. The megatrends that John Naisbitt identified in 1982—especially participation, decentralization, networking, multiple options—may represent bold new departures for top management, but they have been essential features of feminine culture from the beginnings of human history. Perhaps that is why these practices have been dubbed "motherisms" by Naisbitt and his associates—common-sense applications of humanistic principles to business. In the same vein, Thomas Peters and Robert Waterman, Jr., in their "search for excellence," have summed up the eight attributes that represent excellence in management as "motherhoods." Among these are such elemental "feminine principles" as Listen intently and regularly; Don't be afraid to make mistakes; Respect the individual.

The synergistic approach is shaking up even the sacred doctrine of competition, which has always occupied an exalted place in American economic theory. In the name of competition, every enterprise becomes a game, in which human values are depreciated and winning is the only thing that matters. "This view of the world must inevitably have contributed to producing widespread alienation and materialism," economist David Slawson writes in *The New Inflation*, "and these are indeed attributes of American society that have been widely noted." Moreover, competition is not the only strategy for increasing productivity, as traditional economic theory would have it. Slawson suggests that "cooperation, the opposite of competition, is also a spur to industriousness. Most industrial tasks within a business organization are done much more in a spirit of cooperation than competition.''⁴

In feminine culture, the synergistic approach has been simply a way of coping and surviving. Cooperation among women is an essential source of mutual support, particularly during the early child-rearing years and in times of crisis. As family caretakers, women have always understood that the family is a system in which the welfare of the whole depends upon the interaction of the separate parts; it is a symbiotic arrangement, a model of interdependence and cooperation.

THE JOINING OF OPPOSITES

The yearning for wholeness has been the enduring hope of humankind and the inspiration for much religious and mythic thought. The transcendence of opposites toward a unity, a cosmos without duality, has been the goal of higher thought, the acme of religious experience in Eastern philosophies and in Western mystical traditions. Many cosmologies emphasize the importance of balance and exchange between differing, even polar views: Heraclitean philosophy, Kabbalism, Oriental cosmology, mystic traditions in Judaism and Christianity as well as in many primitive societies. It is the final joining of opposites that is nearly always the basis of universally sought religious ecstasy, the experience of unity and undifferentiated bliss.

This is what Jung has called the *coincidentia oppositorum*, a state of rapture, healing (''wholeness,'' ''holiness'') that is in most religious traditions equated with paradise. (Lately, brain research has suggested the physiological basis for this experience: the simultaneous and synchronized activity of both hemispheres in the brain, across the division of the corpus callosum, literally making ''the two into one.'') This is a condition depicted in our most profound and potent symbols: the holy marriage, the joining of the sacred couple—Juno and Jupiter, Siegfried and Sieglinde, the androgynic images that unite male and female to make a complete totality, suggesting the ultimate religious and physiological drive toward achieving transcendence over polarization.

The desire for the unification of opposites represents for many feminists a vision of a new world order, liberated from the domination of the masculine "yang energy." In a position paper, "The Power of Yin," Barbara de Laney asks: "Can we achieve a new orientation of consciousness embracing values traditionally disparaged as 'feminine'?" She argues that yang thinking has resulted in "competition, material growth at any cost, and social and environmental dominance and control . . . becoming manifest in the form of diminishing natural resources, serious ecological disruptions, and increasingly unmanageable social inequities and injustices—not to mention the threat of thermonuclear power games, the ultimate manifestation of excessive 'virility.' " Feminine consciousness, she continues, is "an essentially humanistic consciousness emerging from the feminine tendency to cherish, to nourish, to preserve. No longer inexorably bonded to reproductive functions, the emerging new woman is increasingly turning her female energies to the much larger tasks of nurturing the species and preserving our threatened life support system. This implies a different kind of creativity—a holistic creativity which is sensitive, above all, to the requirements of life-oriented growth and process."

PATHWAYS TO A NEW ERA

In today's torn and conflicted world, the age-old yearning for human community seems farther away than ever before. Much of the energy and creativity that could be invested in life-oriented growth is committed instead to the planning and preparation for death and destruction on a scale of magnitude that stretches the limits of the imagination. Even a confirmed optimist can hardly be unaware of the powerful forces at work today that run directly counter to the humanizing course of feminization.

The qualities of feminine culture that offer the promise of a more fulfilling way of life can be perverted and used to prop up the failed modes of thought and behavior that have scarred the landscape of the past. In the workplace, women's skills and energies may be used as a cheap source of labor, as in the case of immigrant groups. The family metaphor may be turned against women if they continue to be associated with traditional family imagery, which will assure that they remain subservient to the dominant male model in the public world. Women's gift of emotional expressivity increases their vulnerability to what sociologist Arlie Russell Hochschild calls "the managed heart." The flight attendant who provides the illusion of security, the solicitousness of the social worker, and the omniscience of the health administrator—"each of these nontheatrical actors belong to a class of workers likely to grow substantially in the next decade, and each is required by the nature of her job—for these jobs are now held mostly by women—to express synthetic feelings and often to suppress more authentic feelings."5

The new "humanistic management," which offers hope for a more humane, more participatory corporate environment, may return to its old ways if there is a turndown in the economy. In health care, many doctors and hospital administrators believe that rising health costs will bring a continuing depersonalization of medicine and the denial of quality health care to the elderly and the poor. The spread of fundamentalism and its unholy alliance with politics has the potential of promoting dogmatism and sectarianism and furthering the institutionalization of the human spirit. The peace movement and the development of a planetary consciousness are vulnerable to a rise in tensions between the superpowers, and are always in danger of being crushed by the military-industrial complex.

Yet there are some hopeful indications for the future that reflect the continuing influence of feminization on both the "soft" and, to a lesser but increasing extent, the "hard" areas of American culture. The trends presenting what can be considered the most significant pathways to the future are:

Science:

The entry of women into scientific research will strengthen the reaction against so-called objective science, a reaction already generated by such concepts as Einstein's theory of relativity and his recognition of intuition "supported by being sympathetically in touch with experience"; by Heisenberg's "principle of uncertainty" in subatomic physics; by quantum theory; by the decline of androcentrism; and by the reaction against Cartesianism—"I think, therefore I am"—which has led in Western culture to the identification with mind apart from the rest of the organism. The new science will eventually merge with philosophy, fortifying its roots in the mysticism of the ancient Greeks with the sophisticated investigations of modern physics, mathematics, and biology.

Work:

A service/information economy presages the decline of massive hierarchical structures. Mammoth, centralized institutions will be replaced by smaller, decentralized units that have the flexibility needed for maintaining a continuous flow of information and responding to changing service needs. The eventual replacement for hierarchy will be networks, a pattern of relationship that suits the feminine temperament, with its proclivity for connectedness, far better than the divisive pecking order of the hierarchical ladder.

An emerging socioeconomic vision projects an economic system in which

> an imposing but ultimately dangerously unstable structure of vast rigid beams and girders has been replaced by a honeycomb of flexible production cells, not only giving resilience to the domestic economy but facilitating its adjustment to a stronger, more stable international order. . . . In the more communal arrangements

of work that become possible under flexible specialization, new social relationships will arise, reducing the gulf between boss and worker, encouraging the introduction of machinery that magnifies rather than dwarfs the creativity of its user.[6]

The measurement of the working day in terms of "metric time," the most common being the eight- or nine-to-five schedule, will gradually give way to flexi-time as the needs of working mothers challenge rigid work schedules. The time clock may, in fact, be consigned to the ash heap of history as the development of technology converges with new leisure-oriented lifestyles to bring about a variety of work schedules that can be adapted to individual needs. The full-time job will be replaced by job-sharing and by periods of intensive work alternating with stretches of idleness; as new values and lifestyles lead more and more people to reject the sanctity of the work ethic, part-time work will become the norm. (In Europe, this is happening already: since 1974, half of the new jobs have been part-time. A report published in the French newspaper *Le Monde* notes that "flexibility has become the byword in both the private and the public sector lately, as a means of reducing unemployment. And for many people, flexibility means freedom".)[7]

The work-home gap will be narrowed as a result of two disparate developments: the modem-equipped computer, which will eliminate the need for the office as a centralized communication and production area; and the revival of interest in craftsmanship. Futurists, Alvin Toffler for one, see the return of work to the home as home computers are tied in to the office and as consumers seek more custom-made, "home-grown" products such as hand-knits, jewelry, quilts, ceramics. Craft-based, skill-intensive production will emerge as the new mode of production, not only in such traditionally craft-oriented enterprises as fashion and home furnishings but within the heavy mass-production industries that will be seeking to create more flexible, adaptive work arrangements in order to survive in the economy of the new era.

Family:

A 1984 study of the family by Family Service America, a nonprofit national organization, foresees a continuing erosion of the traditional nuclear family with its wage-earner husband, homemaker wife, and dependent children. The divorce rate will maintain its present high level, but "a widespread consciousness of what children go through during divorce may exert a subtle pressure to keep the divorce rate from growing higher than it is." There will be a high remarriage rate, resulting in an increase in "blended families."

Single-person households will continue to grow, due to young people living alone, people separated or divorced, and surviving spouses of a marriage. There will be an increase in single-parent families and in homosexual couples. This "greater sexual freedom," according to the report, "will occur against a backdrop of weakened religious, social, and legal taboos." The family redefined as "two or more people joined together by bonds of sharing and intimacy" will gain widespread legal and social recognition.

An increasing number of families will share facilities and services, prompting zoning changes for new and converted housing that will permit common kitchens and playrooms for single-parent families. A new type of extended family will come into existence, in which traditional kinship bonds will be supplemented or replaced by the voluntary ties of friendship and mutual support. Fathering will become much like mothering, and both roles, through extension to stepchildren, adoptees, and children born of surrogate mothers, will acquire broader social and psychological dimensions; nurturing will be accepted as a masculine attribute.

Children will have "aunts," "uncles," "cousins," "grandparents" to whom they are related through social, communitarian linkages rather than through biology. The concept of family will expand, encompassing people of diverse ethnic, sexual, and cultural orientations. We will be entering a posttribal phase that will erase many historic stereotypes and barriers; as people intermarry and intermix at work and play, they will be perceived for what they are as individuals rather than through the distorted lens of arbitrary group membership. Pluralism will begin at home.

Politics:

The feminine influence on this "hard area" of American culture will change the face of politics by the end of this century. Political analyst William Greider believes that we are about to see "the most significant and promising political change of the eighties, one that could produce a radical reordering of American politics. Collectively, given all their discontents and desires, women are becoming the new antiestablishment force in politics. And they have a natural advantage that outsiders assaulting the established order normally lack: women are the voting majority." Because women are "closer to human development than men," California Assemblyman John Vasconcellos sees women contributing to politics the qualities of "cooperation, compassion, and receptivity that politics desperately needs."

Even before the choice of Geraldine Ferraro as the Democratic candidate for vice-president, the feminization of politics was being hailed as "the greatest political upheaval of the century." It is probably no coincidence that Ferraro is a hybridized woman, combining a strong commitment to family and to feminine values and concerns with a reputation for toughness and professionalism in her legal and legislative work. Ellen Goodman takes note of Ferraro's "sense of personal balance. She grew during that time, but she didn't grow out of herself. She remained mother, wife, daughter, and woman as well as candidate. Loyal as well as ambitious. She didn't carry clean laundry to her kids on the trail for the publicity but for the perspective. She didn't go home on weekends for rest as much as for roots. She didn't do the grocery shopping to attract the woman's vote but to retain her own sense of reality." Ferraro's historic candidacy has made it plausible for women to aim for high political office. "We are concerned with the visibility of women candidates," says Republican Elisabeth Griffin, head of the Women's Campaign Fund. "Ferraro's candidacy means it is going to be a more natural, a more ordinary event to see women running for these offices."

Though women, like men, vote their economic self-interest, polls have shown consistently that women depart sharply from men on war-and-peace issues. The divergence has been attributed to women's inbred pacifism as well as to biology. Marjorie Lansing, a political scientist at Eastern Michigan University, sees it as an expression of women's life-protecting role: "Women create life and are unwilling to destroy it. Women see solving conflict in a different way than men—they try to work out peaceful negotiations."

As women learn to play the game of politics, they will reshape this male arena to their own style. There will be a greater reliance on informal relationships, especially networks. The model will be the network in Washington, D.C., referred to in chapter 4, which cuts across party lines to recruit women for positions in the government. Women's networks will become increasingly international, following the lead of the Sisterhood Is Global Institute, established in 1984 as the "first global feminist think tank." The institute, which has been compared to diplomatic and intellectual groups like the Brandt Commission and the Club of Rome, focuses on such problems as female illiteracy, hunger, and the threat of nuclear war. Another recently formed group, the Feminist International Network for Peace and Food, sees itself as a women's United Nations. Informal groups like these will proliferate at local, national, and international levels, developing a grass-roots base that will drain the political initiative away from the unwieldy, bureaucratized official political structures. As Lech Walesa wrote when he was released from internment, "We must not seek governmental power. What we must do is create the sort of democratic structures in our society that any government would have to respect."

In electoral politics, as image overwhelms substance, the political parties will become indistinguishable from each other, which will hasten their decline. But as we move into a media culture, women will develop more sophisticated fund-raising and communication skills and, although they will learn to blend substance with image, the feminine predilection for the tangible and concrete suggests that the greater emphasis will be on substance.

There will be less pomp and ceremony and more substantive accomplishment in the legislative area. "Men left to themselves are going to engage in almost endless ceremonial acts," reports Jack Weatherford, an anthropologist who, in a scholarly study of Congress, has found much in common with his research in Kenya and other non-Western societies. "The women in Congress work, and they work like Trojans. They don't engage in nearly as much ceremony." Weatherford offers an illustration of needless, pointless ceremony in the signing of a bill: "The President, with each stroke of his signature, uses a different pen to hand out to congressmen as souvenirs. A simple three-second act has been extended to an hour-long ceremony."

Another example is the taboo on calling anyone by name on the floor of Congress. One must refer to "the Gentleman from Virginia" instead of the name that member goes by, and a member must request and be granted permission to extend his remarks, even if he or she wants only two more minutes. Weatherford believes that all this excessive ceremonial posturing may be fine for men at meetings of the Moose Lodge, but it impedes the process of governing the country. Comparing some of our congressmen with shamans who "put on a good show but don't effect many cures," he concludes that "women everywhere are doing brute work. . . . Men are the ones with the excess time to devote to status games."

As the feminization of the political process replaces empty showmanship with legislative accomplishments, there will also be more openness in government, less of the suspiciousness and conspiratorial style associated with the masculine approach to politics. (John Dean has admitted that, if the wives of the Watergate conspirators had been told by their husbands what was going on, "those things would never have happened. It was just a bunch of men . . . making those kinds of plans.")

Women will bring into politics a new concept of power, "empowerment," a mutual strengthening that will replace domination through manipulation and force. Hannah Arendt has described this type of power as "the ability not just to act but to act in concert. Power is never the property of an individual; it belongs to a group and remains in existence only so long as the group keeps together." It is a subtle form of power, often hidden or disguised, yet it is often more effective than overt power. (In traditional African societies such as the Ndembu, women are conspicuously absent from the ceremonial events—the war dances and curing rituals—but anthropologist Edith Turner, who studied the Ndembu for several years, discovered that it is in "the local hearths of the women's huts that the center of village life is really located." Nevertheless, many anthropologists and even the Ndembu themselves are unaware of this, because "they're looking at the most public places for the 'action.'") This quiet, pervasive form of power that women have been bringing into public life through such traditional organizations as the League of Women Voters will be complemented by a more open, assertive style as feminist organizations like NOW do battle on economic and political fronts. Power will be redefined from power *over* to power *with* others.

The Arts:

The visual and performing arts will continue to narrow the gap between the artist and the art consumer. With additional leisure time at their disposal, people will paint, sculpt, write, compose, and perform music as hobbies, bringing the everyone-an-artist dream closer to reality. In television, industry executives predict that as the number of female producers, directors, and writers increases, the "run-jump-chase" shows will give way to programs of greater interest to women, those that delve into relationships. "There will be a larger body of this type of program material produced for program buyers, male or female, to choose from," says TV executive Barbara Corday. She sees men and women in television continuing to educate each other—the men learning from women in the human-relations area, the women learning from men about business.

The Peace Movement:

In the politics of peace lies the most awesome challenge and, at the same time, the most promising opportunity for women to bring about a change in the course of human history. Because women value the individual over abstractions, they experience patriotism as identification with humanity, transcending the jingoistic, flag-waving xenophobia that throughout history has exacted an enormous price in blood and suffering from the human species. It is the sense of community that the Greek village woman felt for the unknown mothers in England whose sons she sheltered.

"Peace is patriotic" is a slogan found on signs carried by women protesting the nuclear arms buildup, and one that has been adopted by male peace activists. (Retired Admiral Gene La Rocque incorporates it in many of his speeches and TV appearances on behalf of the Center for Defense Information.)

Ultimately, as the peace movement becomes sexually integrated and reaches into all sectors of society, it will be not through treaties or rhetoric or "star wars" technology that lasting peace will be achieved, but rather through the transformation of the narrow nationalistic mind-set into what Jonathan Schell has described as a "generous, large-spirited statement which lifts one out of one's private concerns and reinforces one's attachment to the community in which one lives. It might well serve as a staging ground for building the broader loyalties that we must develop if we are to survive."

Women's time-honored dream is of a world in which violence and war have been abolished and conflicts are resolved through negotiation. In lore and legend, this utopian vision has drawn upon women's special strengths and powers: the withholding of sex, as in *Lysistrata,* or the prophesying of dire events, as in *The Trojan Women*. The utopian communities described in the writings of women have banished armies and weapons, violence and exploitation, dominance and supranationalism.

Translating such visions into reality will require the combined efforts, energies, and unyielding commitment of both sexes. In one scenario, the peace movement will become international and will promote interchanges between people from all parts of the world. Global tensions will be alleviated as "the enemy" is perceived as consisting of people whose commonality is as strong as their differences, and who share a common hope for their children—a chance to grow up in a peaceful world. This trend toward internationalization will be reinforced by both the nuclear threat and the growing economic interdependence of nations.

Spirituality:

Americans will continue to turn away from the dictates of organized religion and will draw upon their own spiritual resources. Dr. William McCready, program director of the National Opinion Research Center at the University of Chicago, views this shift as a major change in the nation's religious character. "The transition is not from authority to anarchy but to conscience. For many people, it is an uncomfortable, messy transition." His studies over the past decade show that "Americans don't respond to moral imperatives. . . . They've been told to trust their own consciences, and that's what they're doing."

The shift to personal religion is an inevitable response to the principle of uncertainty that has replaced earlier models of certain and irrefutable knowledge. "The extraordinary insight of modern physics about the way the world really works," says journalist Flora Lewis, whose specialty is foreign affairs, "is that the world is a mass of uncertainties piling up into likelihoods." A sense of uncertainty and unpredictability has been pervading the psychosocial as well as the scientific sphere, as the complexity of contemporary life and the growing sense of a universe out of control have increased our feelings of personal helplessness. The vision of a secure American future buoyed by America's position of world leadership died in the defoliated fields of Vietnam.

Uncertainty is, of course, much more difficult to live with than certainty, and Lewis reminds us that "it requires respect for and a degree of deference to other peoples' observations and ideas.'' It also demands of us, she continues, ''a new kind of courage—the courage of restraint and tolerance. Without it, we may abuse human achievement in the service of our own destruction.'' It is incompatible with the dogmatic, doctrinaire, I-am-right-you-are-wrong kind of thinking that has always dominated religious orthodoxy.[8]

In this unfolding environment of uncertainty, the feminine experience will give women an advantage. Uncertainty is bred into the very tissue of feminine culture. For a woman, the development of identity is entwined with relationships, which grow and fluctuate with the passage of time. Assisting in the development of a child is surely a ''mass of uncertainties piling up into likelihoods.'' Children are constantly changing and responding in surprising, unpredictable ways, and mothering requires an undeviating sensitivity to the child's changing needs and interests.

The ''messy and uncomfortable'' transition to personal religion will be less messy and uncomfortable for those who have integrated the feminine values of respect for one's self and others, as well as tolerance, vulnerability, and adaptability into their personal belief systems. Reliance on the self rather than on a prescribed body of doctrine emanating from a supreme authority can mean the realization of freedom and the strengthening of personal resources; but it can also bring on feelings of anomie, of disconnection and disorientation. When the individual conscience is the ultimate authority, a value system based on cooperation, compassion, and intimacy becomes an essential source of spiritual sustenance for both sexes.

Identity:

The rise of personalism together with the decline of the work ethic will lead to a shift in self-identification from doing to being. We will define ourselves by our passions and commitments rather than by the way we earn our living. In the variable, uncertain world of the future, the rigid, fixed roles and personality models of the past, determined by such arbitrary criteria as gender, ethnic derivation, or nationality, will give way to a more fluid, open-ended identity. Social historian Robert Jay Lifton has characterized this flexible persona as "protean," from the Greek mythological character Proteus, who was able to change his shape with ease from wild boar to lion to dragon to fire to flood.

Though Lifton does not identify the protean personality as female, he could well have done so, for while rigidity and fixity have been associated with masculine culture, shape changing is integral to feminine experience. Leonie Caldecott relates the story of a woman who comes to visit Meister Eckhardt, the fourteenth-century theologian and mystic, and when asked to identify herself replies that she is neither girl nor woman nor husband nor wife nor widow nor virgin nor master nor maid nor servant, explaining why each role is an inadequate description of her true self. "Since I am all of these, I am neither one," she says. "I am just something among somethings, and so I go." Returning to his pupils, Meister Eckhardt observes that he has just listened to the purest person he has ever known.[9]

Another way of looking at the emerging identity was suggested in our discussion of the hybridized, or integrated, personality. This requires a flexible, expansive perception capable of blending the spiritual with the mundane, independence with interdependence, vulnerability with courage, receptivity with decisiveness. Philosopher George Simmel describes this personality type as one that is able "to act as a thoroughly differentiated, individualized being, and at the same time to act as a unity containing in some deep stratum the forces of all differentiated qualities in a state of complete diffuseness," and he ascribes this capacity only to "those women who are gifted with the genius of femininity." But in fact, this differentiated-integrated identity will describe more and more of the men and women of the future, who represent a merging of the most creative and adaptive attributes of feminine and masculine culture. It is these new men and women who are in the most favorable position to act as mold breakers, for they are the illuminators and forethinkers, the carriers of the ideas and values that will define the shape and direction of the new era.

Feminine culture has shown that it can infuse a failed, run-down system with new energies and vision. The rethinking of obsolete myths and stereotypes, the challenge to entrenched values and styles of behavior—all of this is a healthy and urgently needed response to a world that is dangerously out of control and is losing its sense of what it means to be human. It is a response that comes out of the life experience of the demeaned, suppressed half of humanity.

But women's culture, which offers us our brightest hope for a saner, more peaceful world, will fulfill its promise only if women carry their values into the public world and are not co-opted by the more powerful masculine culture that dominates that world. The history of cultural assimilation suggests that when two cultures are in contact, the weaker one is either rejected or absorbed by the more powerful one. If it is absorbed, it ceases to exist, and an entire way of life is lost. The members of the weaker group lose their unique identity and heritage, and more significant, they lose the possibility of identification with their own kind.

Those women today who are reaching for change, for "liberation" in its most obvious, immediate sense, are often too wildly eager to discard all that has been associated with their formerly trivialized and restricted possibilities. Like immigrants newly arrived in America, who in their rush for assimilation jettisoned their entire heritage in order to obliterate anything that marked them as different or foreign, so too are women rushing out of the sheltered atmosphere of domesticity, often abandoning in the process of masculinization all that has come to be associated with the warm, graceful, emotionally expressive aspects of their humanity.

Feminine and masculine culture must work in tandem to bring about new ways of living together that will affirm our dignity and creativity as individuals and our commonality as inhabitants of an interdependent planet. The world we live in can no longer operate on the traditional value system of masculine culture; the ruthless competitiveness, the unchecked individualism, and the exercise of power through violence have brought us to the brink of self-destruction.

But the will to survive, which may be nature's way of saving us from ourselves, is at work in the personal and social transformations occurring in mainstream culture. A growing number of men are learning that the values and attributes that have been disdained as feminine are the essential human resources for personal growth and satisfying relationships; as more men join their ranks, the promise of a bright and peaceful future will come closer to realization.

The process of feminization has shown us the way to achieve a balanced and humane society. Our health and wholeness, our hopes for a peaceful and compassionate world will be determined by our response to this unprecedented opportunity for individual and social change.

REFERENCES

CHAPTER 1

On the Threshold

1. Elizabeth Janeway, *Powers of the Weak.*
2. Carol Gilligan, *In a Different Voice.*
3. Jean Baker Miller, *Toward a New Psychology of Women.*
4. Daniel Boorstin, *The Americans: The Democratic Experience.*

CHAPTER 2

Feminine as a Second Language

1. Jo Durden-Smith and Diane deSimone, *Sex and the Brain.*
2. Barrie Thorne and Nancy Henley, *Language and Sex: Difference and Dominance.*
3. Jessie Bernard, *The Female World.*
4. Jon Stewart, "Mantalk/Womantalk," *San Francisco Sunday Examiner and Chronicle,* November 27, 1983, California Living section.
5. Lilli Lenz, "Perceived Identity Shifts in Asian and Southeast Asian ESL Students," (M.A. diss., San Francisco State, San Francisco, 1983).
6. Marianne La France and Clara Mayo, *Moving Bodies.*
7. Robin Lakoff, *Language and Woman's Place.*
8. Thomas J. Peters and Robert H. Waterman, Jr., *In Search of Excellence.*
9. Lakoff, *Language and Woman's Place.*
10. Betty Lehan Harragan, *Games Mother Never Taught You.*

References

CHAPTER 3

Feminine Friendship: The Art of Intimacy

1. Philip Slater, *The Pursuit of Loneliness*.
2. Robert Bellah et al., *Habits of the Heart*.
3. Carroll Smith-Rosenberg, "The Female World of Love and Ritual: Relations Between Women in 19th-Century America."
4. Jessie Bernard, *The Female World*.
5. Margaret Mahler, Fred Pine, and Anni Bergman, *The Psychological Birth of the Human Infant*.
6. Nancy Chodorow, *The Reproduction of Mothering*.
7. Daniel J. Levinson et al., *The Seasons of a Man's Life*.
8. Robert Brain, *Friends and Lovers*.
9. Lillian B. Rubin, *Intimate Strangers*.
10. David Michaelis, *The Best of Friends*.
11. Robert Bell, "Friendships Between Men and Women," *Psychology of Women Quarterly*, Spring 1981.
12. Steve Tesich, "Focusing on Friends," *New York Times Magazine*, December 4, 1983.
13. Stuart Miller, *Men and Friendship*.
14. Elliott Engel, "Of Male Bondage," *Newsweek*, June 21, 1982.
15. Miller, *Men and Friendship*.
16. Ciji Ware, *Sharing Parenthood After Divorce*.
17. David Behrens, "Confusion," *Ms*, August 1984.

CHAPTER 4

New Networks: Feminine Power Goes Public

1. David Broder, *The Changing of the Guard*.
2. Lois Banner, *Women in Modern America*.
3. Dorothy Hammond and Alta Jablow, *Women in Cultures of the World*.
4. Patricia Caplan and Janet M. Bujra, *Women United, Women Divided*.
5. Alan Lomax, "A Note on a Feminine Factor in Cultural History," in *Being Female*, ed. Dana Raphael.
6. John Naisbitt, *Megatrends*.

7. Anna Quidlen, "Women's Networks Come of Age," *New York Times Magazine,* October 21, 1984.
8. Mary Scott Welch, *Networking.*
9. Quoted in Quidlen, "Women's Networks Come of Age."
10. Anne M. Costain, "Representing Women: The Transition from Social Movement to Interest Group," in *Women, Power and Policy,* ed. Ellen Boneparth.
11. Naisbitt, *Megatrends.*

CHAPTER 5

Humanizing the Workplace

1. Rosabeth Moss Kanter, "Women and the Structure of Organizations," in *Another Voice,* ed. Marcia Millman and R. B. Kanter.
2. Karen Pennar and Edward Mervosh, "Women at Work," *Business Week,* January 28, 1985.
3. Emily Stoper, "Alternative Work Patterns and the Double Life," in *Women, Power and Policy,* ed. Ellen Boneparth.
4. Lionel Tiger and Heather T. Fowler, eds., *Female Hierarchies.*
5. Kathleen Hendrix, "Influx of Women Changing the Workplace," *Los Angeles Times,* September 14, 1984.
6. Hilary Rosenberg, "Ms. Broker Comes into Her Own," *Financial World,* August 31, 1983.
7. Betty Friedan, "Feminism Takes a New Turn," *New York Times Magazine,* November 18, 1982.
8. Willis Harman, "Work," in *Millenium,* ed. Alberto Villoldo and Ken Dychtwald.

CHAPTER 6

Reshaping the Family

1. Marvin Harris, *America Now.*
2. Elizabeth Janeway, *Powers of the Weak.*
3. Robin Fox, *Kinship and Marriage.*
4. Philippe Aries, *Centuries of Childhood.*

5. Dorothy Hammond and Alta Jablow, *Women in Cultures of the World*.
6. Paula Webster, "Matriarchy: A Vision of Power," in *Toward an Anthropology of Women*, ed. Rayna R. Reiter.
7. Barbara Ehrenreich, *The Hearts of Men: American Dreams and the Flight from Commitment*.
8. Anita Shreve, "The Working Mother as Role Model," *New York Times Magazine*, September 9, 1984.
9. Lila Leibowitz, *Females, Males, Families*.
10. Joseph Giordano, "A Stepfather Tries to Find His Role," *Ms*, February 1985.
11. Elizabeth Mehren, "Psychologists Scrutinize Males," *Los Angeles Times*, August 29, 1984.
12. Vicki Jarmulowski, "Blended Families," *Ms*, February 1985.

CHAPTER 7

Feminizing Health Care

1. Adrienne Rich, *Of Woman Born*.
2. John McPhee, "Heirs of Family Practice," *New Yorker*, July 23, 1984.
3. Perri Klass, "Bearing a Child in Medical School," *New York Times Magazine*, November 11, 1984.
4. Gale Maleskey, "What Can We Learn from the Women's Health Movement?" *Prevention*, January 1984.
5. Sue Fisher, "The Decision-Making Context: How Doctors and Patients Communicate,' in *Linguistics and the Professions*, ed. Robert J. di Pietro.
6. Ellen Goodman, "Doctor-as-God is Dead or Dying," *Los Angeles Times*, July 5, 1984.

CHAPTER 8

The Third Coming: In Search of a New Spirituality

1. Simone de Beauvoir, *The Second Sex*.
2. Elaine Pagels, *The Gnostic Gospels*.

3. Carol P. Christ and Judith Plaskow, eds., *Womanspirit Rising*.
4. Lilli Lenz, "The Feminine Principle of 19th Century America: A Study in Schizophrenia," research paper, 1982. University of California at Santa Cruz, Santa Cruz, California.
5. Barbara Walker, *The Woman's Encyclopedia of Myths and Secrets*.
6. Mary Beard, *Woman as a Force in History*.
7. Mary Gerzon, *A Choice of Heroes*.
8. Wendell Beame and William G. Doty, eds., *Myth, Rite, and Symbols: A Mircea Eliade Reader*.
9. Kenneth Briggs, "America's Return to Prayer," *New York Times Magazine*, November 18, 1984.
10. Elaine Sciolino, "A Time for Challenge," *New York Times Magazine*, November 4, 1984.
11. William James, *Varieties of Religious Experience*.

CHAPTER 9

Revitalizing the Arts

1. John Russell, "There Is No Such Thing as Women's Art, Just Good Art," *New York Times*, July 24, 1983.
2. Barbara Rose, *American Art Since 1900*.
3. Joseph Meeker, *The Comedy of Survival*.
4. Judy Chicago, *Through the Flower*.
5. Lucy Lippard, *From the Center*.
6. Linda Dahl, *Stormy Weather*.
7. Mel Gussow, "Women Playwrights: New Voices in the Theatre," *New York Times Magazine*, May 1, 1983.

CHAPTER 10

Protecting Life

1. Nancy Huston, "Tales of War and Tears of Women," in *Women and Men's Wars*, ed. Judith Stiehm.
2. Helen Kazantzakis, *Nikos Kazantzakis: A Biography Based On His Letters*.

3. Tillie Olsen, interview in *Publishers Weekly*, November 23, 1984.
4. Center for Defense Information, Washington, D.C., "Nuclear War Prevention Kit," 1985.
5. Morris Janowitz, *The Reconstruction of Patriotism: Education for Civic Consciousness*.

CHAPTER 11

New Men, New Women

1. Barbara Ehrenreich, "A Feminist's View of the New Man," *New York Times Magazine*, May 20, 1984.
2. Andrew Hacker, "Women vs. Men in the Work Force," *New York Times Magazine*, December 9, 1984.
3. Robert Duncan, *The Noise*.
4. Mark Gerzon, *A Choice of Heroes*.
5. Adrienne Rich, *On Lies, Secrets and Silence*.
6. "Women in the Workforce," *Los Angeles Times*, October 8, 1984.
7. Germaine Greer, *The Obstacle Race*.
8. Elaine Showalter, "Women Who Write Are Women," *New York Times Book Review*, December 16, 1984.
9. Evelyn Fox Keller, *A Feeling for the Organism: The Life and Work of Barbara McClintock*.
10. Korn/Ferry International, executive search firm, Los Angeles, survey "Profile of the Successful Woman Executive," 1982.
11. Dana Raphael, *Being Female*.

CHAPTER 12

Beyond Feminism

1. Sherry Turkle, *The Second Self*.
2. Evelyn Fox Keller, *A Feeling for the Organism*.
3. Eric Flamholtz, *Management Magazine*, Fall 1982.
4. W. David Slawson, *The New Inflation*.
5. Gail Sheehy, review of *The Managed Heart*, by Arlie Rus-

sell Hochschild, *New York Times Book Review*, October 23, 1983.

6. Robert Heilbroner, review of *The Second Industrial Divide, New York Times Book Review*, January 6, 1985.
7. Michel Hertaux, *World Press Review*, January 1985.
8. Flora Lewis, "The Quantum Mechanics of Politics," *New York Times Magazine*, November 6, 1984.
9. Leonie Caldecott, "The Dance of the Woman Warrior," in *Walking on the Water*, eds. Jo Garcia and Sara Maitland.

BIBLIOGRAPHY

Allgeier, Elizabeth Rice, and McCormick, Naomi B. *Changing Boundaries: Gender Roles and Sexual Behavior*. Palo Alto, CA: Mayfield Publishing, 1983.

Arendt, Hannah. *On Violence*. New York: Harcourt, Brace & World, 1969.

Aries, Phillipe. *Centuries of Childhood*. New York: Vintage, 1962.

Auerbach, Nina. *Communities of Women*. Cambridge: Harvard University Press, 1978.

Banner, Lois. *Women in Modern America*. New York: Harcourt Brace Jovanovich, 1974.

Beame, William, and Doty, William G., eds. *A Mircea Eliade Reader*. New York: Harper & Row, 1976.

Bellah, Robert, et al. *Habits of the Heart*. Berkeley: University of California Press, 1985.

Bernard, Jessie. *The Female World*. New York: Macmillan, The Free Press, 1981.

Beard, Mary. *Woman as a Force in History*. New York: Octagon Books, 1981.

Bleier, Ruth. *Science and Gender*. Elmsford, NY: Pergamon Press, 1984.

Boneparth, Ellen, ed. *Women, Power and Policy*. Elmsford, NY: Pergamon Press, 1983.

Boorstin, Daniel. *The Americans: The Democratic Experience*. New York: Random House, 1973.

Boston Women's Health Collective. *Our Bodies, Ourselves*. New York: Simon and Schuster, 1985.

Brain, Robert. *Friends and Lovers*. New York: Basic Books, 1976.

Broder, David. "Networks." Chapters 5–11 of *The Changing of the Guard*. New York: Simon & Schuster, 1980.

Caldecott, Leonie, and Leland, Stephanie, eds. *Reclaim the Earth*. London: The Women's Press, 1983.

Caplan, Patricia, and Bujra, Janet. *Women United, Women Divided*. Bloomington: Indiana University Press, 1979.

Capra, Fritjof. *The Tao of Physics*. Boulder, CO: Shambala Publications, 1975.

Chicago, Judy. *Through the Flower*. New York: Anchor Books, 1982.

Chodorow, Nancy. *The Reproduction of Mothering*. Berkeley: University of California Press, 1975.

Christ, Carol P., and Plaskow, Judith. *Womanspirit Rising*. New York: Harper & Row, 1979

Cousins, Norman. *Human Options*. New York: W. W. Norton & Co., 1981.

Dahl, Linda. *Stormy Weather: The Music and Lives of a Century of Jazzwomen*. New York: Pantheon, 1984.

Davidson, Mark. *Uncommon Sense*. Los Angeles: J. P. Tarcher, 1983.

de Beauvoir, Simone. *The Second Sex*. New York: Alfred A. Knopf, 1953.

di Pietro, Robert, ed. *Linguistics and the Professions*. Norwood, NJ: Ablex Publishing, 1982.

Dreifus, Claudia. *Seizing Our Bodies*. New York: Vintage, 1978.

Duncan, Robert. *The Noise*. New York: Ticknor & Fields, 1984.

Durden-Smith, Jo, and deSimone, Diane. *Sex and the Brain*. New York: Warner Books, 1983.

Edwards, Margot, and Waldorf, Mary. *Reclaiming Birth*. Trumansburg, NY: Crossing Press, 1984.

Ehrenreich, Barbara. *The Hearts of Men: American Dreams and the Flight from Commitment*. New York: Anchor/Doubleday, 1983.

Fox, Robin. *Kinship and Marriage*. New York: Penguin, 1967.

Fromm, Erich. *Escape From Freedom*. New York: Avon, 1969.

Bibliography

Garcia, Joe, and Maitland, Sara. *Walking on the Water*. London: Virago Press, 1983.

Gerzon, Mark. *A Choice of Heroes*. Boston: Houghton-Mifflin, 1982.

Gilligan, Carol. *In A Different Voice*. Cambridge, MA: 1982.

Goldberg, Philip. *The Intuitive Edge*. Los Angeles: J. P. Tarcher, 1983.

Goldenberg, Naomi. *Changing of the Gods*. Boston: Beacon Press, 1979.

Gordon, James S. *Health for the Whole Person*. Boulder, CO: Westview Press, 1980.

Greer, Germaine. *The Obstacle Race*. New York: Farrar, Straus, Giroux, 1979.

Hammond, Dorothy, and Jablow, Alta. *Women in Cultures of the World*. Menlo Park, CA: Cummings Publishing, 1976.

Harragan, Betty Lehan. *Games Mother Never Taught You*. New York: Warner Books, 1977.

Harris, Marvin. *America Now*. New York: Simon & Schuster, 1981.

Henley, Nancy M. *Body Politics*. Englewood Cliffs, NJ: Prentice-Hall, 1977.

Huizinga, Johan. *Homo Ludens: A Study of the Play Element in Culture*. Boston: Beacon Press, 1972.

James, William. "The Religion of Healthy-Mindedness." Lectures IV and V of *Varieties of Religious Experience*. New York: Random House, 1902.

Janeway, Elizabeth. *Powers of the Weak*. New York: Alfred A. Knopf, 1980.

Janowitz, Morris. *The Reconstruction of Patriotism: Education for Civic Consciousness*. Chicago: University of Chicago Press, 1985.

Kazantzakis, Helen. *Nikos Kazantzakis: A Biography Based on His Letters*. New York: Simon & Schuster, 1968.

Keller, Evelyn Fox. *A Feeling for the Organism: The Life and Work of Barbara McClintock*. New York: W. H. Freeman & Co., 1983.

Kuhn, Annette. *Women's Pictures: Feminism and Cinema*. London and Boston: Routledge & Kegan Paul, 1982.

Lakoff, Robin. *Language and Woman's Place*. New York: Harper/Colophon, 1982.

La France, Marianne, and Mayo, Clara. *Moving Bodies*. Monterey: CA: Brooks/Cole Publishing, 1978.

Leibowitz, Lila. *Females, Males, Families. A Biosocial Approach*. Belmont, CA: Wadsworth Publishing, Duxbury Press, 1978.

Lerner, Gerda. *The Female Experience*. Indianapolis, IN: Bobbs-Merrill, 1977.

Levinson, Daniel, et al. *The Seasons of a Man's Life*. New York: Ballantine, 1978.

Lippard, Lucy. *From the Center*. New York: E. P. Dutton, 1976.

Maccobby, Eleanor Emmons, and Jacklin, Carol Nagy. *The Psychology of Sex Differences*. Palo Alto, CA: Stanford University Press, 1972.

Mahler, Margaret; Pine, Fred; and Bergman, Anni. *The Psychological Birth of the Human Infant*. New York: Basic Books, 1975.

Maxwell, Florida Scott. *Women and Sometimes Men*. London and Boston: Routledge & Kegan Paul, 1957.

Meeker, Joseph. *The Comedy of Survival*. New York: Scribner, 1974.

Michaelis, David. *The Best of Friends*. New York: William Morrow, 1983.

Miller, Jean Baker. *Toward a New Psychology of Women*. Boston: Beacon Press, 1976.

Miller, Stuart. *Men and Friendship*. Boston: Houghton-Mifflin, 1983.

Millman, Marcia, and Kanter, R. M. *Another Voice*. New York: Anchor/Doubleday, 1975.

Moffatt, Mary Jane, and Painter, Charlotte, eds. *Revelations: Diaries of Women*. New York: Vintage, 1975.

Naisbitt, John. *Megatrends*. New York: Warner Books, 1982.

Ochs, Carol. *Women and Spirituality*. Totowa, NJ: Rawman & Allanheld, 1983.

Pagels, Elaine. *The Gnostic Gospels*. New York: Random House, 1979.

Peters, Thomas J., and Waterman, Robert H., Jr. *In Search of Excellence*. New York: Harper & Row, 1983.

Raphael, Dana. *Being Female*. Paris: Mouton Publishers, 1975.

Reiter, Rayna R., ed. *Toward an Anthropology of Women*. New York and London: Monthly Review Press, 1975.

Rich, Adrienne. *On Lies, Secrets and Silence*. New York: W. W. Norton, 1979.

Rich, Adrienne. *Of Woman Born*. New York: Bantam Books, 1981.

Rosaldo, Michelle Zimbalist, and Lamphere, Louise. *Woman, Culture and Society*. Palo Alto, CA: Stanford University Press, 1974.

Rose, Barbara. *American Art Since 1900*. New York: Holt, Rinehart & Winston, 1975.

Rubin, Lillian R. *Intimate Strangers*. New York: Harper & Row, 1983.

Ruzek, Sheryl Burt. *The Women's Health Movements: Feminist Alternatives to Medical Control*. New York: Praeger, 1973.

Slater, Philip. *The Pursuit of Loneliness*. Boston: Beacon Press, 1970.

Slawson, David. *The New Inflation*. Princeton, NJ: Princeton University Press, 1981.

Smith-Rosenberg, Carroll. "The Female World of Love and Ritual: Relations Between Women in 19th Century America," *Signs*, Chicago, IL: University of Chicago Press, 1975.

Sobel, David S., ed. *Holistic Approaches to Health*. New York: Harcourt Brace Jovanovich, 1979.

Sorrels, Bobbye D. *The Nonsexist Communicator*. Englewood Cliffs, NJ: Prentice-Hall, 1983.

Starr, Paul. *The Social Transformation of Medicine*. New York: Basic Books, 1982.

Stiehm, Judith, ed. *Women and Men's Wars*. Elmsford, NY: Pergamon Press, 1983.

Thorne, Barrie, and Henley, Nancy. *Language and Sex: Difference and Dominance*. New York: Newbury House, 1975.

Tiger, Lionel, and Fowler, Heather T., eds. *Female Hierarchies*. Chicago: Beresford Book Service, 1978.

Tufte, Virginia, and Myerhoff, Barbara. *Changing Images of the Family*. New Haven: Yale University Press, 1979.

Turkle, Sherry. *The Second Self*. New York: Simon & Schuster, 1984.

Villoldo, Alberto, and Dychtwald, Ken, eds. *Millenium: Glimpses into the 21st Century*. Los Angeles: J. P. Tarcher, 1981; distributed by Houghton Mifflin.

Walker, Barbara. *The Woman's Encyclopedia of Myths and Secrets*. New York: Harper & Row, 1983.

Ware, Ciji. *Sharing Parenthood After Divorce*. New York: Bantam Books, 1984.

Welch, Mary Scott. *Networking*. New York: Harcourt Brace Jovanovich, 1980.

Wheelwright, Jane H. *Women and Men*. San Francisco: Jung Institute Publication, 1978.

Woolf, Virginia. *Three Guineas*. New York: Penguin, 1938.

INDEX